The Spice Box

An Anthology of Jewish Canadian Writing

SELECTED BY GERRI SINCLAIR &
MORRIS WOLFE

LESTER
&ORPEN
DENNYS
PUBLISHERS

Canadian Cataloguing in Publication Data

Main entry under title:
  The Spice Box

ISBN 0-919630-75-8

1. Canadian literature (English) — Jewish authors.*
2. Jews — Canada — Literary collections.
I. Sinclair, Gerri, 1948-.   II. Wolfe, Morris, 1938-

PS8235.J4S64   C810′.8′08924   C81-094755-2
PR9194.5.J4S64

Every reasonable effort has been made to trace ownership of copyright materials. Information will be welcomed which will enable the publisher to rectify any reference or credit in future printings.

Design: Jack Steiner Graphic Design
Spice Box photo: George Simhoni
Production: Paula Chabanais Productions

Printed and bound in Canada for:

Lester & Orpen Dennys
78 Sullivan Street
Toronto, Ontario
M5T 1C1

We are grateful to a number of individuals and institutions. The idea for the book was Malcolm Lester's. Simon Fraser University and British Columbia's Youth Employment Programme provided us with a research assistant, Heather MacNeil, and office space. Barbara Balfour assisted with research in Toronto. The Multiculturalism Program, Government of Canada, was generous in its support. And a number of friends and colleagues offered us advice — and consolation — along the way. To all, much thanks.

Jacket photo shows silver spice box, Central European, 19th century: filigree two-tiered turret with four gilded bells and four flags on square base and four feet. Small gilded cupola is surmounted by bell-tower and ball-and-flag finial. From the Cecil Roth Collection, courtesy of Beth Tzedec Museum, Toronto. Photo by George Simhoni.

CONTENTS

INTRODUCTION

In a 1909 study of Canadian immigrants, *Strangers Within Our Gates*, J. S. Woodsworth reported that the first task Jewish immigrants set themselves on arriving in Canada was "to acquire a knowledge of English." Canadian Jews, Woodsworth observed, devoted themselves to learning their new language with remarkable intensity:

> It is almost pathetic to see old men, after their day's work, coming to night school to read from children's primers; and this is not merely that they may do business, for at once they plunge into all kinds of intellectual activities. They are omnivorous readers. Our librarians tell us that the young Jewish people patronize the public libraries more than any other class. They establish literary societies, social and dramatic clubs and political associations. They glory in their literary traditions.

Woodsworth's sympathetic description of Jewish immigrants differed greatly from the popular view to be found in the pages of newspapers and magazines of the time. A *Saturday Night* editorial in 1906, for example, stated that Jews "come to us from countries where they have endured centuries of oppression, have had beaten out of them almost the last vestige of self-respect." Consequently, the editorial continued, "they are poor material for use in the big job of nation making that we have on our hands."

As it turned out, Woodsworth was right. Jews made — and continue to make — a contribution to Canadian life out of all proportion to their numbers. Nowhere has that been more true than in our literature. *The Spice Box* is a celebration of that contribution.

When we began working on this anthology, we had no firm groundrules about how many writers should be in the collection, or what aspects of Jewish life should be covered and from what points of view. We just wanted to bring together the best writing we could find, by established and beginning writers, in whatever form — poetry, fiction, non-fiction — on the subject of being Jewish in Canada. At first we even left open the question of whether writers

Introduction

who *aren't* Jewish might appear; J. S. Woodsworth is, after all, only one of many non-Jewish Canadians who have written well and sensitively about the Jewish experience. But in the end we elected to concentrate on works of Jewish writers.

This is not to say that we approached our assignment without any definite plans. We knew that certain writers would undoubtedly find a place in the collection: A. M. Klein, Leonard Cohen, Irving Layton, Miriam Waddington, Eli Mandel, Adele Wiseman, Mordecai Richler, Shirley Faessler, Henry Kreisel, Phyllis Gotlieb. In these cases we, as editors, had the job of deciding which work or works to include. No doubt some readers will disagree with our decisions; there were few easy choices. (For example, we picked an excerpt from Adele Wiseman's novel *Crackpot* over one from her more celebrated work *The Sacrifice* because we felt the former had not received the recognition it deserved.)

In addition to these ten writers, we supposed that we might find twelve or fifteen others whom we wanted to include in the book. In fact, *The Spice Box* contains works by almost forty authors — and there could have been far more. The wealth of material brought us many pleasant surprises. We were familiar, for instance, with the translations of the Yiddish poems of Rochl Korn and J. I. Segal, but we had not come across the translations of Solomon Ary's haunting prose. Nor were we acquainted with the work of several other writers who appear here: poets Lela Parlow and Avi Boxer, or short-story writer Abraham Boyarsky, whose tale "A Birthday Party" is characterized by a gentle pathos which gives way, at its conclusion, to a cry for unmitigated vengeance. And we'd forgotten Larry Zolf's delightful essay about his father's assumption that Canada was some sort of penal colony to the American dream.

Our original plan was to use the familiar pedlar's cry, *Rags, Bones, Bottles*, as the title of the book. It was as pedlars, after all, that many Jews began their new lives in Canada. (Indeed, one of the editors of this anthology has, framed and hanging in his living-room, two pedlar's licences issued to his father: one in 1922, to "Lazar Wolfowitz," who had recently arrived in Canada from Poland; and one in 1933, to the now respectably named "Louie Wolfe," who in a real-life game of snakes-and-ladders had lost a small business and was desperately trying to start all over again.) But several contributors urged us to reconsider the title; they felt it was too negative. Helen Weinzweig argued, for example, that if one extreme of prejudice cast the Jew as Rothschild, the title *Rags, Bones, Bottles* evoked the equally false stereotype of the Jew as beggar.

It was our publishers who suggested calling the book *The Spice Box*. At first we hesitated, because Leonard Cohen had used a similar title — *The Spice-Box of Earth* — for an early collection of poems. But we decided that the full title, *The Spice Box: An Anthology of Jewish Canadian Writing*, was sufficiently different to avoid confusion. And the spice box is a longstanding reminder of the bittersweetness of Jewish life, for not only is it an object of ritual art (and a collector's item) but it plays an important part during *havdalah*, the ceremony which concludes the Sabbath. According to Jewish belief, an additional soul inhabits the body during the Sabbath. When the sun sets on Saturday night and the additional soul departs, devout Jews console and fortify themselves by inhaling the fragrance of the family spice box.

Centuries of hatred have forced Jews to define themselves, to know who they are. As a result, they have the longest memories of any people in the world — while Canadians, on the other hand, have the shortest. "It's only by our lack of ghosts/we're haunted," says Earle Birney in "Canlit." In sharp contrast, A. M. Klein describes the pervasive influence of his Jewish ancestry:

> Not sole was I born, but entire genesis:
> For to the fathers that begat me, this
> Body is residence. Corpuscular,
> They dwell in my veins, they eavesdrop at my ear,
> They circle, as with Torahs, round my skull. . . .

Indeed, Jews have never lacked ghosts to haunt them; the spectres of pogroms, the Holocaust, and the Arab-Israeli wars circle round the pages of this anthology.

But this may be changing, at least in North America. According to a recent survey conducted by the American Jewish Committee, there has been a significant decrease in anti-semitism in the United States (and in Canada too, one assumes) over the past seventeen years. The number of those who believe that Jews "have a lot of irritating faults" has declined from forty-eight per cent in 1964 to twenty-nine per cent today; those who think "Jews are less honest than non-Jews" has gone from thirty-four per cent to twenty-two per cent. The effect of this declining prejudice, and of growing assimilation, can be observed in the contents of *The Spice Box*. For although we set out to arrange the material in a sequence which would reflect the transition from the old world to the new one, this sequence also reveals a trend away from a strong awareness of Jewish identity towards a sense of growing ambivalence. J. I. Segal's jubilant poem about a mad red-haired fiddler, "At My Wedding," gives way to Ray Shankman's rueful "Wedding Poem" about conventionality. The subject of Tom Wayman's "Jews" is, ironically, the irrelevance of racial and social classifications: for him, "family" means self and friends, nothing more; everything else — religion, class, race, tribe — is meaningless. Similarly, Avrum Malus declares himself a modern Jew: for his daily ritual he dons, not *tefilin*, but running shoes.

Not all our selections deal directly with Jewish life. Helen Weinzweig's computerized world in "Hold That Tiger" contains no explicit Jewish content. Yet in its Kafka-like quality it clearly suggests a Jewish sensibility and voice. For, by and large, Jewish culture is the record of a continually displaced people attempting to find a home for themselves in a hostile environment.

Critics like Northrop Frye and Margaret Atwood argue that a similar struggle has given rise to the imaginative voice of Canadian literature. Mordecai Richler takes the point further. "To be a Jew and a Canadian," he says in his essay "Hunting Tigers Under Glass," "is to emerge from the ghetto twice." Tom Marshall agrees; in his book on A. M. Klein he observes that "there is a sense in which the Jews are the most Canadian of Canadians: history has forced them to experience the conflicts and tension that all sensitive Canadians experience — but to an intense degree." In a country where every individual is a member of an ethnic group (at least, so concludes the Royal Commission Report on Bilingualism and Biculturalism), the Jew becomes a kind of Everyman — a stranger trying to fit into an alien geography and culture. Thus the Montreal streets of Ludwig, Layton, and Richler; the Toronto ghetto of Erna Paris; the Winnipeg North End of Wiseman and Waddington; the small town of Torgov; and the prairie towns of Maynard, Mandel, and Currie, all share essentially the same mindscape.

Some writers — Robert Kroetsch and Eli Mandel, for example — argue that region is no longer so much a function of place as it is of voice. It is the dislocated voice of the modern Jew that speaks more and more insistently in the second half of *The Spice Box* — a voice clearly audible in Miriam Waddington's "The Nineteen Thirties Are Over":

> . . . but I walk
> carefully in this land
> of sooty snow; I pass the
> rich houses and double
> garages and I am not really
> this middle-aged professor
> but someone from
> Winnipeg whose bones ache
> with the broken revolutions
> of Europe, and even now
> I am standing on the heaving
> ploughed-up field
> of my father's old war.

The Spice Box invites you to join us in following the many voices of Canadian Jews as they make their sometimes funny, sometimes poignant journey from the *shtetls* of Europe into the mainstream of modern Canadian life.

Morris Wolfe
Gerri Sinclair
August 1981

Solomon Ary

THE PACT

Bailka was a fiery beauty, with dark auburn hair and blue-green eyes. Her mouth was dainty, her nose delicate, her breasts perfect. Her manner was always happy, lighthearted. When she was only thirteen, the boys in the neighbourhood already took notice. They could see she was in a class by herself.

Bailka's parents had no money. Her father, Red Zalmon, owned a cab, and earned barely enough to make ends meet. He was tall and well-built, with red hair and dark eyes, but he had the look of a desperate man. Something always seemed to be troubling him. Still, he and his wife had one great joy in life — their daughter, Bailka. When she walked to the village with her friends, Red Zalmon would sit in the cab, staring after her, his mouth half-open in a smile of pure pleasure. For her sake, he scrimped on every-thing, wouldn't even take a shot of whiskey. All this so that his Bailka should want for nothing.

When she turned fifteen, she met a young fellow of the same age, and right off they went everywhere together. He was tall and handsome, and he wore fine clothes. His pockets always jingled with money. His family was well set up with a shop in a prosperous part of town. Of course, the idea of having a cabbie in the family was not to their liking, and they tried to discourage the romance. But their son wouldn't listen. He said that he and Bailka were meant for each other.

In the evenings he would come to take her out for a stroll, and all the village mothers would come and sit in front of their houses to watch. "May no evil befall them," they'd sigh, beaming at the young couple. "What a lovely pair they are!" "It should only happen to our children.... "

So it went, for over a year. Then suddenly the young fellow stopped coming around. Bailka's mother never left the house, and the girl herself was not to be seen. Red Zalmon sat in his cab, drunk, and sometimes he was seen weeping bitterly.

No one wondered what happened. No one had to ask. At that time, in Poland, there was a strict moral code for women. All it took was a few guys to spread the word about having sex with a girl, and the cops would start a "black book" on her. She'd be known as a prostitute. Every month she would have to report to a doctor to check for venereal disease.

The game that was most popular with some of the guys went this way. A fellow would go out with a girl, and convince her that he really loved her and that they would marry someday. But in the meantime, he'd want to have sex with her. And the girl, being in love, would believe him and do as he asked. So her fate would be in his hands. Later, he might decide that he was through with her. Then there would be an outcry — but so what? It would all be forgotten soon enough.

Sometimes the game was played with a different angle. A guy might want to show his friends that he wasn't just anybody — that he knew how to win a girl and then drop her. So he'd get in cahoots with another fellow. This other fellow would come to a certain place at a time agreed upon, and there he would "surprise" the couple while they were having sex. The friend would then threaten the girl with public disgrace before her family and friends unless she'd put out for him too — at least that once. If the frightened girl gave in to his demands, she'd be caught in a net from which there was no escape. By the time another "friend" had asked for "just one time," there would be quite a few guys who knew about her. They'd make threats to expose her to the cops, and talk of the "black book," warning that she'd be no better than a common whore. Gradually she would become known to all the guys, and after that to the street thugs. Then, finally, she'd be forced into having sex with a whole gang at a time. On those occasions, two guys would walk out in front, with the dejected girl between them, and the others would follow about twenty feet behind, all of them joking loudly, as though they were on their way to a carnival. One thug who was almost always there in the gang was Shmuelkeh Baraban, a short, broad-shouldered guy with a pock-marked face. He was the favorite "hit man" for the younger set of gangsters in town, because he took such pleasure in beating up people.

When a bunch of guys planned an operation like that, it was called "a pact."

Bailka became the victim of one of those pacts. No matter how she twisted and turned she could see no way out of the trap. She was terrified of telling her parents, and of course her handsome sweetheart had vanished. She was abandoned to the streets. Once,

Shmuelkeh Baraban tried to force her to take his penis in her mouth. In her fury, she bit off a piece of it. The cops took him to the hospital and that's how Red Zalmon got the news. He went wild with rage, and beat his daughter so that no one could recognize her. Bailka's smiling face was seen no more.

The young fellows didn't take much notice of the loss, or of the drunken Red Zalmon. But they did take the time to make up a little song, which they laughingly hummed around town:

> *A knife will stain the foreskin red,*
> *Let Bailka bite it off instead!*
> *Ay, diddle diddle dum....*

Translated from the Yiddish
by R. Malmquist and Sacvan Bercovitch

Rochl Korn

GENERATIONS

For My Daughter

Loving another, yet she married my father.
That other portrait faded with the years.
From her album paged in musty velvet
Shimmered forth his paling, yellowing smile.

To watch her embroider a towel or tablecloth:
She pricked the vivid silk with her nostalgia.
The stitches flowed like narrow streams of blood.
The seams were silvered with her silent tears.

And my grandmother — how little I know of her life! —
Only her hands' tremor, and the blue seam of her lips.
How can I imagine my grandfather's love of her?
I can will myself to believe in her suffering.

No letter remains, no, not a scrap of paper
Did she will us; only old pots in the attic
Crudely patched: tangible maimed witnesses
To a dead life: the young widow, the mother of five.

So she planted a luxuriant garden
That would embrace the newly barren house
And her new barrenness. So the trees grew,
Obedient to her will, in perfect rows.

Now my daughter is just sixteen
As I was on that quiet day in May
When I became pregnant of a single word
Scented with lilac, the remote song of a bird.

A few letters, and what is called "a slender volume":
These are the relicts of my life. I lacked perspective
On happiness, so I ran ever faster
To escape the happy boundaries of my fate.

4

Listen, my daughter, never go in pursuit!
It all lies *there*, in the woven strands of blood.
How the straight trees whisper in grandmother's garden!
Only listen! These dim echoes in my poem ...

But what can sixteen years conceive of sorrow?
And pensiveness? the tremor of old lives?
For her, only the eternal beginnings.

Where she goes, old shadows kiss her footprints.
Somewhere, in white lilac, the nightingale
Gasps out his fragile song

Which ends always with the note of eternal beginning.

Translated from the Yiddish
by Carolyn Kizer

TO MY MOTHER

in place of the stone that would have marked her grave

Now you are gone and I live
all the days that were taken from you.
You flow into me so peacefully
as if I long ago became the shore to your dream.

I am more modest and discerning, mother.
I have all of autumn in me,
and in the leaf-fall of my days
I hear the sorrow destined to me.

I know that every journey to good fortune
ends with our return to childish tears,
our doorway in the ruins,
true to us when nothing else is.

And I know the heart's withholding;
how we wait for a glimpse a word a sound
and are left at the edge of our darkness
like an empty stalk in the summer sun.

And I know the word is only the spoor
left by errors that root themselves
in the untilled ground of our being, and the word is my
    bridegroom,
mated to me, binding me to the least light of day.

I know a great deal now, as if through folds
of earth you laid your hands on my head,
but even now, all I know stands poor and shamefaced
before your innocence.

Only you were fated to guide the wisdom of the heart
whole to the threshold of the lips,
so that the word would be home and daily bread
for all who were turned away by love.

Only you
trusted tears
to lead you to the very start of pain
no longer able to hide from itself.

And only you, only you were given
the encircling gaze, like a roof, like a wall,
that took into itself everything abandoned and alone,
from a sick swallow to a shamed, outstretched hand.

I have turned back from all my journeys to good fortune
to the deepest, the ultimate source of sorrow
and to the great innocence of your love:
it is stronger than death and my own loneliness.

Translated from the Yiddish
by Seymour Levitan

TEACHING YIDDISH

The children from my neighborhood
all come to me to learn Yiddish:
I tell them not to open their books,
I want to look at them and read
their faces as if they were pages
in a book; I want to know and be known,
so this is how I talk to them
without ever saying a word.

Dear boys and girls, Yiddish sons
and daughters, I want to teach you
what you've come to study but first
I have to learn how to read you I
have to write you and describe you
as you are and I don't really want
to be your teacher but an older
brother; so what shall we do?

First I think I'll read a story
by Sholem Aleichem just to see how much
you know about Yiddish laughter.
If you can laugh with real Yiddish flavor
at one of Sholem Aleichem's stories
I won't need further proof;
you'll do well with chumish in Yiddish
and even with gemorah in Yiddish,
and with literature naturally —
in what but Yiddish?

But you're laughing already
even before we get to Sholem Aleichem's
Motl Paisie the Cantor's son:
so today we're having our first lesson
in Yiddish laughter and all around me
shine your open faces and your lively eyes;
so let's tackle Sholem Aleichem head on
and go into a huddle of laughter.

Translated from the Yiddish
by Miriam Waddington

AT MY WEDDING

At my wedding
a red-haired madman fiddled
on the smallest gentlest little fiddle;
he played his sweet lament
and fabled song
while other fiddlers watched in dumb amazement.

Where did he learn it,
this red-haired simpleton?
When you consider that he lived and worked
in backward villages,
and played only at drunken gentile brawls;
if you can picture it, he could hardly
scratch together a handful of holy words —
not even to save himself.
As for sleeping, he bedded on a wooden bench,
and if a servant
gave him radishes from the master's garden,
he was fed.

It was at my wedding this poor devil played,
no one could stand still, yet all were rooted,
ears in the air like pointed spears,
while the little fiddle tenderly caressed
and fiercely scored the people,
tore them to bits, flayed them and drew blood
to all their veins
until strung as taut as violin strings
the old folk, doddering, cried out for mercy.

Translated from the Yiddish
by Miriam Waddington

Adele Wiseman

HODA*

Out of Shem Berl and Golda came Rahel. Out of Malka and Benyamin came Danile. Out of Danile and Rahel came Hoda. Out of Hoda, Pipick came, Pipick born in secrecy and mystery and terror, for what did Hoda know?

In the daytime her frail and ever-so-slightly hump-backed mother, or so they described her to blind Danile before they rushed them off to be married, used to take Hoda along with her to the houses where she cleaned. And partly to keep her quiet, and partly because of an ever-present fear, for she felt that she would never have another child, Rahel carried always with her, in a large, cotton kerchief, tied into a peasant-style sack, a magically endless supply of food. All day long, at the least sign of disquiet, she fed the child, for Hoda even then was big-voiced and forward, and sometimes said naughty things to people. Rather than risk having an employer forbid her the privilege of bringing the little girl to work, Rahel forestalled trouble. Things can't go in and out of the same little mouth simultaneously.

Hoda for her part enjoyed eating. She was on the whole a good-natured child. Even in the moments when her jaws were unwillingly at rest she was content to let her flecked ash-grey eyes linger contemplatively on the yellow and white dotted kerchief sack for what she felt were long periods of time while she restrained herself from disturbing her mother at her work. When at last she could refrain no longer, for she was only a child after all, Hoda would give vent to a surprisingly chesty contralto. "Ma-a-a," she would rumble, "Maa-a-a-a-ah!"

Rahel would rise quickly from her knees, wipe her hands, untie the kerchief, and give her daughter another little something to chew on. It amused some of her employers to see this continuous

*Chapter One of Adele Wiseman's novel *Crackpot*.

10

process, and they entertained themselves by feeding the child too, just to be able to comment, in what Rahel mistook for admiration, on how much she could put away. Hoda herself never refused these gifts of food, though there was something of aloofness, even of condescension, in her acceptance, as there is with some zoo animals that people feed for their own amusement. It was as though in allowing them to play their game she was not necessarily accepting their terms of reference. Occasionally a woman with kindly intentions would scold Rahel for letting her little girl get so fat. Rahel misinterpreted the kindly intentions and resented these critics who wanted her to deny her child. She saw in it simply another sign that it is the way of the rich to deny the poor, and continued to make sure that her child was bigger and more beautiful every day. Why else does a mother crawl on her knees in the houses of strangers?

Still others of the women whose homes she cleaned took advantage of the presence of the sack and allowed themselves to assume that since she had brought her own food they didn't have to provide any lunch for Rahel. Such days were hard for her, for she was too embarrassed to remind her employer that lunch had been agreed on between them when they discussed terms. At the same time she would rather starve than take food from her daughter's mouth, of which she considered the yellow sack to be a simple extension, as her own breasts had been once. So she worked through the long day of cramping hunger pains, tasting only her distaste, but still feeding Hoda all the while, automatically and without resentment.

Work was not easy to find, for she did not look very strong, and besides people did not like the idea of a Jewish woman hiring herself out to do what they considered to be demeaning tasks. On the other hand people felt sorry for her, hump-backed, with a blind husband sitting at home and a fat child to lug about. And they knew, for such things get around, though Danile and Rahel never spoke of it in public, how badly Danile's wealthy uncle had treated them when he had discovered that he had been tricked into sponsoring the immigration to the new world of the skeletons in the family closet. "Whaddaya want from me?" he told his wife, as they argued the matter night after night in bed. "Nobody told me they were cripples. Duds!" And he cursed his opposite number, Rahel's rich uncle in the old country, who had negotiated the affair with him so handsomely, and had, it turned out, at small expense rid himself of a chronic burden. "No wonder he's rich," raged the uncle of Danile, with a fine mixture of chagrin and admiration.

In effect, Uncle Nate had thrown them out, though he hadn't actually had to go that far, for Rahel, gentle always in her actions, though not necessarily in her judgements, had not waited for him to behave as badly as he gave indication that he was capable of doing. Gauging very quickly the temper of the uncle's household she had gone out, found and rented the shack, and moved her family into it. Then, since she had no other skill, she went among the neighbours and offered herself as a charwoman. In this at least she had plenty of experience. At home in the old country, before her unexpected marriage, she had been the one who had cleaned house and looked after the long line of little sisters her mother had conceived of her soldier father when he sent word he was in the vicinity and she made her periodic visits to the woods and fields near the camps where he was stationed.

At first, only the enemies of Uncle Nate took her in to clean for them, as a way of embarrassing the big man. But these people wanted at one and the same time to show that they were made of finer stuff than Nate and to make sure that Rahel did not expect special treatment, just because she was a Jew and related to wealth. Consequently they were the hardest to please, and Rahel ended up by doing most of her cleaning for people who were not much richer than herself and who would occasionally hire her, perhaps once or twice a year, when they needed a thorough turning out of their homes.

Sometimes, for all that her mother tried to prevent it, Hoda would get into trouble. There was one woman, for instance, who made fun of the child's chesty call of "Maa-a-a-a!" by counterpointing it with a nasal "Baaa-aaa!" like that of a catarrhal sheep. She repeated the game several times during the day. Each time the child turned unblinking eyes on her, with a solemnity that made her laugh, and continued to contemplate her ruminatively over her snack. Finally, the tease made the mistake of coming too close, and making her noise right in the little girl's face. With a lunge surprisingly swift in one who was almost wider than she was tall, Hoda clamped her teeth on her tormentor's nose, producing immediately a sharp improvement, if not in the pitch, at least in the sincerity of her utterance, an improvement which the child acknowledged at once with a hearty, wicked chuckle.

That was bad enough, but what was worse as far as Rahel was concerned was that she couldn't extract an apology from her normally tractable daughter. Hoda watched silently, growling in her throat behind her crust, her grey eyes smouldering, while her mother apologized and placated. She submitted passively while her mother spanked her to assuage the wounded nose of her employer, and even let out a theatrical bellow during the process, though all concerned knew that Rahel's hand landed very lightly, and the employer's humour had anyway taken a magnanimous turn by now and she was just as theatrically begging her cleaning woman not to beat the child on her account. She even brought a cookie as a peace offering, in token of forgiveness, and Hoda was pragmatic enough to accept the offer, with an ambiguous grunt which might have been taken to indicate forgiveness too.

When night came and Hoda was put to bed her blind father told her the good stories. These were real life, not yes and no and hush and shame shame say sorry. Daddy told her who she was and where she came from and what had happened. Real things.

"No," said Danile, "You wouldn't believe our luck, for on the surface aren't we the unluckiest people in the world? But study things, study and you'll see. God only seems to punish."

Listening from the kitchen, where she was cleaning up the supper dishes, Rahel argued in her mind as she would never do out loud.

God only seems to punish but your suffering is real, Danile.

"By the time I was seven years old," continued Danile, in that voice of his that was filled with awe, so that one thought he was about to reveal some wondrous accomplishment, "Yes, when I was not much older than you are now my little Hodaleh, I was already going blind."

Hoda snuggled closer. Danile rejoiced, holding her, his child, a big, soft, tangible circumference, all warmth and movement.

"I would stumble over things; the world shrank; there was fog everywhere. My mother said, 'Danile, what's the matter with you child, can't you see where you're going?' And I said, 'No, Mamma.' "

Hoda shuddered. Her father's voice always sounded strange when he said that part. "No, Mamma," not like a daddy voice at all.

" 'Danile, what's the matter with you?'

" 'I don't know, Mamma.' "

Why do you talk about it so much? thought Rahel. *Why does she have to know such things? She's strong and healthy. Nothing will happen to her, while I live.* But Rahel shuddered, too, sensing her own fragility.

"When my mother understood that I really couldn't see, she was furious, not so much with me as with herself. She said it was her own fault for not having watched over me carefully enough. She cursed the negligent moment when she must have left me long enough for me to turn my innocent eyes upward and look too boldly at the sun. Only a child or a fool will be bold enough to try to see into the sun, and for this the sun with his pitiless stare must have punished me. 'Why did you have to stare at the sun?' she used to ask, after all the journeys and medicines and incantations had failed to help me. 'What did you think you would find there? Foolish boy.'

"And I used to ask myself the same thing. I didn't know why I had stared at the sun, or when, even, though I knew I must have done as my mother said. Why then had I wanted to see into the sun? And what did I see? And why am I punished for it? Even now I sometimes think that if I knew what I had seen I wouldn't mind the punishment so much, though of course I know it's a nonsensical thought. God blinded me for reasons of His own, and the loss is nothing to the gain. For if I had not been blind and your mother had not been a little crooked many wonderful things would not have happened and you would probably never have been born. Shouldn't I call that luck?"

Hoda chuckled a happy assent.

Rahel had carefully placed another split log in the stove. Now she slammed the full kettle noisily on the hottest part so that it splashed and hissed. *Only a child or a fool....* All her life, all her childhood and all her girlhood she had prayed, at times with an almost demented intensity, for that deformity to disappear. For years she had gone nightly to bed, forcing herself every night to picture and to believe in the picture of herself arising the next morning and simply, luxuriously, stretching herself straight as everyone else did. That skew of her body wasn't really hers; she wasn't really that way. If they hadn't done that to her when they were in such a hurry to drag her into the world she would have been just like anyone else. Then suddenly, unexpectedly, perversely, her prayers had been granted. But instead of the miraculous disappearance of her deformity the humiliating miracle of her marriage had taken place, marriage to a man who would never be able to see her twisted body. Why then did he insist on crying it forth as a source of pride, as her particular, lucky charm? This was what exasperated Rahel, this and the fact that he wasn't even accurate about it. To listen to him you'd think she had God knows what between her shoulders, with his little crookedness and his humps and his lumps. And then there was also the high-handed way he had of dismissing it sometimes. There is a difference between having your deformity minimized and having it belittled. Rationally, she knew Danile was trying to do neither, knew and reproached herself because her objections were in themselves often contradictory. Still, it wasn't a hump on her back; it wasn't, properly speaking, really on her back at all. It was her right shoulder that was hiked up, but it didn't hunch her over. It just threw her somewhat out of kilter. Actually, it wasn't a hump at all. If she hadn't happened to be so small in build it might not even have been so noticeable, or so her mother had often said. A tall woman can carry these things off. But it was no use trying to point all this out to Danile. He wasn't interested in the anatomical fact. And in a way, if you followed his way of thinking, exclusive of all the other ways which the world knew and accepted, he was right. You can't hedge a miracle.

Once only Rahel had tried to argue with her husband over his interpretation of their fate. And he had explained to her, as though it were the key to all enigmas, that it stands to reason that God's open hand can be as terrible as His fist. Unconvinced, she had nevertheless felt petty and ashamed of the peevishness of her nature as compared with the generous innocence of his own.

"My father," he was saying now, "though he was only a tailor by trade, was a wise man. He used to say, 'It's God's will. You have a fine memory. Not many could have picked up so much by ear as you. And if you can't see the Holy Work you can hold it at least, feel it, keep it close to you, live with it. Even so you can be blessed.'

"I often ask myself, *How did he know?* For didn't the Book lead us past the barriers into the new world? Have I ever told you that story?"

"No," lied Hoda promptly.

"Danile," called Rahel. "Enough already. Put her to bed."

"No, Ma!" bawled Hoda.

"Just a minute more," said Danile. "I'm in the middle of a story. You and your mother were really the heroines of that one," he continued to the child, but speaking with transparent cunning, loudly enough to make Rahel smile in spite of herself.

"We had come all that long way, right to the edge of the big ocean I was telling you about, and one day your mother was talking to some woman, another immigrant, and this woman says to her, 'You don't think they're going to let you into the new world, you and your husband? They want only whole people in America.' An ordinary man, you understand, travelling with a child and a woman with a slight hump, well maybe. But a blind man too? No. You see my child, the new world is almost like heaven. They want you to be perfect before you get there, at least on the outside. In heaven of course they are more interested in what you are inside.

"Anyway, what did your mother do? From the day of our marriage, when they brought us home from the graveyard and we talked together for the first time, she had insisted that I was to go about like a modern Jew, beardless. Every day she shaved me herself. Now she comes running to the hut where we men slept, and she says to me, 'Danile, you must grow a beard. When our turn comes for the immigration examinations you must look like a serious scholar.'

"*What's this about a beard?* I ask myself. *Why all of a sudden a beard? A beard she wants? All right, I'll grow her a beard.* So I grew my beard. And while we waited for our summons she lectured me, over and over.

"'Remember, Danile,'" he imitated his wife's voice, to the delight of the child. "'Remember, Danile, the child on one arm, the book in the other hand, and held up to your face, as if you can't be pulled away from it for such trifling things as examinations and interrogations.'

"And when the time came at last I did exactly what she said, because when your mother says, she says. But I was so nervous I kept asking her, 'Is it all right, Rahel? Does it look all right?'

"And she would whisper back, 'It's fine, it's fine, only turn the page sometimes.'

"Well, that's all very easy when you're sitting down. But after a while we had to get up and move with the line, from one crowded room to another, each one more crowded and hotter than the last, and in each one my little daughter was growing bigger and heavier. Would you believe it, I could actually feel you grow? I knew my little girl was going to grow up but I didn't expect I would actually catch her in a growing moment. Let me tell you my juicy one it wasn't so easy to hold you that way, nonchalantly in one arm, growing as you were right there and then into such a sturdy little vessel. We had to wait a long time. My arm began to ache. I began to ache all the way down one side. I had to shift and heave you every time your mother reminded me to turn the page. Finally, I couldn't hang on to you with one arm any longer. You had simply grown too heavy. So I tried to slide you over so both arms would take some of the weight. Just then they called our names.

"Your mother grabs me under the arm to guide me, but pretending it's because she's frightened to leave my side, and also a little bit, probably, from the way she's pressing against me, to try to hide her shape. So she's dragging my tired arm one way, you're sliding the other way, and the book I'm supposed to hold in front of my face is sitting on my hand under your little behind. When I finally struggle it out and poke it up on the other side of you I hear your mother's voice whispering, 'It's upside down, Danile!'

"By this time I'm in such a sweat I don't know if she means the book is upside down or my daughter. So I begin to feel you around surreptitiously, and that's when you decide to let us all know which side is up. I must have wakened you with all that shifting and sliding, because suddenly you begin to roar out, blood-curdling bellows, like it seems to me I've never heard you cry before. That doctor couldn't believe it. 'Only nine months old?' he says. 'She's going to be a healthy citizen.' My heart jumps when I hear this. We're already citizens together. And while I'm soothing you and bouncing you with new strength and you, thank goodness, won't stop yelling, your mother deals with the officials. On their part they are in such a hurry to get rid of us they become even blinder than I am.

"'Yes that's fine, that's all. You can go.' When I heard those words I felt such a surge of friendship, I wanted to stop and thank them, but your mother wouldn't let me; she dragged me right out of there. When she got me out on the street she began to cry; 'What for? Now is no time for tears.'

" 'Oi, Danile, Oi Danile, the Book is still upside down!'

"But upside down though it was, and held by a blind man, it led us safely into this land. You see how right my father was? The Book is holy; knowledge is a wonderful thing if you know how to use it, even ignorant people, like your mother and myself. Sometimes I sit with the Book in my hand and think how close the Almighty has let me come to wisdom while I must remain so far. And yet, He lets His words come to our aid in His own way."

"All right, Danile," called Rahel, "Enough now. Let the child get to sleep."

"No ma!" bawled Hoda.

"Not that I'm completely ignorant," Danile continued, as though trying to correct a false impression. "While he lived my father would take me every day to the synagogue and I would learn with my ears, just as your mother and you take me now on the way to work. My ears are quicker than many another student's eyes. Often I heard far more than they could see. 'That's Reb Simcha coming in the door, scraping his feet so: chuff chuff chuff.' Or I'd call out, 'Shahmus, bang on the rail there, and shout for the women to keep quiet upstairs. Maya the herring is having an argument with Petya long-finger's wife.' And sometimes the Rov himself, not just the Shahmus, would shout up to them on my say-so: 'Women up there, Maya and Gitl! Be quiet! Aren't you ashamed to be arguing in the House of God?' And they would be silent in shame and in wonder that he had recognized and called them by name."

Hoda liked the funny parts. The quickness of her father's ears, though she had never seen them move, was a source of great pleasure. When she came home with her mother from work, while they were still blocks away from the house, she would try to coax her mother up on her toes, so that they should approach the house without him hearing. And when he called out, invariably, "Who's there?" as the door creaked open, she would rush forward with mingled disappointment and delight.

"You heard me! You heard me!"

And Danile would reply, "Oh no, I didn't hear you; I heard a tiny little mouse go 'squeak squeak squeak!' When did you come in?"

Rahel waited for them to finish laughing to call Danile finally away before he could begin to speak again. Left alone he would go on as long as the child demanded. Such was his nature. She could still remember those first few bewildering days of her marriage, which had been also the last few days of her mother-in-law's life. When Malka, known perversely in the town as Benyamin the tailor's needle, because she was so stout, had raved in her sickness, it had been Danile she had raved about, and his blindness, and the brightness he had stolen from the sun on the day of their contest, that brightness which she swore he had stored in him for ever, for he had a nature of extraordinary sweetness. Of course that was a mother's view. That same sweetness made some people feel that there was something unnatural about him, as though he were a little feeble-minded and incapable of truly understanding the gravity of his own plight. And incapable too, perhaps, thought Rahel, not for the first time, of feeling the insult of being married off to one they called a hunchback, a man as handsome as he, and under such circumstances too. And yet, he too had some cause to consider himself lucky, even to her way of thinking. If the plague hadn't carried her off so soon he might have found himself married to Selma the idiot, who slept in the fields and covered her head with her skirts when she heard a man approaching. Who would be looking after him now?

What more do you want from life, Rahel? she often asked herself as she went about her work, her mind not foreign to a certain private irony. *You have been nurtured by the open hand of God Himself. Who would have believed that even plagues can be good for somebody?*

As Danile told it, "What's a plague? A sickness. A cholera. In a plague everyone is blind together. It runs about of its own accord, invisibly, attacking without respect, rich and poor, high and low, good and bad. Plague has no favourites, except, so they say, it has a little bit more respect for Jews than for other people. It's true, it kills fewer Jews, and that's a fact. The others say to themselves, 'Look at that, the Jews are only lightly brushed by the plague; so few of them fall, while we are being carted off in wagonloads. It must be true they have a God!'

"But their priests and their leaders don't like that. So they say to them, 'Beware the Jews. They make evil magic that sends the plague your way. To get rid of the plague you must get rid of the Jews.' That's when these people become a plague in themselves, through their ignorance. When I stop to think of it, in actual fact your mother and I, with God's help, really saved the town from a double plague. Because of course it's all a lot of nonsense. They could see for themselves the only magic we made was the same magic they were making. We drew the same circles around our houses with charcoal to keep out the sickness. We too hung cloves of garlic and lumps of camphor in sachets around our necks for they have great strength in them to ward off plagues. You can smell their power. The only difference was that we had our God and no magic works without Him, and they want everything to come easily and if it doesn't come they go berserk.

"Well, that was in the old town, in the old country, where your grandmother lives still, and all your aunts, and maybe even your grandfather by now, though when last we heard he was still serving the Czar, poor man. If things hadn't gone so badly for him, and the Czar hadn't got such a murderously tight hold, how much easier life might have been for your mother's family. The trouble is there are so many things to look out for in life, and your grandfather, Shem Berl, is a simple, trusting soul. They put a paper in front of him and tell him to sign his release from the army, after ten long years, so he signs. Can he help it if he can't read Russian? So they toast him *tovarich*, and he finds he's signed on for another five years. So he serves his time honourably, as fine a tinker as you could meet in any army in the whole world, and when it comes time for his discharge they say to him, 'All right, Shem has served his time. Now what about Berl?'

"So he says, 'I'm Shem Berl.'

"But the Czar's tail won't hear of it. 'Two names, two soldiers for the Czar from your family! Shem has served and Berl must serve!' So Shem Berl called on both his dead grandfathers, after whom he was named, for double strength, and he served again.

"When the time came for him to be discharged a third time, he swore up and down he would sign no more papers. No one could hold him now. He was going home. And home he came, at last, to his wife, to his family, to his responsibilities. When he arrived he found the whole family in a turmoil, his wife biting her lips, his sisters wailing, his mother in hysterics. They had come, those brutes, to demand that his baby brother, who had grown up in his absence, should now serve his time. His mother was convinced the Czar had cast his evil eye all the way from Petersburg especially on her boys. She knew once her little Mendl was dragged off to the army he would never return, for if Shem Berl was desirable to the Czar, Mendl must be half again as desirable, for he was the joy of her old age.

"What was Shem Berl to do? His wife begged him; his daughters pleaded with him; his brother-in-law, your rich uncle Laib who sent us here, threatened him, but your grandfather shouldered his pack once again and gave himself as a substitute for his brother.

"That's how it came about that in the time of the plague, luckily for us all, he was far away, for had he been home he might not, poor man though he was, have allowed them to take his daughter, even for the sake of the dowry. He had too much pride. But now was not the time for pride. Now was a dreadful time. Even sitting at home, for my mother would not allow me out of the house, and hearing the stories of what was happening, and the cries and the groans of the sick and the bereaved in the streets, and without ever imagining the part I was to play, I knew that such frightful events were meant to show something, if only a man had the wisdom to understand. People fell to their beds like wheat in the fields, tossing and turning and flinging themselves about senselessly like grain being winnowed in God's private machine. Many flew straight into the afterlife, where the Almighty must have made a very fine loaf of his harvest, for some of the town's best never stood upright in this world again.

"They tried everything to fight it. Soon there was not a clove of garlic to be bought anywhere in our district at any price. Nothing helped. The sickness held its breath and fell upon people and turned them inside out before the strength of the medicine could take hold. It leaped over the black rings of safety and raged within the barriers as fiercely as without. Once it had forced its way into a person it burned, it flamed, it tore out everything he had inside of him and sent it blazing out both ends.

"I know. I heard it. I think I actually heard it enter our house. I know I heard it edging into my mother's voice. I could hear it in her breath. I heard it wrestling with her. I heard her pleading with it. I heard its cry of triumph when she fell writhing on the bed. At first she tried to help herself. Then she couldn't. She could only struggle. That wretched smell grew stronger. Her cries went on and on. I wanted to help her, but she kept screaming, 'Don't come near me, Danile! Stay away! Don't you come near me!' in such a voice, as though I were another enemy. I didn't know what to do. I wanted to fetch help, but she screamed at me not to leave the house. The plague was all over, out there, waiting for me.

"Not to come, not to go, not to be able to see, not to know what to do. I went to the door. I shouted out, 'People, help! People, have mercy! People, save my mother! Help us!' No one listened. No one came. I wept. I asked my God why He had made me less than a man. Then I took my Book, and I held it in my hands, and I sang. To drown out her suffering I sang, not to hear her cries so nakedly and so that she should not hear me weeping I sang all the holy words that I knew, ignoramus that I am, over and over again, in the strongest voice I have so that perhaps, if nothing else, the power of the words and the strength of my voice alone would sustain her with the help of God.

"And she was still alive when they came. At first, when they burst into the house, and they cried out joyously, 'She's still alive!' I thought that they had come to try to save her. But that was not to be. They were glad for another reason.

"You see my child, these plagues do not concern simply individual persons. They are not simply a matter of this one collapsing and that one dying and of one blind boy's sorrow. Things had by this time reached a point where the whole community was threatened, not only by the epidemic itself but by the madness of the surrounding peasants. They were jealous because the Jews were not dying off as quickly as they, and word had come that unless by some miracle the sickness could be banished they would fall on us and destroy what the disease had not dared to touch.

"It was a time for desperate measures. The beautiful ones of the town came together to confer, those who were not too frightened or too afflicted, the wise and the holy and even one or two of the rich. Among them was your mother's uncle.

"When all else fails there is an action which can be taken, a gesture which, made properly and with God's blessing, can restore the forces of life where only the forces of death reigned before. The beautiful ones knew that the time had come to make this gesture.

"Now the thing to do is to take the two.... "

Rahel noticed that Danile always hesitated slightly at this point, as though even he were flinching at what he was about to say. But the hesitation was so slight it was perhaps perceptible only to her, or perhaps she only imagined that he was flinching too.

"...they take the two poorest, most unfortunate, witless creatures, man and woman, who exist under the tables of the community; they dig them up, he out of his burrow in the woods, she from the heap of rags in which she crouches, and they bring them together to the field of death. It is the tradition to take the craziest and the most helpless you can find. Who else would go? But after all the community is trying to do them a favour too. The town provides the bride with a dowry, furnishes, if they are homeless, a little mud hut for them, and undertakes to look after them. Everything is done just as for a proper wedding, which they would never have been able to afford for themselves. Indeed, usually they did not have the wit to know what it was all about anyway, and wandered off to their own separate burrows afterwards.

"So the beautiful ones decided that now was the time to marry off such a pair and lift the curse of the plague and the threat of the pogrom from our heads. But whom to choose? There was a shortage of idiots in our community that year. The man the children called Golgol had been killed in a pogrom the year before. When everyone else was barricaded behind doors and the bandits were approaching he suddenly ran out from somewhere, beckoning to them and shouting in the friendliest fashion, 'Kill Jews! Kill Jews!' Strong as an ox he was. He was still running and they were still shooting bullets into him long minutes later. And the unfortunate Selma, a true grotesque; I remember her from when I could still see; she too had been taken off by the plague.

"So your mother's uncle spoke up. He reminded the others of his eldest niece, far from an idiot, of course, a very intelligent girl, and not even homely; and furthermore, he dared say, and who would dare deny? from a decent family; indeed she was herself a hard-working, good-natured girl, as who should know better than he, the child of his own sister? Hers was merely the slightest deformity; nevertheless if the town were to offer a reasonable dowry, he himself would contribute to the cost of a marriage not dishonourable. He was in a position to influence his sister; she would see the sense in it, and the community would, naturally, in gratitude, keep their pact with the Almighty and continue to take care of the couple, if, that is, a suitable mate could be found. He's a clever man our uncle. And we can't blame him entirely. He had daughters of his own to provide with dowries.

"Then someone else remembered that I had been seen at the door of our hut, weeping and pleading with the world to come to the aid of my mother. My father was dead, my mother dying, my prospects poor. If by chance my mother was still alive I would be a logical groom. If my mother was gone already it would be too late. The situation was too desperate for them to be able to wait over a period of mourning.

"That was when they came running to our house. At the same time the uncle hastened to speak to your poor grandmother. What could she do? If it was anything like the way it happened to me she did not get much time to think about it. Nor did your mother. They carried her off for the examination, saw that she was whole, that is healthy, and took her to the ritual bath."

Rahel squirmed but dared not interrupt. If the child asked for an explanation here, then she would really put her foot down, she promised herself. Why he had to go through every little detail she didn't know, she really didn't. But Hoda was too engrossed at this point to ask questions.

"As for me," Danile was saying, "before I knew it I was being led — no, dragged — no, carried from the house. It was a hot day, clammy. I struggled like a wild thing, slithering about in their hands and my sweat. They had a hard time holding me. They tried to explain what we were about to do but all I knew was that I should not be leaving my mother now, without a voice to cry out for her. 'Have mercy on her,' I pleaded with them, over and over again.

" ' Yes, yes,' they made me hear them finally. 'Don't worry. She will be taken care of. The plague will disappear if you come with us now. God will aid us, if you will come.'

"Their words forced me to begin to realize what it was all about. I had been begging for God's help. Dared I refuse to play my part? Perhaps it was fated. If this was so I must be calm. My heart must cease flinging itself about. I must no longer weep like a child. I must make no sound. I must pay attention, yes, perhaps for the first time in my life. There was a question being asked and soon, soon, perhaps even now, I and only I would be called on to reply. But how reply? Who was I? What was my attention worth? Strain though I might, I would never suffice. All I could know was my immeasurable ignorance. *Very well,* I thought, *if that is all I can know let me know that at least.* And even as I was floundering thus, words fell away. I became one living alertness. Nothing could pass me by. Everything that existed had to pass through me, even the breeze that sprang up and whispered in my face as we approached the home of the dead. They led me carefully here, for there were many newly dug graves. I trod on damp clumps of newly turned sod that seemed to move beneath my feet like living things. That was so; there was no stillness anywhere. There was only movement, anticipation, the breath of the universe. And I was no longer a blind boy being led beneath the canopy to meet his unknown bride in the village of the dead. Do trees have eyes? What can the stars see? I saw what they saw and I knew what they knew then. Don't ask me what it was, I couldn't grasp the wholeness of it for long, but for one moment I knew, I acquiesced, and I was known.

"Since that moment I have never been truly afraid, not in the holy way, with the fear a man might wish for. Ordinary fear I knew again, and soon. Who marries without tasting that? That returned when I felt Rahel at my side and knew she was trembling too. Who was I to have a bride trembling beside me? I was so frightened I don't even remember how it went, what they said, how I replied. I fumbled for a long time with a ring and a soft little hand that kept disappearing. It was not so much that I couldn't see, but all of them, the ring, my hands, her hand, wouldn't stop moving, all in different directions. Finally, a gentle little voice took pity on me, as she has taken pity on me ever since. 'Let me,' she whispered, and all was well."

Danile knew that Rahel did not entirely approve of his habit of giving the child a detailed version of these events. But once he had begun to speak it was hard for him to leave off trying to describe the way it had felt and what it had meant. If he told too much, well, those things the child wouldn't understand anyway. They would pass her by. But because he felt a little guilty about it, he always tried, when he suspected he might have talked too much, to round off his tale with a compliment to Rahel, to smooth the edge of her disapproval. It was by way of a little gift, and as he spoke he meant it, discovering as he went along the truth in every word he said; but it was often so awkwardly dragged in, or else so triumphantly emphasized, that it managed, by its very incongruity, to make her laugh when she would have liked to scold.

Hoda herself would accept no abridgements or truncations. If he varied his description she would backtrack with him, collating the versions. Sometimes Danile had a hard time remembering what he had said last time. But the child did not forget.

"What did the sun say?" demanded Hoda.

"The sun? What did the sun say? Well now, oh yes, the sun peeked in under the canopy while the ceremony was going on and he said, 'Look at that. He's found himself the prettiest pair of eyes in the whole village.'"

Hoda laughed her satisfaction. "And what happened when you came home?"

"I said to your mother, 'I'm sorry, my mother is sick.'"

"And she replied, 'Yes, I've heard.' And straightaway she set to work looking after us both, as though it were meant to be and it had always been."

"But did Bobba really die?" asked Hoda, who fought and strained through her grandmother's illness, every time her father described it, trying to keep her alive.

"Yes. She lived long enough to make it possible for us to save the community, but when the turning point came in our fortunes she did not have the strength to climb back to life. Who would have imagined that would be possible? My beautiful mother. She was the sturdiest woman in the village. Why, even when I was fully grown, and they say I am quite a tall man, I couldn't get both my arms all the way around her. You take after her. I can tell by the feel of you."

"I wouldn't die," said Hoda.

"Of course not," said Danile hastily. "Only in build, not in fate, please God."

"You see what you get?" muttered Rahel.

"And the plague went away?" asked Hoda, checking off the familiar items to make sure.

"Yes, of course," said Danile. "That was the wonder of it. Almost immediately, the plague began to disappear. Some people even got well again, and that's a sure sign of the power of our wedding."

"And the pogrom went away?"

"There was no pogrom. The plague left them too."

"What happened then?" Hoda was persistent.

"Well, then we settled down. Everybody was very grateful to us, at first, anyway. They saw to it that we had food to eat. And then of course your mother is such a good housekeeper that she stretched out what we had."

"And then?"

"And then time passed. Well, you can't blame people entirely. While the danger is there they will do anything, be grateful to anybody. When the crisis is past they begin to forget how it felt; they have other problems and the obligation begins to seem as much of an imposition as the original danger. I don't know; it's hard to figure it all out. There seems to be something not quite altogether between time and place and feelings and events. The pieces don't match up; they won't hold still, the right time, the right place in life, the right feeling, the right length and strength for each. It never lasts long enough or it comes too late, or it doesn't matter any more to one and it matters too much to another; there are just too many pieces, each reaching for the others, and each being swept along in a different direction. You can't blame people. They don't know enough to be able to piece it all together. They can't even hold still themselves. That's why I want you to go to school, and study. When your moment comes, I want you to be prepared to know what it means."

"So what did you do?" asked Hoda, in a voice which, to her mother, sometimes seemed to have a kind of inexorable sternness; as though the child already knew enough to disagree, or at least to keep her own counsel.

"Do? Nothing really. We kept alive." Danile too was sometimes made vaguely uneasy by the intensity with which the child kept after the story, though he could not resist her interest for long.

"What about my sister?" asked Hoda.

"What about her?" said Danile, stalling, for he could feel Rahel's disapproval in the air. Why shouldn't the child know that she had had a sister? Why shouldn't the poor little thing have her brief existence acknowledged?

"Malka," Hoda prompted.

"A name for my mother," said Danile tenderly. "Who could foresee such luck? And she was perfect, absolutely perfect. I ought to know. Didn't I hold her in my two hands with your mother buzzing at me to be careful, please be careful, as though I had to be told? Even the midwife said she was perfect. Whatever they said afterwards and for whatever reason the Almighty snatched her away again so soon, she was not a crippled child."

Of course she wasn't! A familiar resentment boiled up in Rahel, smarting in her eyes. *Perfect, perfect.*

"She was delicate, yes," Danile went on; "too small, too thin, too exhausted with the effort of being born too soon to be able to continue to pump her own life for long. That's what the midwife said, or something like that. When she stopped breathing, your mother and I said nothing to each other, but I knew that we both had the same thought. Perhaps it simply wasn't meant for people like us to bring children into the world. That thought was black enough, but when our uncle came to offer his condolences, we found out that it was not such a new idea. Many people had been thinking the same thing all along."

Rahel could not contain herself. "You wouldn't have thought they would take such an interest," she burst out, "from the way they had been forgetting all their fine promises to us. For all they cared we could have starved a dozen times over. Whenever someone felt in extra need of a good deed to be recorded with the One Above to offset something he felt guilty about below, he'd throw a coin our way, or send some food from the bottom of his table. For this we were dragged through the streets to stand miserable among the dead."

Hoda stirred as her mother spoke. Her mother seldom joined in the stories, but when she did something happened to them; new feelings came into them that made her uneasy. For some reason that she could not fathom, because her mother was the softest, safest person in the world, the stories hurt more when her mother helped to tell them.

"It's true," said Danile gravely. "If it were not for your mother running to the baker's and sitting up with the dough all night while it was rising, to prevent it from spilling all over the ovens, weeks would have gone by without us tasting either a piece of bread or the bite of herring she earned in the marketplace by day."

"And now," Rahel continued as though to herself, so that the child had to crane to hear, "my fine uncle comes and in so many words he congratulates us for having the good sense to lose our child. In spite of hard times, he tells us, the town is willing to continue to support us. But there are some people who are grumbling that we are taking advantage of them. There are some who say that wards of the town have no right to raise a family at the town's expense. And there are some who say that it is not fair to bring more crippled children into the world for others to take care of. Crippled! Oh of course, says uncle, he personally is not one of these people, but he can see their point. And we can see his point well enough. If the town should decide that we have forfeited the right to even the pretence that they are helping us, the burden would be his."

"Well, we can't entirely blame … " said Danile.

"No wonder she did not have the strength to go on breathing," continued Rahel in a whisper, "with the weight of the disapproval of all those beautiful people lying down on her. No wonder she couldn't breathe."

"So I said to him," said Danile quickly, to distract the child from the fact that her mother was weeping. "I said, 'We are not wards of the town. We are wards of the One Above, entrusted to the town.'

"And he said, 'Since when are you such a big philosopher? You sit and talk to the Book all day with nothing to worry about. Everything is brought to you. Has the Book begun to answer you already, that you're splitting hairs with me?'

"Not that I can blame him entirely; what he said was true. But it was no answer. And I wanted to tell him so. I wanted to tell him that we did not need the town's help if they chose to go so against the spirit of our covenant. But I was afraid that he would reply as he had the right to, that it was all very well for me to sit and play at being proud, for I had a frail and delicate creature, his own niece, working day and night to support me. A man like me is in no position to tell a man like Uncle anything at all. So I kept silent, and since he is not really such a harsh man through and through, he likes simply to have his own way, but wants no hard feelings if he can help it, when he left, to show that all was well between us, Uncle gave us a very generous tip."

"We couldn't afford to throw it in his face," sighed Rahel.

"I'm surprised you didn't," said Danile. "Do you know that same rich uncle never dared say a word to your mother against her father? With your grandmother he would curse and rave, but when your quiet little mother was around, not a word about Shem Berl the soldier. Well, we too can be charitable. So we kept the money. Why should we deprive him of a generous gesture to his credit Above? Poor Uncle. If only he could have foreseen the result of his visit he might not have ended it with such an expensive flourish. He would have kept his hand in his pocket and saved the money for our travel fare. It's a fact, if he had not come and upset us that day, you might never have been born. But that very night you began to knock on the door of life, saucy little one that you are. Had we not been so disturbed and unable to sleep we would probably never have heard you. Instead, while your mother and I lay weeping, you called out to us, and we heard you say, 'Where is it written that the townspeople, even the most beautiful ones, can give orders to the source of life? What is meant to be will be!' And though we were afraid to take the risk of so much disappointment again, in the end we could not resist your voice."

"And you opened the door?" asked Hoda, beaming expectantly.

"Yes!"

"And I came?"

"And you came."

"And Uncle was mad?"

"Mad? Mad enough to cudgel that clever head of his and do us a real favour at last. Who ever thought that blind Danile too would live to see the new world?"

"And I didn't even die!" Hoda laughed triumphantly, her voice trumpeting out, as though her arrival and survival were a signal victory for the forces of virtue. Danile could not resist her laughter and laughed with her, with something of the same triumphant innocence in his voice. Rahel, who could not laugh so easily, was nevertheless strangely touched. Her impulse, always, was to protect these two, but at times she had the not entirely comfortable feeling that they could, in some ways, take care of themselves far better than she knew. But that was something else, something apart from the twenty-four real hours a day during which they needed her, the real life, feet-on-the-ground, world-on-your-shoulders, hours. Perhaps that was what her hump was for, to balance the world on. Rahel found herself laughing too. *If that's what it's for I'm not complaining. Just let me lug my load around a little longer.*

Twenty-four real hours, a hundred little things an hour. If she hadn't been attentive to what was happening in the real world, and quick to react, she might still be going from one grocery store to another, trying to find a nugget of camphor like the one that she was even now sewing a little bag for, to hang around Hoda's neck. The minute she had heard talk of the danger of an epidemic of infantile paralysis in the city she had known what to do. Straight to the grocer! She had paid a whole dollar! And even so the grocer had told her she was lucky that he still had a few cubes left. There had been a rush on camphor in drug and grocery stores all over the city. Well, thank goodness; far-flung and strange in its ways though it was, the new world was not so entirely barbaric as to be without some acquaintance with the life-preserving medicaments.

A. M. Klein

PSALM XXXVI: A PSALM TOUCHING GENEALOGY

Not sole was I born, but entire genesis:
For to the fathers that begat me, this
Body is residence. Corpuscular,
They dwell in my veins, they eavesdrop at my ear,
They circle, as with Torahs, round my skull,
In exit and in entrance all day pull
The latches of my heart, descend, and rise —
And there look generations through my eyes.

ONCE IN A YEAR*

Once in a year this comes to pass:
My father is a king in a black skull cap,
My mother is a queen in a brown perruque,
A princess my sister, a lovely lass,
My brother a prince, and I a duke.

Silver and plate, and fine cut-glass
Brought from the cupboards that hid them till now
Banquet King David's true lineage here.
Once in a year this comes to pass,
Once in a long unroyal year.

*From a longer poem, *Haggadah*.

SONNETS SEMITIC
V

Now we will suffer loss of memory;
We will forget the tongue our mothers knew;
We will munch ham, and guzzle milk thereto,
And this on hallowed fast-days, purposely ...
Abe will elude his base-nativity.
The kike will be a phantom; we will rue
Our bearded ancestry, my nasal cue,
And like the Gentiles we will strive to be.
Our recompense — emancipation-day.
We will have friend where once we had a foe.
Impugning epithets will glance astray.
To Gentile parties we will proudly go;
And Christians, anecdoting us, will say:
"Mr. and Mrs. Klein — the Jews, you know.... "

AUTOBIOGRAPHICAL

Out of the ghetto streets where a Jewboy
Dreamed pavement into pleasant Bible-land,
Out of the Yiddish slums where childhood met
The friendly beard, the loutish Sabbath-goy,
Or followed, proud, the Torah-escorting band,
Out of the jargoning city I regret,
Rise memories, like sparrows rising from
The gutter-scattered oats,
Like sadness sweet of synagogal hum,

Like Hebrew violins
Sobbing delight upon their Eastern notes.

Again they ring their little bells, those doors
Deemed by the tender-year'd, magnificent:
Old Ashkenazi's cellar, sharp with spice;
The widows' double-parloured candy-stores
And nuggets sweet bought for one sweaty cent;
The warm fresh-smelling bakery, its pies,
Its cakes, its navel'd bellies of black bread;
The lintels candy-poled
Of barber-shop, bright-bottled, green, blue, red;
And fruit-stall piled, exotic,
And the big synagogue door, with letters of gold.

Again my kindergarten home is full —
Saturday night — with kin and compatriot:
My brothers playing Russian card-games; my
Mirroring sisters looking beautiful,
Humming the evening's imminent fox-trot;
My uncle Mayer, of blessed memory,
Still murmuring *maariv*, counting holy words;
And the two strangers, come
Fiery from Volhynia's murderous hordes —
The cards and humming stop.
And I too swear revenge for that pogrom.

Occasions dear: the four-legged *aleph* named
And angel pennies dropping on my book;
The rabbi patting a coming scholar-head;
My mother, blessing candles, Sabbath-flamed,
Queenly in her Warsovian perruque;
My father pickabacking me to bed
To tell tall tales about the Baal Shem Tov —
Letting me curl his beard.
Oh memory of unsurpassing love,
Love leading a brave child
Through childhood's ogred corridors, unfear'd!

The week in the country at my brother's — (May
He own fat cattle in the fields of heaven!)

Its picking of strawberries from grassy ditch,
Its odour of dogrose and of yellowing hay —
Dusty, adventurous, sunny days, all seven! —
Still follow me, still warm me, still are rich
With the cow-tinkling peace of pastureland.
The meadow'd memory
Is sodded with its clover, and is spanned
By that same pillow'd sky
A boy on his back one day watched enviously.

And paved again the street: the shouting boys,
Oblivious of mothers on the stoops,
Playing the robust robbers and police,
The corncob battle — all high-spirited noise
Competitive among the lot-drawn groups.
Another day, of shaken apple trees
In the rich suburbs, and a furious dog,
And guilty boys in flight;
Hazelnut games, and games in the synagogue —
The burrs, the Haman rattle,
The Torah dance on Simchas Torah night.

Immortal days of the picture calendar
Dear to me always with the virgin joy
Of the first flowering of senses five,
Discovering birds, or textures, or a star,
Or tastes sweet, sour, acid, those that cloy;
And perfumes. Never was I more alive.
All days thereafter are a dying off,
A wandering away
From home and the familiar. The years doff
Their innocence.
No other day is ever like that day.

I am no old man fatuously intent
On memories, but in memory I seek
The strength and vividness of nonage days,
Not tranquil recollection of event.
It is a fabled city that I seek;
It stands in Space's vapours and Time's haze;

Thence comes my sadness in remembered joy
Constrictive of the throat;
Thence do I hear, as heard by a Jewboy,
The Hebrew violins,
Delighting in the sobbed Oriental note.

GENESIS*

For many years my father — may he dwell in a bright Eden! — refused to permit in his presence even the mention of that person's name. The mere imminence of an allusion to my uncle soon brought my father to an oblique deliberative ominous knuckle-combing of his beard, a sombre knitting of his brow, and froze at last his face to the stony stare Semitic. The tabu was recognized, and the subject was dropped.

Not that my father was by nature a furious man; he was, as a matter of fact, kind and gentle and of a very forgiving disposition; but on this question he was adamant, as unappeasable, as zealous for the Law, as was the Bible's fanatic Phineas. It was not necessary, he said, that in his house, which was by God's grace a Jewish house, there should be jabber and gossip about "the renegade", "that issuer to a bad end"; in our family we had names better distinguished with which to adorn conversation; we didn't have to be reminded of the branch lopped from the tree; the children could attune their ears to seemlier discourse; and — let it be God who judged him.

At this everyone would fall into a reminiscent sad silence, particularly my mother, who would brood awhile on the fate of her younger brother, and then, banishing wilfully her unhappy thoughts, would fix the wisp of hair errant from beneath her perruque and would rise to serve tea, in glasses, each with its floating moon of sliced lemon.

My uncle's name had not always been so unwelcome beneath my father's roof. I remember well how important a part, a magic incantatory part, his name played in the early days of my childhood. I was making my first acquaintance with the letters of the Hebrew alphabet — the old Tannenbaum, round little pygmy of eighty, bearded to the breastbone, was my teacher — and I recall how it was his custom, as I struggled with the vowel signs — those beneath the letters, like prompters prompting, and those beside

*Chapter One of A.M.Klein's
 novel *The Second Scroll*.

the letters, like nudgers nudging, and those on top, like whisperers whispering — how it was his custom to encourage me forward from each mystic block to the next with repeated promise of pennies from heaven. The angel who presided over my lesson, he would say, would drop down candy money if I did my lesson well. The angel kept his word, of course, and as his unseen coins suddenly hit and twirled on the big-lettered page, my mother would sigh, and exclaim: "Oh, that he might be like his uncle Melech, a scholar in Israel!"

I never saw my uncle Melech, but reports of his Talmudic exploits kept sounding in our house and there made a legend of his name. To Montreal, to our modest address on the Avenue de l'Hôtel de Ville, there came from Volhynia letter after letter, penned in the strange script of eastern Europe — all the sevens wore collars — letters twittering the praises of the young man who at the age of twenty had already astounded with his erudition the most learned rabbis of the Continent. Dubbed the *Ilui* — the prodigy of Ratno — it was in these epistles written of him, amidst a clucking of exclamation marks, that he had completely weathered the ocean of the Talmud, knew all its bays and inlets, had succeeded in quelling some of its most tempestuous commentators; that one had not imagined that in these latter days it were possible that such a giant of the Law should arise, one had not thought that one so young could possibly excel sages twice and thrice and four times his age; but the fact was none the less incontestable that the most venerable scholars, men as full of Torah as is the pomegranate of seeds, did time and again concede him the crown, declaring that he was indeed as his name indicated, Melech, king.

Nor was he, as are so many of the subtle-scholarly, any the less pious for his learning. The six hundred and thirteen injunctions of Holy Writ, or at least those that remained binding and observable in the lands of the Diaspora, he sedulously observed; punctilious he was in his ritual ablutions; and in his praying, a flame tonguing its way to the full fire of God. He was removed from worldly matters: not the least of his praises was that he knew not to identify the countenances on coins.

My parents were very proud of him. He represented a consoling contrast to the crass loutish life about us where piety was scorned as superstition, and learning reviled as hapless, and where Jews were not ashamed to wax rich selling pork. This last was a

barb aimed by my father at his cousin, a man of religious preten-
tions, yet by trade a pork-vendor, whom my father delighted to
mimic, showing him in the act of removing an imaginary pork loin
from its hook, slapping it onto its wrapping paper, and then, so as
to wet the paper — this was the fat of the jest — licking his fingers
enthusiastically.... Surrounded by such uncouthness, it was good
to have the recollection of the young Talmudist cherishing Torah
in its integrity, continuing a tradition that went back through the
ages to Sura and Pumbeditha and back farther still and farther to
get lost in the zigzag and lightning of Sinai.

Curious to know what this paragon worthy of my emulation
looked like, I asked my mother one day whether she had a photograph of Uncle Melech. "A photograph!" My mother was shocked.
"Don't you know that Jews don't make or permit themselves to
be made into images? That's the second commandment. Uncle
Melech wouldn't think of going to a photographer." I had to
content myself, aided by my mother's sketchy generalities, with
imagining Uncle Melech's appearance. Throughout the decades
that followed, this afforded me an interesting pastime, for as the
years went by and I myself changed from year to year, the image of
Uncle Melech that I illegally carried in my mind also suffered its
transformations.

When the first sign came that such a retouching of the photograph would soon be necessary, we did not know it for what it was.
I was ten years old, it was the Feast of Rejoicing in the Law, and my
father was at the synagogue when the letter from Uncle Melech
was dropped through the slot over our threshold. My mother, who
could not read — her respect for learning, I often thought later,
stemmed largely from this fact — anxious to know who was speaking to her from afar, immediately dispatched me, with the letter,
to my father. The synagogue was brightly illuminated throughout,
even in those parts where no service was going on. On the tables
reserved for study, there lay holy books, some of them still leafy
with twigs of myrtle between the pages, last remnants of the
Succoth ritual, serving now as bookmarks; but in the centre of the
synagogue, about the *almemar* and before the Ark of the Covenant, there was sound and exaltation. Wine had been drunk, and
the Torah was being cherished with singing and dance.

As every year, the old Kuznetsov was already ecstatically exhilarated; his beard awry, his muddy features shiny pink, his very
pockmarks hieratic like unleavened bread, he was dancing — a

velvet-mantled scroll in his arms — with a fine other-worldly abandon, as his friends clapped hands in time. The cantor kept trilling forth pertinent versicles, answered by the congregation in antiphon. A year of the reading of the Law had been concluded, a year was beginning anew, the last verses of Deuteronomy joined the first of Genesis, the eternal circle continued. Circular, too, was the dance, a scriptural gaiety, with wine rejoicing the heart, and Torah exalting it to heights that strong wine could not reach.

My father, a copy of the Pentateuch before him, stood watching the sacred circle, smiling. Not a demonstrative man, he felt that joy had worthier means of expression than hopping feet; a shrewd man, too, he could not resist the reflection that most of those who were now jubilant with Torah either did not see Torah from year's end to year's end or, seeing, looked on it as knowingly as did the rooster on the page of the prayer of *Bnai Adam*. None the less, my father stood there smiling, smiling and happy, happy to see Torah honoured even if only by hearsay.

I showed him the letter. "From Uncle Melech," he said, "that's a good letter for Simchas Torah." We withdrew to a more secluded spot in the synagogue. Looking up over his elbow as he read it, I saw that a number of words on the thin sheets were carefully, though not illegibly, blocked out, as if laid out in little coffins. I noted, too, that as my father read, from page to page his mood changed. The elation of a few minutes before left him. His nostrils widened and soon his lower lip was quivering. Tears slid down his face, to get caught, shining, in the hairs of his beard.

I looked up at my father, whom I had never seen weeping before, nor ever did again except for the time, two years before his passing, when on the High Holidays he joined in the prayer: *And in our old age cast us not aside, as our strength fails forsake us not....*

"A pogrom," my father said quietly, "a pogrom in Ratno."

That night as from my bed I eavesdropped on the conversation of my father and mother, I learned the details of Uncle Melech's letter — of how the Balachovtzes, driving ahead of the fleeing Bolsheviks, had entered Ratno, and of how, summoning to their ranks the peasants of the region — yesterday's friends and neighbours — they had robbed and pillaged and murdered. The marked-out blocks on the letter, I gathered from the snatches of talk, from the choked sobbings that came in the dark of my room to my pillow, were the names of those who were no longer among the living: the old rabbi, Rabbi Heshel; Israel Meyer, the shochet, slaughtered with his own knife; our cousin Aryeh Leib, Yentel Baila's son; both daughters of Braina, the potter's daughter; and others, and others — names that I had heard often before, connected with some holy parable or comic anecdote, which now moved about my bedstead like ghosts.

There was also something else in that letter to which not much attention was paid that night: Uncle Melech's tone of bitterness. It was unmistakable. It is true that he quoted passages from the Bible enjoining resignation, but he also quoted Jeremiah: *Wherefore doth the way of the wicked prosper? Wherefore are all they happy that deal very treacherously?*

The letters from Uncle Melech that followed during the months thereafter contained no further reference to the massacre. Nor were they, as they had always been, any longer marked by witty allusion, or novel interpretation of Gemara, or parable and homily. Beginning with formal and flattering salutation, they reported that his health was good, inquired after ours, and in the more recent letters sought information about life in Canada. It was clear that something grave had taken place, not only in the four cubits of my uncle's ambience, but in his very soul. My father discussed with my mother sending him a ticket to come to Montreal. This was a sacrificing gesture, for my father's savings were meagre; my mother feigned to propound all the arguments against such generosity, and finally my father sent a letter to Uncle Melech in which he made the suggestion that he would pay for his transportation and that he should leave forever the land of *Fonya Swine*.

To that letter there came no reply.

It was about a year later that there were brought to our house, on a Saturday night, two strangers, just arrived from Halifax, where they had debarked after their ocean voyage from Ratno via Liverpool. Their suits were cut different from ours. They wore caps. Their faces were lined and always held serious expressions except when they patted my head and I discovered that they had sunflower seeds in their pockets. They spoke with a great and bitter intensity.

They had been in Ratno at the time of the pogrom. It was before the High Holidays, and everyone was waiting for the occasion to win from the Lord through prayer a happy and prosperous new year. Then they came — the drunken riffraff eager for sport, thirsty for blood. Those of the Jews who could, fled, hiding from Ivan's wrath in cellars, in barns, in the forest, nostril-deep in water. But the old and the unimaginative, the helpless and the trusting, remained behind, and it was from among them that the victims were taken. "My own father was hanged before my eyes!" cried out the younger of the two strangers. "I know the men. I will yet return. Revenge!" He broke into an uncontrolled sobbing. It was contagious.

Murder by murder the pogrom was reconstituted for us by the passionate strangers. As my father inquired after relatives and old friends and as the strangers reported them well or among those perished for the Sanctification of the Name, it was a gruesome census that was being taken in my home. To make sure that the letters we had had from Uncle Melech were really his and not those of some good friend continuing the fiction of his life, to assure herself about her brother, from whom she had had no recent intelligence, my mother asked about Melech Davidson. "The *llui*? Didn't you hear?"

From the expression on my mother's face the stranger who spoke gathered that he was touching flesh. He hesitated, and then sought to change the subject.

"I'm his sister!" my mother importuned. "You've got to tell me! What are you hiding? Woe is me!" She knitted her fingers together and bent them backward. "Woe is me, and bitter! Him, too? But we got letters from him!"

"No, no, not that at all. The *llui* is, thank God, well. But he, too, received his portion of the calamity. You can imagine what kind of bandits they were who beset us. Your brother had the *chutzpa* to intercede on behalf of the old rabbi, Rabbi Heshel; he begged for his grey hairs, for his sanctity. 'Away, dog!' the commander shouted at him. *'Pashol von!* You're all Bolsheviks. All Jews are Bolsheviks!' When the young Melech persisted in his plea, pointing out that good Jews couldn't be Bolsheviks, that Bolshevism uprooted our religion, that Rabbi Heshel was altogether a saint who didn't mix in worldly affairs, Melech was taken out and publicly flogged for his Jewish impertinence. He's recovered now. He was ill for a while, but he's well now. In fact, two weeks before we took the train from Ratno, he left the town."

"And he wrote us nothing about it, my poor brother! My fallen crown!"

At first we had only rumours of Uncle Melech's destination.

That he was playing with the idea of leaving Ratno we knew from his inquiries about Canada, but that he would finally choose as he did came to my father like a thunderbolt.

Uncle Melech had joined the Bolsheviks! To my father this was tantamount to apostasy. Here again I must rescue my father from the writings of his son; my father was no pharisee who stood shocked at a man's changing of his political convictions (they were not really political convictions that were involved, since Uncle Melech was always but an apolitical subject of the Czar). Nor was my father a man to be startled by rebellion; he had himself rebelled against the Romanovs — through flight. But Bolshevism ——

Bolshevism meant the denial of the Name. My father's notions about the philosophy of Marxism were very primitive. Occasionally on Sundays, when there was a rotogravure section, he would buy the *Jewish Daily Forward* and read with an incredulous skepticism the theoretical articles which that journal featured. Invariably he would drop his paper with the helpless comment: *"Hegel-baigal!* The way these men do stir up a stew!" Considered from the point of view of common sense, the thing was simply ludicrous.

His antipathy to the dialectic, I am afraid, stemmed also from a nonintellectual source: his gratitude to the land of his adoption. This land hadn't given him much, mainly because he hadn't been a taker, but it had given him — this was no cliché to my father — freedom. Whenever one of his Ratno compatriots took it in his mind to run down Canada and its capitalismus, my father would withdraw a coin from his pocket and point to the image thereon engraved: "See this man, this is King George V. He looks like Czar Nicholas II. They are cousins. They wear the same beards. They have similar faces. But the one is to the other like day is to night. Nikolai might be a *kapora* for this one. After Nikolaichek you shouldn't even so much as whisper a complaint against this country!" This patriotism, it is to be admitted, was essentially pragmatic; it never did reach the fervour of his Canadian friend Cohen the cabinet-maker, the Cohen who had carved the ferocious lions guarding and upholding the Decalogue in front of the Ark of the Covenant in the *Chevra Thillim,* the martial Cohen who always bore on his person a Union Jack fringed with *tzitzith* and who threatened at the slightest provocation to fight the South African War over again; but it was none the less a loyalty solidly grounded, and one that was not likely to be impressed by a *pilpul* that drew all its examples, not from Canada, but from the Russia he had abandoned.

In that Russia, he agreed, it was high time that the Czar and his crew came to a black end. But Bolshevism — that had corollaries which were anathema. Soon malice began bringing my father the heinous details of Uncle Melech's conversion. Uncle Melech, it was reported, had shaved his beard. Uncle Melech, it was stated, was with the Russian cavalry; an imaginative gossip went so far as to add that Uncle Melech had made his phylacteries part of his horse's harness. Uncle Melech, it was whispered, ate pork. He broke the Sabbath. He had become a commissar and was especially active with the zealots of the Society of Godlessness.

My mother would try to defend her brother's action — what he had lived through, she said, had upset his judgement — God spare us all such a testing! But it was an unconvinced defence and one that knew, even while it was being made, the arguments of its rebuttal. For it was clear that other people, too, had witnessed the pogrom and yet had not turned from their faith; many, moreover, had perished, while Uncle Melech had been saved; and even of the perished — what was man, to question the will of God?

We never again spoke of him in our house. But as the years passed I had no further need to rely upon my domestic sources for information; I could always pick up the latest news about him from the townsfolk of Ratno now resident in Montreal, whom I would meet at recurrent festivals and funerals. I was by this time attending the university and already had been conditioned to look at Marxism with a most unfilial impartiality, and so the reports of Uncle Melech's progress in the Communist Party not only failed to disturb me but indeed filled me with a secret pride. From these reports, received during the late twenties and early thirties, I made myself a new image of the uncle who together with angels had stood invisible and auspicious over my Hebrew lessons. It was a strange metamorphosis, this, from Talmudic scholar, syllogizing the past, into Moscow student, conspiring a world's future. It is true that Uncle Melech never did rise to high office in the Communist bureaucracy — his clerical antecedents stood against him — but his talents, both linguistic and polemical, were immediately perceived and appreciated. He attended, during the late twenties, various schools in Moscow, and thence he blossomed forth as Comrade Krul, the international authority upon the decadence of European literature. Throughout these years we received of course

no letters from him, and I heard of him and his exploits but twice:
once when a dialectical essay of his appeared in English transla-
tion, and again when I read an account of the strike that he had
organized among the employees of the Warsaw Bourse, where he
had succeeded in keeping commodity transactions at a standstill
for over a week.

It was the essay, however, that really interested me, for it
constituted a remarkable instance of what happens when the
Talmudic discipline is applied either to a belletristic or revolutionary praxis: Krul's quotations from European writing had the
thoroughness, and in a sense the quality, of a concordance, and his
argumentation was like nothing so much as like the subtilized airy
transcendent *pilpul* of Talmud-commentary commentators. As for
his matter, it was a series of curious alternations between pro-
phetic thunder and finicky legalism; often he lapsed into parody,
yet here and there one would be startled by either the justness of
the irreplaceable word or the daring of the high imaginative flight.

The German invasion of Poland trapped him in Kamenets, not
far from Ratno, where he was enveloped by the great smoke that
for the next six years kept billowing over the Jews of Europe —
their cloud by day, their pillar of fire by night.

Seymour Mayne

FOR A. M. KLEIN (1909-1972)

So you made the N.Y. Times
with your death — a column,
mimic of your poetic mine,
the richness of your vision —
And rising behind Montreal's gothic
french and english, *Yerushalayim*
with her gates, with her orifices
and one destined for the catatonic
master of madness.
                    Your city
rose to the north, and green
like Safed the hills lay at your feet
to be sung into the carpets
upon which your Adam first tripped.

Unlike the first Patriarch
you did not return to your Canaan
flowing with the gilt honey
and gleaming canvas milk
that poured and mixed
for your ad-libs
and libations.
                And in the blankness
of our north you finally stared
as if blind — the motes were cold
and flaky, and suddenly symmetrical
brittle hands, five-fingered prongs,
mercurial, piercing and dipping
into every outraged sense, and silencing
you with the deepest suffering —
the gagged tongue
limp and mute
unable to call itself back.

What due had you then you thought —
a knot of poems, a scheherazade
of a thousand witless dervish rockings,
stale-linen turbans *davening*
under the aureate arcs?
                        And near
where you tried to live again,
beneath the bridge of Outremont Park
where I came with cutting skates in my youth,
a second troll haunted
his princely self and stopped up
his dusky mouth with fear
in the mathematical snowy nights.

Now we know why all your equations
were equivocal — a pundit's brilliance,
yet disguising the grand with the puny —
of double voices speaking, gasping,
apostrophizing from the round zero of the mouth
rings to the empty ear's circle
and woven labyrinthine laurels
over the vacuous glycerine of the sunken eye.

Henry Kreisel

UNCLE JACOB*

They had hardly finished dinner when Bernhardt and Herman came bursting in, breathing heavily because they had run all the way. They threw themselves at Jacob without paying much attention to the others. Bernhardt wore a pair of knickerbockers and Herman had on short leather pants and a dark-green *Bauernjanker*.

"Did you get our letter, Uncle Jacob?" they asked, both speaking at the same time.

"And are you going to take us to the Prater?"

"We know a lot of places there."

"And I bet you've never seen what we're going to show you there, 'cause nobody knows about those places except us."

"Yes, and one of the side-shows has got a new program, all new. They got a knife thrower, and *die Dame ohne Unterleib*. She's a woman that hasn't got any lower body at all. Gee, I'd like to see that."

"Yes. We're going to see all that, but first we're going to show you our cave in the Krieau."

"Mhm. We're going to let you crawl in, but you've got to promise us that you won't tell anybody where it is or how you get in there, 'cause it's secret, see? Are you going to promise, Uncle Jacob?"

The mother said, "Quiet, children. Quiet, please."

"We discovered that cave, and only three people in the whole world know about it. You'll be the fourth, Uncle. We're going to show it to you because you'll be going away from here soon and you won't have a chance to tell anybody. But you mustn't let a word slip out of your mouth while you're here. And you know, when you're in the cave you can see everything that's going on outside, but anybody that's walking around outside can't see you at all when you're hidden inside."

"That's true, Uncle. That's the kind of a cave it is."

"Children! Children!" cried Manya, holding her hands to her

*Chapter Ten of Henry Kreisel's novel
The Rich Man. The year is 1935.

ears. "Quiet! Quiet! Uncle is eating. Don't bother him now. Let him eat."

They ceased talking abruptly, and it was as though a heavy rain of machine-gun fire had stopped, making the stillness yet more pronounced.

"All right, all right," said Jacob laughingly, "we'll go in about an hour, and you will show me everything."

"One hour!" they exclaimed, and their voices had the long-drawn ring of disappointment. "One hour! But that'll be too late."

"What do you want?" said Manya. "It's only just after one o'clock. Everything is closed yet in the Prater."

"Not on Sundays," said Herman. "They open early on Sundays. And we want to go to a lot of places. Besides, our cave is a far way off, and we want to sit in it when we get there. So we've got to leave here early."

"All right, all right. You'll have plenty of time." Manya's voice was becoming irritated. "Now sit down, and be quiet."

Reuben reached for a knife and cut two big slices of cake for the boys. "Here," he said, calling them. "Eat this and sit down quietly for a while."

"Are you going to come with us soon?" said Herman filling his mouth with a big piece of cake.

"Very soon," said Jacob.

"They come, and the whole house is upset in a minute," said Manya, looking at the mother. "Sometimes I'm glad I have no children. At least it's quiet in the house."

"Is your mother at home?" Reuben asked. "And have you eaten dinner?"

"Yes," answered Bernhardt, "we've eaten long ago. Mama and Papa are both at home. Mama is sitting like this." He walked over to a chair and assumed the pose of a person reading, "and Papa is making a sketch of her. My papa can draw well, Uncle Jacob, and I'm going to be a painter when I grow up. I'm going to be a famous painter with pictures hanging in the big galleries. And I'm going to send you a picture all the way to Canada. You're going to like that, won't you, Uncle Jacob?" He spoke with such conviction and in such earnestness that one was almost ready to believe that he would be a great painter some day.

"I'm going to be a carpenter," said Herman, his mouth full of cake. "You know what, Uncle? I'm going to make you a big chest of drawers out of mahogany wood and polish it real nice for you."

"Oh, you don't know what you want to be," came Bernhardt's disparaging remark. "You change your mind every day. Last week when the man came to fix our broken window, you watched him, and then you said you wanted to be a glazier because you liked the way he cut the glass and kneaded the putty with his knife."

"Yeah, I know," admitted Herman. "But I didn't want to be that, long. I'm going to be a carpenter, I know for sure, 'cause I like it."

"You only like it because you watched a man planing a piece of white wood, and another was polishing a chest and he made it all shiny. You change your mind every week, but I don't."

"Well, you're eleven. I bet when I'm eleven I'll still want to be a carpenter."

"All right," said Bernhardt. He got off the chair and walked over to the sofa on which Herman was lounging. "All right, then. What do you want to bet for?"

Herman considered a moment. "I bet my honour against yours," he said then firmly. "If I've changed my mind and want to be something else when I'm eleven, you can have my honour."

"All right," said Bernhardt.

They shook hands.

"Uncle Jacob," said Bernhardt, "did you hear what the bet was?"

Jacob's sides shook with laughter. "Yes," he said.

"All right. Now you've got to part our hands."

They came up to Jacob, their hands firmly clasped.

Jacob looked at them with a puzzled expression on his face.

"How shall I do it?" he asked.

"Just part our hands," said Herman impatiently.

Jacob took hold of their wrists and pulled their hands apart. The bet was concluded.

"Are you going to come with us now?" asked Herman.

"Let your uncle finish his dinner in peace," said Manya. "He'll go with you when he is ready."

"Oh, but he's finished his dinner long ago," said Herman. "I c'n eat much faster'n that, can't I, Bernie?"

"Sure you can. I can, too."

With suspicious eyes they watched Jacob smoking a cigarette. At last he rose. "Reuben," he asked, "you will come with us?"

"Oh, no," broke in Herman, exchanging a swift glance with his brother. "Uncle Reuben can't come with us today. We can't show him our cave. We can only show it to you 'cause you won't stay here long enough to tell."

Reuben smiled. "Go with them, Jacob," he said. "Go with them. They want you for themselves. What do they want me for? They've known me all their lives."

"Come on, Uncle," they said.

The boys walked on either side of him, talking rapidly, and both at the same time, so that Jacob had a great deal of difficulty understanding what they said, and no chance at all of saying anything himself. His difficulty was further increased by the fact that they began talking in the broad Viennese dialect as soon as they were in the street, and Jacob could only get every tenth word or so. It was obvious, however, that they were talking about their cave, describing it carefully, sketching its position and the way of approach, emphasizing again and again that he was the fourth person to be let into the big secret, and making it quite plain that he was to regard this as a great honour and distinction, indeed the greatest privilege which they had in their power to bestow upon anyone.

Suddenly Herman stopped. "Look Bernie. There's Holzinger," he said, pointing his finger at a small boy who was hopping along curiously on the other side of the street. He took three big steps, and then he stopped. And then he made three very small ones, just setting one foot in front of the other, and stopped again. He completed the process of moving himself forward by hopping three paces. Then he started the cycle all over again.

Herman formed his hands into the shape of a long o and placed them in front of his mouth. "Oh, Holzinger!" he shouted. "Holzinger!"

The little boy lifted his head slowly and peered across the street.

"Holzinger," shouted Herman, "Come across here! This is my uncle! The one I told you 'bout! The one that's just come from Canada!"

Jacob laughed. Putting his fingers to his lips, he cautioned, "Sssh! Not so loud!"

A few people stopped and glanced at Jacob and passed on. Holzinger came running across the street. He was exceedingly short-sighted, and on his little snub-nose he had a pair of thick, round, metal-rimmed glasses.

"Hello, Herman," he said. His voice was hoarse. "I'm hoarse," he said. "Where are you going?"

"This is my uncle. The one I told you 'bout. The one that came all the way from Canada. The rich one. The one that gave the soldiers to me, and the fountain pen to Bernie." He took Jacob's hand and held it, moved by a subconscious desire to show that Jacob belonged to him.

Jacob chuckled, his face beaming with pleasure. He was not embarrassed at all. The boys stood there, radiating charm and happiness. Holzinger opened his eyes wide, and let his lower lip curl down. He moved his head very slowly, letting his eyes wander carefully over Jacob, observing every detail.

"Is that him?" he asked. He was evidently very much impressed by what he saw. He scratched his head. He had red hair. Then he rubbed his nose. "He's got white shoes," he observed, addressing himself to Herman.

"I know," said Herman.

Holzinger finished his critical examination. "Where are you going?" he asked.

"We're going to show him our cave, and then he's going to take us to the Prater and to all the shows, and he's going to let us ride on the merry-go-rounds."

"Say, c'n I go with you?" Holzinger asked timidly. "I mean just to see the cave?"

Herman shook his head sadly. "No, you can't. We can't show you the cave. Bernie an' I discovered it. Only my father's seen it except us, and now we're going to show it to our uncle. But nobody else can see it."

"I got a cave too," said Holzinger. "If you show me yours, I'll show you mine."

"Oh, but ours is much better. And besides, my uncle wants to be with us."

"Wait'll my uncle comes," said Holzinger, pouting. He looked up at Jacob once more, and then he left them, walking slowly, with head bent, rubbing his nose with his finger.

They went on, and soon they came to the same broad, tree-lined avenue along which Jacob had walked with Reuben. But instead of walking along it, they crossed it and went on beyond.

Here, only five minutes from the poor district in which Jacob's family lived, there were no houses, but only open ground and meadows, so that it seemed as if one had left the city and were out in the country.

Not many people were about at this early hour of the afternoon. Jacob and the boys walked along the gravelled pathways, flanked on both sides by cultivated lawns. They passed the Rotunde and the exhibition buildings, and then the race-track which lay desolate and hot in the midday sun because no races were run that day. Jacob shuffled alongside the boys. They had grown silent suddenly, and led him quietly. They had now walked about fifteen minutes, and Jacob was beginning to wonder where they were leading him. He looked about, searching in vain for merry-go-rounds.

"Boys," he asked at last, "where are we going? Where are the shows? There is nothing here."

"I know," said Herman. "We're going to show you our cave first. Then we can sit in it for a while, then we'll show you all the other things."

They turned sharply to the right, swerving from the cultivated lawns.

"This here is the Krieau," said Herman proudly. "Now you've got to walk real slow and careful, Uncle, and you've got to look around you to see that nobody follows us, see, 'cause we don't want anybody to find out where our cave is."

Jacob laughed. The children looked at him quickly, their eyes berating his improper conduct. They walked slowly, their bodies bent forward, and now and again they stopped, pretending to have heard a noise. Occasionally they did hear something, and then they fell flat on the ground, though the noise of crackling twigs and shuffling footsteps was usually produced by no one more startling than a woman pushing a baby carriage on the beaten pathway. Jacob of course did not go down on the ground, but remained standing, and since the bushes were not very high there he could see the people who walked by and they could see him. One woman stopped, startled by the figure in the bushes, and looked at him with an astonished expression as though she wondered what he was doing in there.

The children, stretched flat on the ground, tugged at his trousers and whispered furiously, "Uncle, get down, Uncle! Look, Uncle, the way we do! It's easy, Uncle!"

But he only laughed, and after two or three attempts they gave up urging him on.

Herman was rather disappointed. "When we took Papa in here," he said, "he went down just like we did." And turning to his brother, he added, "Somebody's gonna see us and come after us and find out where our cave is."

The brush grew thicker now, and soon it reached over their heads. Interspersed among the bushes were birch trees, and the ground was a maze of roots and leaves and twigs. Here and there wild lilac sprigs blossomed, and Jacob plucked a little sprig and put it through his buttonhole. He tripped a few times when his foot got caught in the noose of a root, but then Bernhardt, who walked behind him, got hold of his arm and prevented him from falling. Jacob tried to keep his eyes screwed to the ground, but now the sharp edges of shoots and branches began to whip his face so that he did not know whether to keep his head down or up. His suit became covered with leaves and twigs and clinging things of all kinds.

"Children!" he begged. "Children! Enough for today! I've seen enough for today."

"Oh," said Herman, "but you haven't seen our cave yet. You haven't seen anything yet. Oh, Uncle, you aren't getting weak, are you? You're not soft, are you? Oh, please, Uncle, you're making a lot of noise. Walk soft and careful, Uncle! Try not to tread on a twig when you see one. Somebody's sure to hear us and come after us."

In spite of his discomfort Jacob had to laugh. He stumbled along, his arms stretched out wide before him, parting the brush furiously, and the sweat trickled down in big drops from his forehead.

At last they came on to a clearing, and Jacob could stand up straight. He inhaled deeply. The boys dashed across the clearing and disappeared in the bushes on the other side. Jacob walked slowly, enjoying the sensation of walking along in a normal posture.

Suddenly Herman's head appeared, framed in a mass of leaves, and he shouted, "Come on, Uncle, run across, Uncle! Somebody's gonna see you."

And Jacob, startled by the voice, obeyed the command quickly and without questioning, like a soldier stealing through the enemy's positions. He cut a funny figure as he shuffled across the clearing, flat-footed, taking short, rapid steps, panting and perspiring, his belly wagging quickly up and down. But strangely enough, he did not mind it now. He was indeed beginning to enjoy this little adventure. For a moment he was a young boy again and thought back to the time when he had discovered hide-outs and had played with his friends.

He was across the clearing now, and the bushland swallowed him up again. He ruffled the hair of the two boys as soon as he came to them, an action which brought him a reprimanding look from both.

They pushed along, and he pressed on with them, no longer half-hearted and grumbling, but now in the game with all he had, ducking when they ducked, dodging imaginary foes when they did, and pretending with them that dozens of silent eyes, peering from behind every tree and every bush, were following them to find out the secret of the cave.

Suddenly the boys stopped, motioning him to be silent. Herman went on alone, carefully parting leaves and brush, sharply scanning the terrain about him. After a few minutes of perfect silence, broken only by twittering birds and scampering squirrels, he raised his hand and beckoned them to come.

"We're getting close to the cave," whispered Bernhardt.

Herman went on, and they followed him. At last he said, pointing his finger, "This here is the cave."

It was not really a cave, but simply a deep hollow in the otherwise flat stretch of ground, surrounded by a dense mass of bramble bushes and brush. From a nearby depository the boys had lugged three big, flat-topped stones, which they used as seats. They had also slightly parted the twigs on one side, thus making an opening through which they could look out, but could not themselves be seen.

"This is our cave," said Herman when they were finally in it. "Do you like it, Uncle?" He was happy and proud. Columbus could not have been prouder after he had discovered America. "We discovered it. Do you like it, Uncle?"

Jacob looked around. "Yeah," he said. "It's all right."

"Sit down, Uncle," said Herman.

Jacob took a handkerchief from his pocket and dusted the stone before he sat down. The march had quite exhausted him. He wiped the perspiration from his forehead. Then he took off his shoes and emptied the sand and the stones which had accumulated there.

At a given signal Herman and Bernhardt crawled up to him.

"Now you've got to promise that you won't tell anybody how you got in the cave," said Herman. "We should really have put something over your eyes, but you're our uncle."

Jacob looked from one to the other.

"You've got to give us both your hands," said Herman.

Jacob held out his hands.

"Now you've got to say it," said Herman.

"I promise," said Jacob.

"You've got to say it all," said Bernhardt.

Jacob looked puzzled. "I promise," he repeated.

"No," said Bernhardt. "You've got to say, I promise I won't tell anybody where the cave is, and I'll be a true confederate."

"I promise I won't tell anybody where the cave is, and I'll be a true confederate," said Jacob.

"Now you're one of us," said Bernhardt.

"Yes," echoed Herman. "Now you're one of us."

"I'm glad," said Jacob. "I'm really glad."

The boys crawled back to their stones and sat down.

"Now there are four big confederates," said Herman. "There's us and our papa and you, Uncle. And then — there's Holzinger and Steiner and Freud and Gruber. But they're only small confederates. They're our friends, but they can never really get inside the cave."

"Yes, but our papa is still the greatest confederate," said Bernhardt, "and nobody can ever become as great as he."

"Our mama would be one, too," said Herman, "but naturally we can't have girls, so she can't be in, although Mama isn't really a girl, she's a woman, and that's not the same, is it, Uncle?" His voice had the tone of someone answering his own question even while asking it.

Jacob said, "Well, children, tell me what you do. Do you go to school?"

"Sure," said Bernhardt. "School will be over soon for this year. I'm going to finish the first year of the *gymnasium*. I'm learning Latin already. Do you want to hear me say something in Latin, Uncle? *Patria nostra olim provincia Romana erat*. Do you know what that means, Uncle? It means: Our country was once a Roman province." He paused to let his words sink in. "Herman is still in public school," he went on, "and he's got two more years to go before he can enter the *gymnasium*. I've only got seven more years to go before I finish, and then Papa said he's going to send me to the College of Art if I still want to go. Papa said he's going to see that we can do all the things he wanted to do, but could never do. I love him."

"I do, too," said Herman, sitting with head bowed, and staring down on the ground. "So far I like geography best of all. And whenever I want to, Papa sits down at the table, and we have a big atlas at home where all the countries are painted in with different colours, and then he tells me all about the foreign countries, Papa does. Mama likes it, too, and sometimes she comes and sits down, and listens, too. When I'm big, Uncle, I'm going on a ship. I'd like to be a sailor."

Bernhardt looked quickly at his brother. "You just said at Grandma's place that you wanted to be a carpenter. You lost your bet now."

"No, I didn't," Herman shot back. "I c'n be a carpenter on a ship, can't I?"

"No, you can't. You lost your bet."

"I can so," Herman cried aggressively. "I didn't lose my bet."

"Yes, you lost your bet. I've got your honour."

"You have not!" Herman jumped up, ready to throw himself at Bernhardt.

"You lost your honour," Bernhardt jeered.

Herman sprang forward and hit him. Bernhardt struck back. In a second they were rolling on the ground, tightly interlocked, wrestling furiously.

"Children! Children!" cried Jacob. He tried to part them. He went down on the ground too, dirtying his suit. After a great effort he pulled the boys apart. They stood there, scowling at each other. Jacob was hardly able to restrain them from rushing again at one another. They were straining like wild horses to shake off his hands.

"A fine pair of partners you are," said Jacob. "What kind of a federation have you got? You make a federation and then you fight."

They became calmer, and he let go of their arms. Reluctantly, and still glaring at each other with hostile eyes, they went back to their stones and sat down.

"You still lost your honour!" hissed Bernhardt.

"I did not," Herman snapped back.

"Children, children," Jacob begged them, "I'm not going to be a confederate if you're going to be like that. And if you keep on fighting, I'm going to tell where the cave is, that's what I'll do."

"Oh, no, you're not!" they both cried, and immediately they banded together again. Herman stretched out his hand, a sign of submission, and Bernhardt took it.

Jacob smiled. "That's right. That's what I like to see."

"You're not going to break your word?" they asked.

"No."

"It doesn't mean anything if we fight," said Bernhardt, "honest it doesn't, Uncle Jacob. We fight all the time, but we still love each other, don't we, Herman?"

"Sure," said Herman. "Sure we do."

"You can fight and still love each other," said Bernhardt, his elbow propped against his knee and his hand cupping his chin. "Mama and Papa said so, too. Mama and Papa often argue, and often they shout at each other and are angry. But it is always all right after a while. And once, when Papa left angry and slammed the door behind him, Mama stood there and she cried, and I went up to her and put my arms around her like this —— " he bent over and embraced Herman, "and I kissed her and asked her if she and Papa didn't love each other any more, and she said yes, and she said that I must never think like that, and that she loved Papa more than anybody else in the whole world, except us, and that Papa loved her too, just as much. And I know, because I asked him, and he said so. And Mama said that people can love each other very much and still fight and hurt each other, even more sometimes than people who don't love each other at all. She said I'm still a little boy and that I couldn't understand all these things, but that I would some day. But I told her that Herman and I always fight, and yet I love him, and she said that's almost the same thing."

"Sure I do," said Herman. "Sure I love Bernie." And he leaned over and embraced his brother and kissed him on the cheek.

A great tenderness came over Jacob when he saw this. He bent forward and patted the hair of the two children. "You're all right, my boys," he said. "You're all right."

Suddenly the boys sat up straight. Then they leaned their bodies slightly forward and listened intently. They could hear voices not very far off, and the noise of crackling twigs, breaking under approaching footsteps.

"What's the matter?" Jacob asked.

Herman threw a reproachful glance at him. "Shhh," he whispered. "Not so loud. Somebody's coming this way, can't you hear? I bet they heard us, 'cause we talked so loud. I — I just hope they miss our cave."

The footsteps came closer and two or three voices were audible now, conferring in a whisper. The boys lay flat on their stomachs, peering out through the peep-hole. They hardly dared to breathe. They were almost choking with tension. Even Jacob held his breath and ducked his head quite low. Suddenly he was very much concerned about the whole thing and found himself wishing, almost praying, that whoever was approaching might miss the cave and go past it. The footsteps were quite close now, and the leaves on the bushes rustled and swished as they were being brushed aside by a vigorous pair of hands.

"Somebody's coming right at us," Bernhardt whispered sadly. "They've found the cave."

Herman was almost in tears. "Let's fight them," he said clenching his teeth.

"It's no use," said Bernhardt. "I bet they're stronger than we are. Let's make a pact with them."

"No," Herman said firmly. "Let's fight them."

The boys stood up, and Jacob stood up with them. Together they prepared to face the intruder.

Now the last screen of protecting leafage gave way, and the figure of a lad of about sixteen appeared and stared down at them. He was very tall and tough-looking. His shirt was torn and his trousers were ripped and had holes in them. He put his hands into his pockets, and his right, stockingless foot beat the ground. He leaned his head a little to the side and puckered up his mouth into a contemptuous grimace. For a while he peered at them in silence. Instinctively Jacob put his arms around Herman and Bernhardt and drew them closer to him.

"Go away," Jacob said. "What do you want here?"

The lad paid no attention to him. Suddenly he began to laugh. "Eh, fellers!" he shouted, turning his head a little, "Look what's in here! Chris', look what's in here! Eh, fellers, where the hell are y'? Come 'ere. There's two little shrimps in 'ere, an' a ol' man. And the ol' man's got a white suit. I bet you never seen a guy wit' a white suit. First time I ever seen a feller wit' one."

Again the breaking of boughs and twigs, and the rustling noise of parting leaves. Then three little boys scrambled up. None of them looked older than thirteen. The big lad was evidently their leader. Silently, and obviously in great wonderment, they gazed down at Jacob. For the moment Herman and Bernhardt did not seem to interest them.

Jacob felt uncomfortable under the scrutiny of their hungry eyes. "Go away," he said again, moving his hands as if he were chasing flies, "go away."

They did not budge an inch. The big chap asked, "You ever seen a guy wit' a white suit, fellers? Bet a suit like that gets dirty faster'n hell."

"Eh, Ferdl, look," said one of them, addressing the leader of the bunch, "he's got white shoes, too, an' a white shirt. Chris', he's white all over!"

Herman sensed that they were very much impressed, and freeing himself from Jacob's arm, he stepped forward a little.

"Now scram!" he said firmly. "Scram, I tell you, or else my uncle's going to beat you up. You know what? He's just come all the way from Canada, and that's way, way over the ocean, and he lives in Toronto, and that's right next to Chicago, and he c'n beat you up. So scram! My brother an' I were just showing him our cave."

"Ahhhhh!" said the big chap ironically. "Is that so? You was just showing him your cave? Who says it's your cave in the first place?"

"I say. My brother an' I discovered it an' it's secret. So there."

The big lad said, sing-songing the words, "Well, it ain't secret no more, so there. We discovered it too, an' now it's ours."

"It is not," shouted Herman.

"All right, then. Wait'll we get you alone. When the ol' man ain't there." He leered down at them, his eyes squinting. Then a contemptuous and derisive smile spread slowly over his face. "Hey, fellers!" He spoke without moving his head at all. "You know what's in this cave? Two little Jew-boys and an old Jew." He spat.

Jacob's eyes grew large. He drew the children back. All the air seemed to have been cut off. It was almost like being in a small, windowless room, pressed against a narrow corner. He felt the pounding of his heart and he was afraid.

"Let's clear 'em out of the cave, fellers."

"You will not!" cried Herman, his face red with anger. "This is our cave." He could hardly control himself. Reaching behind him, he grabbed a stick, and rushed forward. Before the big lad knew what was happening, Herman had hit him twice over the head with the stick, and then jumped back, seeking protection with Jacob.

"You little rat! Eh, fellers, didya see this? The little Jew-rat hit me. Go on, fellers, jump down an' hit him back."

"Whyn't you jump down yourself?" said one of his friends. "Why d'you send us alla time? I know why. 'Cause you're scared. 'Cause you're scared of the little white ol' man."

"Who's scared?" the big lad yelled, grabbing him by the collar and shaking him.

"Lemme go!" he screamed. "Lemme go!"

Jacob stepped forward. "Go away. Go fight somewhere else. Don't show your faces here again. This cave belongs to the two boys. Now go away."

The big chap released the little fellow from his grip and looked at Jacob. Jacob glowered back at him, trying to give his face a fierce expression. Then he took one more step towards him and the youth drew back a little. Herman ventured closer and brandished his stick.

"This is our cave," he said. "Isn't it, Bernie? We discovered it, didn't we, Bernie?"

"Yes," said Bernhardt timidly. "We did."

"Like hell," said the big lad. "Wait'll we get you alone. We'll knock the hell outa you."

He turned sharply about and strode away quickly. The three little boys jumped up and followed him obediently. The one who had refused to attack Herman lingered behind, and then hurriedly and with great contempt he spat twice, threw himself down on the ground and crawled away as nimble as a weasel. "Ferdl," he shouted, "Ferdl. I spit at 'em!"

Herman wanted to shout something in reply, but Jacob restrained him. His hands were trembling. Suddenly a stone came flying through the air and hit him on the shoulder. He started, and ran out.

"You, you...."

A burst of laughter answered him and the voice of the big bully, shouting hatefully, "Goddam Jews. Wait'll we get you alone."

Then they scurried away rapidly and their footsteps died away in the distance.

Jacob did not go into the cave again. "Come out, boys," he said. "I think we should go now." The incident had visibly shaken him.

"Anyway," Herman said, "we beat 'em off."

"They'll be laying for us now," Bernhardt said softly. "We can't ever come back here now."

"Oh, there are lots of caves around here. We can find another one and hide out there." Herman assumed an air of careless bravado. "Besides, we could've beaten them off even without Uncle Jacob's help."

"No we couldn't," Bernhardt said. "I'm scared."

"Come on, boys," Jacob called again. "I want to get away from here."

"Yes," said Bernhardt, "let's go. There'll be a lot of people in the Prater now."

Jacob breathed easier as soon as they came upon a beaten track, and after that it did not take them long to reach the centre of the Prater. There were great throngs of people around, and they could hardly move. It took Jacob a little while to get used to the noise. The joyous cries of children mingled with the general laughter and merriment. From all sides came the tin-clang of weary Wurlitzers, accompanying the endless circles of merry-go-rounds. In the beer-gardens and in the open-air cafés loudspeakers blared out the latest jazz hits, newly imported from America. It was a mad, whirling, strident cacophony.

The children seemed to have completely forgotten the depressing incident of a few minutes ago, but Jacob could not so easily shake it off. He let himself be dragged along by the boys. Gradually their happy mood infected him too, and he began to work up enthusiasm for the things they were doing. Soon his stocky, droll little figure could be seen swaying to and fro on a merry-go-round horse; he staggered up and down "wiggle-woggle" stairs; he had his hat nearly blown off when they went down a steep on a roller coaster, and he was enjoying himself.

"Le's go now and see *die Dame ohne Unterleib*, and the knife-thrower," said Herman, panting and excited, his face glowing.

"It's over there," said Bernhardt, "We know the clown there."

"He's the funniest clown in the Prater, I think," Herman said.

On a little platform, quickly improvised with a few wooden boards and a rough railing, a man was blowing a bugle, and another kept shouting, *"Kommen Sie Näher, kommen Sie alle näher!"* and he clapped his hands to attract the crowd. "Everybody come close! Everybody come close!"

The crowd gathered round the platform, giggling and talking, shuffling impatiently, like a lowing herd of cattle waiting to be led to pasture.

"As soon's there're enough people here, the clown's going to

come jumping out," Herman said. "You'll see, Uncle. He's funny."
He laughed in anticipation.

"Tra-la-la-la, tra-la-la, tra-la-la-la-la," came a croaking baritone
from behind a grimy red curtain that partitioned the barker's platform from the inside.

"That's him," cried Herman. "That's him."

The man who had shouted and clapped his hands disappeared
behind the curtain and came back dragging the clown by the ear.
The crowd yelled and laughed.

The clown cried, "I'm going to tell my father. I'm going to tell
my father." He had a false nose and his face was painted with a
thick coat of red and white paint, and he wore a patched, vari-
coloured costume. He was a very ordinary clown.

"What's your father?" asked the man with the bugle.

"He's going to say my father's dead," whispered Herman.

"My father's dead," snarled the clown.

"Well, what was he before he was dead?" asked the man with
the bugle.

"He's going to say he was alive before that," whispered Herman,
laughing.

"He was alive before that," bellowed the clown.

"*Nein, du Dorftrottel*." The man with the bugle hit him over the
head. "You idiot. Doesn't anything ever get into that thick skull of
yours? I mean what did he do to earn his daily bread?"

"He ate no bread," the clown cracked. He spoke slowly, drawl-
ingly. "Beer was the staff of his life."

"Oh, you're hopeless. Now listen carefully." The man with the
bugle talked to him now with exaggerated patience. "What did he
(your father, that is), what did he do to earn the money to buy his
beer?"

"That's what my mother always wanted to know too," the
clown said.

The crowd roared with laughter. The clown kept on making
jokes which were ancient and bad, but he had a receptive and
very uncritical audience, ready to laugh at anything, and thankful that they were being entertained free of charge. Herman and
Bernhardt had heard the whole routine so often that they knew it
by heart, but yet they laughed, and their laughter was as fresh and
spontaneous as if they were hearing the jokes for the very first
time.

When the routine was finished, the boys pulled Jacob over to the box-office to buy the tickets. The clown was standing there, shouting and trying to make as many people come in as he possibly could before the crowd scattered.

"*Meine Damen und Herren*," he yelled. "*Eine Weltsensation! Die Dame ohne Unterleib!*"

"Hallo," Bernhardt said to him. "Hallo. You were really funny today."

The clown pushed them inside. Sweat was running down his face and dissolved the paint, and the red and white merged and trickled down in ugly streaks, and he kept wiping his face with his sleeve.

Inside there were a few rows of wooden benches, and a small, crude stage made of rough boards. Then the show began. To the accompaniment of an untuned piano a man threw knives at a girl, narrowly missing her. A youth ate flames and spewed them forth again, and an old and tired magician performed tricks as old and tired as he. But yet the children were fascinated, and Jacob was fascinated, because they were.

And then at last the star of the show — *Die Dame ohne Unterleib*. She was wheeled onto the stage, for she could obviously not be expected to walk on. Great applause greeted her. The fact that the wheelchair was not of the orthodox kind, but looked rather like a big wooden box on wheels, seemed to trouble few of the spectators.

Bernhardt strained forward on the bench. "I saw her," he whispered to Herman. "I saw her a few days ago. I remember her face. She was standing outside, talking to somebody, and she had legs then. I saw her walk inside afterwards."

But Herman, his eyes glued to the stage where the lady was now bowing her head and blowing kisses to the audience, could not so easily be shaken. "It must've been another woman that you saw," he whispered back, "because this one hasn't got any legs. So how could she walk?"

Abraham Boyarsky

A BIRTHDAY PARTY

I knew my mother for a little more than five years after that day, but no earlier or subsequent recollection of her arouses my memory like that late afternoon in November of 1952. We had just emerged from the Canadian Consulate in Frankfurt, Germany. On the sidewalk, Father nudged my sister closer to me collapsing the festoon of our little arms. As she chatted excitedly with Father, Mother squeezed my hand; a solacing warmth, tinged with little rills of cold, spread through my forearm. I had often seen her melancholy and cheerful at once, but never were the emotions of joy and sorrow so visible in her every movement, so audible in her every word. It was like looking at a dying man laugh.

Mother wore a long, green dress and a thin beige sweater that concealed her womanhood. A streak of sunlight glinted on her chestnut hair, and I leaped high to grasp it. Noting my efforts, she raised me in her arms, and planted warm kisses upon my cheeks, that Father had pinched to fluorescence earlier in the day to lend me a healthy appearance.

My mother's love had always had a trace of sadness in it; it tinged her bearing even in the happiest of moments. I had been aware of this other dimension in her for some time, and I felt attracted to it, for I knew that within this other domain rested the things that were truly important to her. Now that we were on the dark side of the road, the glint in her hair was gone, but I continued hopping all the same, to cheer her up with my silliness. She smiled approvingly, but there was still something sad in her eyes, something intangible and lost, something neither my existence nor my actions could ever redress. I glimpsed her cheeks that were strangely florid and I felt deeply rejected: with florid cheeks, she did not need me. Fortunately, I soon discerned a gloomy look in her eyes, a look that only I understood, and I knew instinctively that I had to protect her. But how? In a moment, I had the answer: I would not, under any circumstances, permit my shoes to touch the line-markings on the sidewalks. This is how I would guard her from the dreadful things she and Father murmured about in the darkness. So I fixed my eyes on the sidewalk and marched resolutely forward, continuously adjusting my pace so that the long narrow furrows would bisect the base of my stride's triangle. The lines were the Germans and the only way I could save Mother was by crossing directly over them. I knew that if I should so much as graze one line, Mother's life would be in grave danger. As my parents' chatter bandied overhead, I was overwhelmed by the pleasure of duty, and the knowledge that my mother's life hinged on my every footstep.

My sister, who had just turned seven, noticed my irregular stride and regarded me quizzically. Soon she was trying to mime my steps, but she did not understand what I was doing, for she constantly stepped on the markings. I dreaded the thought of Mother's fate, should it devolve on her.

"Canada! We're going to Canada!" Father repeated exuberantly, white bubbles foaming at the corners of his mouth.

As we walked under the thin foliage of big trees to the deportation camp, Father transmitted our good fortune to my sister and me with crunching hugs that left us breathless. Mother looked lovingly on. With a nod and a gentle tug, she encouraged us to hasten; it was growing dark.

"If I hadn't lied about those dates, we could have gone to America," Father said to her with some regret.

"It doesn't matter — Canada is just like America," Mother said encouragingly.

"Canada? Whoever heard of Canada?"

"It's a good land. We'll leave Germany, that's all that matters."

"Yes," Father assented, then added: "I'll sell chickens there just as I do here. In Canada, people also have to eat. We'll manage."

"Of course, we will," she agreed confidently.

Slivers of purple smoke rose from the invisible chimneys of squatty tenement buildings, uncoiling streaks across the paler sky. Near a building with a gaping hole in the front wall, we turned into a long, dark alley. From there, we came out on a broad roadway with clear, deep markings in the sidewalk, where I enthusiastically resumed my duty. Only when we crossed a street, did I allow myself to look up from the sidewalks, and glance at the familiar houses, some overrun with ivy, others with beds of withered flowers adjoining the rotting stoops. The resinous scent of burning leaves nipped at my nostrils; here and there, in the middle of a lawn, a circular slough of glowing embers crisped in the evening wind. We passed through warm scents of cooking, then, at last, beyond a rubble-covered lot, appeared the piebald walls of our camp. We walked quickly, like people caught in the rain.

II

Our room was at the far end of a long dun-coloured corridor, illumined feebly by a small lightbulb near the staircase. The room was small. Bunk beds faced each other from opposite walls, and a narrow window between them looked out on the quadrangle with its naked trees and flattened yellow grass. The quadrangle, enclosed by four train-like buildings, was mottled with holes. During the day, the camp sounded with the hurried, uncertain activity of wan-faced survivors. After dark, it lay quiet in deceptive repose, seething mutely beneath the winds of memory. The night crowded musty odours upon the camp, odours of senselessness and discontinuity. On warm evenings, or when something important had happened somewhere, apostates of life, some dressed in tatters, mingled in little groups on the quadrangle, sharing a cigarette, a remedy, the name of a phantom town. They huddled close together, and their glimmering eyes, glazed by the ichor of a distempered past, spoke of distant *shtetlech*, of cows and grain, of *cheders* and bazaars. Standing with my nose pressed against the narrow window, I megaphoned my hands around my eyes to diminish the glare from within. On occasion, a bright crescent moon crept up slowly behind them, and I, oblivious of the voices of my parents and sister, sensing that important issues were being discussed out there, gazed into the darkness with awe and gloom. Not until they dispersed, plodding alongside the stone rampart of the quadrangle to the various entrances, did I leave my post. Often, on turning around, I became intensely aware of the smell of cheese. From all along the high narrow ledge that girded the room, hung white sacks of curdling milk, like the sunken stomachs of overfed ducks.

Not until Mother had tucked me in, and, sitting at my side, hummed the enchanting melody that invariably brought tears to her eyes, did I relinquish my thoughts of the men on the quadrangle. Now I had to concentrate on keeping my eyes open for as long as possible; should I close them, Mother would soon stop singing. To keep awake, I would tense my face as hard as I could, but inevitably her soft, soporific tune loosened my muscles and carried me far away.

III

On the day after our successful visit to the Canadian Consulate, Father took me with him to the open market. He lifted me onto his shoulders and carried me through the streets. When we arrived at his stand, in a long row of others, he pulled off a thick leather blanket from the chicken cages, and began calling out in Yiddish and Polish. Customers came up to us and Father stealthily handed them cigarette packages, for which they paid with large sums of money. He handed me a roll filled with soggy cheese. I munched on it as I sat atop the cages, callously annoying the chickens with my swinging legs. Father paced up and down the street, calling to the hurrying pedestrians. From time to time, American soldiers stopped, sniffed about, and strutted on. Nevertheless, business was good this day and Father was excited.

When we came home in the evening, I complained of a stomach-ache. So sharp were the pains that I could not take up my post at the window. The long night brought no abatement. In the morning, Mother took me to the camp infirmary. The doctor diagnosed appendicitis. They operated in the afternoon. It was only late the following day that Mother's melody roused me from my deep sleep. On waking, I discovered countless red pimples, like the blood-shot eyes of little animals, flecking my body in strange patterns. I had chicken-pox, and the pains in my stomach had been one of the symptoms. The operation had been unnecessary.

For ten days, I lay quarantined in a tiny room in the infirmary, the oblique zipper on my tummy tugging at my flesh in all directions. Each morning, three plump nuns, their small wrinkled faces peering through black hoods, crowded around me and blotted out the sun. They caressed my face and hands, and their heavy crosses clinked, entangled, unwound, then oscillated slowly and portentously before my startled eyes. It was only after Mother had told me to spit three times as soon as they left, that I overcame my fear of them.

IV

On the Sunday after my return from the hospital, a large group of familiar people gathered in our room to celebrate the sixth anniversary of my birthday. Women sat on the lower bunk beds while children played on the upper ones. The sacks of curdling milk had been removed. Chaim, an elderly man with thin curly white hair and a flat nose, played on an accordion as he sat hunched under its weight. Hershl, my so-called uncle, who was a partisan with Father, picked out the beat with his long hairy fingers. He had lustrous black hair, parted in the middle and slicked down over his scalp like a silk stocking. Uncle Hershl danced and laughed to Chaim's sprightly tune, but his face looked absurd in jubilation. At the end of the piece, Uncle Hershl, who loved herring and boiled potatoes, blew up a rumpled paper bag and rended it with a resounding whang. Startled women clutched their bosoms, then laughed when they saw Uncle Hershl's ridiculous face. Now that he had entertained the grown-ups, he turned his delicious attention toward the children. He made a besom stand obliquely on its brush of twigs, then stopped up his ears with his little fingers, waving his hands and crossing his eyes in hilarious confusion. When the children, bursting with laughter, could no longer endure his expression, he mercifully pulled out his stained fingertips. Noticing that I was not laughing as hard as the others, he grabbed me around the waist and turned me face down across his lap. "When Uncle Hershl is happy, everyone has to laugh!" he reprimanded me, feigning a slap on my rear end. Convulsed with laughter, no one noticed me untying Uncle Hershl's shoelaces. My sister, however, soon discovered it and pointed it out to him. As he glanced down in proud surprise, I squirmed out of his grasp.

The adults gathered around the little table in the middle of the room and made a toast. I stood outside the dome of their bodies and played with my friends. A plump little girl nicknamed Shpulkes because her clothes were kept together by a vast assortment of safety pins, puttered restlessly about, swinging her arms and scolding everyone. She had a round face with teeth set crookedly between swollen, suppurating lips. Shpulkes roamed through the room attacking anyone who seemed vulnerable. Soon the little monster was upon me, mugging me with her loud presence, spraying my face with moist words. For no apparent reason she kicked me in the shin. It was my birthday party and I was determined to be honoured, so I pulled her hair. She began to wail. Before long, out of guilt, I suppose, I too began to cry.

Our sobs disturbed the adults. Some of them turned disconcertedly to us. A lean woman, with powdered, cadaverous cheeks, picked up Shpulkes and caressed the tight blonde curls on her head.

"Children will be children!" another woman, short and gaunt-faced, declared philosophically with a gesture of dismissal. She smiled reassuringly to everyone as she munched away on a slice of black bread topped high with cottage cheese.

Mother came to me, took me in her arms, and whispered into my ear.

"It's your birthday Avremeleh — you must show everyone that you're a big boy, and you know that big boys don't cry."

She drank my tears and dried the runnels on my cheeks with her fingertips. I leaned my head against her shoulder and was at peace with the world.

"Now, there, there," a stout woman cooed through flaming red lips when it was already over. "There, you see what a good little boy he is. Oh, you can put him down now — let him play with the other children," she advised Mother cruelly.

Suddenly the noise of the adults ceased. All that was heard was a woman whimpering. Mother rushed to the sink to wet a towel, then shouldered her way back to the grieving woman.

"I also lost children — two girls and a boy," I heard Mother say commiseratively, with a cadence that was familiar to me. "We all lost children." A frightening chill seeped out of the unfocused eyes of the adults, dampening the spirits of the children.

"I have no one, but no one — at least you have a husband and children," the woman sobbed irrepressibly. A sombre silence settled over the room, so intense that the children stopped all activity. The guests looked at each other through grilles enfencing their pasts, their anguished faces bespeaking death and loved ones. Then Uncle Hershl, wiping his eyes, reminded everyone that it was my birthday party, and the grieving woman, assenting solemnly, called me to her. I looked up at Mother; her eyes gave me permission, so I stepped up to the woman. She pressed me tightly to her, transmitting the agony in her bosom. Between fading sobs, she dabbed her nose and eyes with a handkerchief. When, at last, the drivel was checked, she gazed searchingly into my eyes. How I wanted to assuage her grief, but I did not know what to say, so I just sat on her bony lap and nodded dutifully.

I was very happy when, at last, Mother said to her:

"Henye, come help me cut the cake."

The woman nodded sadly and followed Mother to the narrow counter near the door. There they sliced up the huge yellow honey cake. Henye went around distributing the narrow wedges, a handkerchief crumpled up in óne hand. I could not eat. Her appetite undiminished by our earlier fracas, Shpulkes gobbled up my portion.

While everyone was eating, I wandered through the crowd. Men extended their hands to me in manly deference and women pressed me to their chests with hugs that were more than hugs. Through the corner of my eye, I saw Father standing apart from the others, mumbling to himself. I approached him. With a suddenness that frightened me a little, he lifted me and stood me up on the table. I looked at the severe faces all around me, and froze under the howl of their silence. Mother was at Father's side, her eyes uplifted and sad. My sister stood quietly at her side, looking so very grown-up in her sedateness. Beyond the circle of heads, I observed Shpulkes sitting on the floor, legs apart, calmly talking to herself.

Father raised the vizor of his cap, wiped the imaginary sweat from his brow, then let out a wistful sigh. Uncle Hershl and Chaim stood at my sides.

"My precious son, we are here to celebrate your birthday," Father began in a faltering voice. Everyone crowded around the table. "This is a happy day for all of us, but for us happiness brings with it sadness. Each moment of happiness reminds us of our mothers and fathers, our sisters and brothers, our children, all those who are not here to share it with us. Each moment of happiness makes us tremble with guilt and shame for being alive. Each moment of happiness brings to mind the unbelievable tragedy that we — the few survivors — lived through. For us, happiness exists only to the extent that it reminds us of all the joy that we lost and shall never have again." Beyond the circle of heads, a woman wept quietly. "This is a happy day, my precious son," Father went on, "and on happy days, we should be happy. But how is it possible, if our world is not a world? How can we forget our loved ones who are no longer with us?" Father's voice broke and he could not continue. Between tearless sobs, he struggled to breathe. When he began to speak again, his voice was quiet and hoarse. "We must never forget! We must keep these memories alive with us! We must engrave these memories upon our children and they upon their children, until the blood of our beloved ones is avenged. And you, my precious son, you who were born after the war, out of tears and misery, you who never saw death with your own eyes, and did not witness the murder of your twin sisters and your brother, you must also remember. Especially you, for you have been granted a good and quick mind. You must never forget that your sisters' little heads were smashed against stone ledges until blood streamed from their eyes and that your brother was trampled underfoot until we could no longer recognize a face, and that your grandfather was shot in the heart and.... My son, we are old and tired people — now you must be the one to remember for us. You are now the guardian of our memories! You are the avenger of our dead!

"When you will grow up, my son, you will return to this wretched land. You will return as a pilot and you will fly low over their cities and you will bomb them. You will bomb them indiscriminately, day after day, until they are as flat and as deserted as our *shtetl*. And if the cries of their dying should reach your ears and if the sight of the destruction should weaken your heart, for you are a Jew, you will remember your sisters and your brother and your grandfathers and your grandmothers, and the vision of their dismembered, rotting bodies, will drive the compassion from your heart! Now promise me that you will bomb their cities! Promise, my son!"

"I promise, Father."

Matt Cohen

THE WATCHMAKER

The watchmaker's gold wallet is embroidered and stamped with a picture of the village green. Dense black hair sits on his head in uncombed clumps and there are small tufts from his nose that melt into his moustache. I see him standing outside of his shop, under the awning, his thick arms tapering down into delicate hands that have been shaped by small motions. At times I think he has no face. There is bone and flesh. There are networks of nerves, veins and arteries that lace through the surfaces. But sometimes he seems to have transformed himself into a blank, a man who sits in the corner and talks to the grandfather clock.

In his coat pocket there is a red satin cushion. This man plays the violin, has small hard calluses on the tips of the fingers of the left hand, is an unbeliever. It would be easy for him to do certain things. He could set all the clocks in his shop to different times. He could grow a beard. He could eat fish sandwiches for lunch or bet on horses. But he restrains himself. He fears that he will reduce his options, lose the mornings under the awning, earn the enmity of his grandfather clock.

His wife would like a new coat. His daughter would like to travel in Europe. He lives in the midst of expectations. So I see him in the summer, under the awning, standing in the shade not even pretending to look for customers. He is pretending he is a shop-keeper. Or he is just letting himself stand blankly for a moment. Perhaps he is unaware of what he looks like. But his wife and daughter must surely catch it sometimes, notice that he has disappeared.

In the winter I sit with him in the corner by the grandfather clock. I try to extract his wisdom, hoping he will dispense it in little lumps.

What is the time? I ask.

Two-thirty, he replies. Then he turns to the grandfather clock and points at his huge pendulum. He laughs and drinks his tea. The clock is large and carved; its works shine like gold behind the glass. It ticks off the seconds. I feel that there are some seconds wasted, some in which I should have been doing something else. I fabricate my mortality. I ask him if he ever feels like that, if what he is doing is sitting by the grandfather clock letting his life escape.

Where to? he says. He turns off his face, he is resting his hand on the wooden side. Where to? he says, immensely pleased with his joke, as if it was some profundity he had eaten for breakfast.

Alright, I say conclusively, then you can invite me for supper.

It is a disaster. His daughter is unsure if I have been brought for her benefit. She refuses to play the piano. His wife, not knowing what to do, asks him to play the violin. It was unanticipated. He is not the kind of man you ask to play the violin. Still, he does it. He draws the bow out of the case first and meticulously brushes the horsehair with rosin. Then he takes out the violin and tunes it. When everything is ready he gets the cushion from his coat and tucks it under his chin. He stands in front of us, as if we are an audience that must be respected. I shall now play a certain sonata, he says. He nods his head and then begins to play.

Doesn't he play nicely? his wife says. It is as if there were a record on. When he is finished the watchmaker puts everything away and sits down. His wife finds this unremarkable.

He is about forty years old. He came to North America from Europe after the Second World War. His accent has intonations of several languages, and when he speaks I feel that everything has been carefully considered in the light of everything. Any man who can survive being turned into a record must know something. What am I going to do? I ask him.

He laughs at me. It doesn't matter.

But, I say, you do something.

Then do something. He pulls out the stool with the chess-board. His hands wrap delicately around the pawns. I wonder if his wife notices it, this delicacy of his hands, or if he is only that way with inanimate things.

From seven to eight every morning I clean his shop. There is a small cupboard with all my appliances. I vacuum the floor, dust off the glass cases, polish the grandfather clock. Then I go home, just before he comes, and stand at the window. The clouds roll by like trains. I stand there invisibly watching the shop. Once a week I stay there until he arrives so he can pay me. In the afternoons I am a visitor, it is different.

Do you have a secret? I ask him point blank. If you don't have one how can you expect me to keep spending all this time here?

Then go, he says. He winks slyly at me and turns to the

chessboard. I see, he says, that you will resign in seven moves.

One morning he didn't come to the shop. He was away for two days. Then he came back, sallow and drawn.

Were you sick?

I had a headache, he said. It was clear that there would be no discussion.

A few weeks later he was away again, this time for three days. I had a headache, he said. It was clear that there would be no discussion. But I persisted.

Alright, he said. I will tell you why I have the headaches. He leaned back in his chair, put his hand on the clock, and closed his eyes.

It was when I was a boy, he said. During the war. We lived in a town that no longer exists. There was my father, my mother and myself. They had seen the war coming, heard stories about what was happening, but when the news broke they were thrown into a panic. The house was in an uproar all the time. One day my mother would send me to school early, to get me out of the house. The next day she would make me stay home and hide in the attic. It went on that way for months. At any moment things would fly off in a different direction. Every day it was said there would be an invasion. Finally my father made up his mind. He told me to pack my things in a small suitcase. Then he took me on a journey. We travelled for two days on a train. We came to a town. You are going to stay with my brother, he said. He is the mayor. No harm will come to you.

But, I said, you never mentioned a brother.

Never mind, he said, I was saving it for a surprise.

He took me to the mayor's house. The mayor was a man much different from my father. He was remote and cold. He patted me on the head as if I was a baby. My father knew I didn't like him but he could do nothing. Everything is agreed, the mayor said. Then my father left.

A week later it happened: there were troops everywhere. In tanks, in jeeps, walking up and down the streets looking for someone to fight. They were billeted in the school and in people's homes. We had a captain at our house. He and the mayor would stay up half the night, drinking and discussing the war. People were always disappearing. There was one time when hostages were shot publicly. The mayor took me to see it. He put his hand on my head and forced me to look. I had no friends except the mayor's wife and there was nothing to do. One day her clock was broken and I fixed it. After that day I fixed clocks and watches. It seemed as if I had always known how. I even fixed the Germans' watches, though somehow I never got them quite right. There was an artillery officer who used to help me when necessary. Eventually the war changed and the Germans left. When the Americans came they didn't want their watches fixed. I asked the mayor when I would be going home.

Your parents are dead, he told me. They were killed two weeks after you came here. So.

And that is why you get the headaches?

No, he said. What I told you was what you expected to hear. If that was enough to give a man a headache the whole world would be in bed. He opened his eyes and patted the clock. The truth is, he said, that it isn't headaches at all. I wake up in the morning and tell my wife to leave the house. I am sick. Then I go back upstairs and lie down on my bed to think. He paused. Don't you want to know what I think about?

Yes, I said.

Good. He leaned back and patted the clock. I will tell you. What I think about is how it happened that my father, a man without a brother, left me at his brother's house. That is unusual, you must admit. It took me a long time to find out but this is what I discovered....

It is impossible to imagine what it was like to be young in Europe when my father was young. He came from a family of no wealth. He was a Jew. The old world seemed to be crumbling yet there was nothing, specifically, that he could have. It was after the First World War. He had been brought up very orthodox and was away from home for the first time. He was studying at a university. But what was he going to do after he studied? Was he going to be a professor? Impossible. A lawyer? How would a man like him, a man of no background, a Jew, get clients? He was a man without a future.

When you have no future the present becomes very important. He met a girl, the daughter of a Jewish merchant. He took her to concerts and had dinner at her house. They went for walks. He felt sorry for himself. He would never be able to afford to marry her. He had a sense that he must destroy something. Yet he was pulled in two directions. The girl was very attractive. She almost loved him. He almost loved her. Perhaps they did love each other. It would be impossible to know; there were other circumstances. They became very involved, going for their long walks in the afternoon. These were secret of course. A respectable girl did not do that in those days, not unless she was engaged. She began to see another man. A man who was older, who would be able to provide her with a house and a life. She felt little for the man but knew that it was inevitable.

My father discovered what was going on. He was young and hopelessly in love with himself, his great despair. The walks grew more frequent. He wrote her passionate letters and said he would kill himself. She was not unmoved by this. They would lie on the grass and my father would describe the various ways in which he might end his life. He would stab himself and shriek her name with his last breath. He would jump off a bridge reciting a poem in her praise. She found this disturbing. It aroused other instincts in her. As he described his suicide my father would caress her, perhaps even kiss her. She would return his kisses.

During this period the other man grew more persistent. He was an established man, a lawyer. He wanted to get married and have children. He couldn't wait forever. He pressed his suit and finally the girl agreed. My father, crushed, did not commit suicide: he left town. A few months later he heard that the man had married — but to a different woman. My father, by now securely in love with his beautiful memory, returned to see the girl. But when he got to the house and knocked on the door, no one answered. Finally he inspected the house. It was clear that no one had been there for months. Everything was out of trim. The curtains were closed.

Disappointed he went to a nearby café to make enquiries. He was told that something terrible had happened to the girl, that the whole family had left town. It was hinted that the girl was pregnant. All suspected that it was the other man. He found out where they were staying and went there. He knocked on the door. The girl's father answered and then, seeing who it was, slammed the door in his face. He knocked again. Go away, the old man shouted.

The next day my father came back. Every day, several times a day, he knocked on the door. Finally they let him in. The girl, of course, was pregnant. Everything was arranged and they got married.

And you were the child?

Yes, he said. I was the child. When the news of the war came my father didn't know what to do. He wanted to hide me somewhere but knew nowhere safe. Finally he hit upon the idea of appealing to the other man, the man who had been engaged to my mother, the man who was the mayor. At first my mother refused. But my father pointed out that there were no other possibilities. There was only one problem. How could he persuade the man to accept me?

He devised a plan. He knew that the other marriage had been barren and that the man had wanted a child. Perhaps he could convince him that he was my true father. It would be a flattering suggestion. Memory fades. My father was very pleased with his gambit. He explained it to my mother. She was curiously silent. It wasn't long before he had the whole story out of her: the man had refused to marry her when he found out she wasn't a virgin.

My father went to visit the mayor. He explained that he had discovered that the child was the mayor's. The danger was obvious. Would the mayor protect it? The mayor refused. What if someone found out he was harbouring a Jew? My father pressed his case. Look, he said, who could possibly know?

You could, the mayor said. If the child is not yours you might well want your revenge.

And so the bargain was made. The day the Germans arrived in my father's town they received a message that there were two members of a Jewish organization, at a certain address. When they searched the house they found guns and knives, the handwritten outline for a pamphlet. My father and mother were waiting in the living room.

And that is what you think about?

No. How can a man think about something like that? It would drive him crazy. He slapped his small hand against the side of the grandfather clock. The truth is that I stay home with my wife. I don't know what's gotten into her. She can't get enough.

His face had disappeared. There was bone and flesh: networks of nerves, veins and arteries laced through the surfaces. He was sitting still, watching the movement of the pendulum. Sometimes it took forever to go from one side to the other. Sometimes it moved so fast that it was almost invisible. Sometimes it stopped altogether.

He stood up. It was time to go home. He put on his coat with the red satin cushion in the pocket.

I see him standing outside the shop, under the awning. I go and visit him in the afternoons and we sit by the grandfather clock, drinking tea and playing chess. He says he has told me all his secrets; but still he tolerates me. I am patient.

Joe Rosenblatt

UNCLE NATHAN SPEAKING FROM
LANDLOCKED GREEN

Wide, wide are the margins of sleep
deep, deep, deep in the flowerbox earth
I sleep ... sleep ... sleep ...
In Carp's ethereal tabernacle
micron lips crackle
spirit embryos gestate
grow jinx wings, umbilical fins, slit gills
cold heart, lung, and lizard's spine
as from a cyanide back bone
flux of shadows strum ... spiritons
from Death's encrusted harp.
Nephew, in this world
no dust remains, no nickle photos of our bones.
We are beyond dust
where spiritons and atoms hum
around a perfect planetary sun.
— such is spectral sex —
from worm to fluorescent penetrant
in the grave, we all swing polar umbra.
Oye, so vengeful is Death's metamorphosis
that I go reincarnated in a minnow's whisper
who once dwelt as a barbaric fishmonger;
and now who can measure my sad physique?

or catch my whisper on a spectrograph.
Yet more soul pinching than worm's acetylene:
There is no commerce in the Netherworld.
Earth Momma, forgive me
for every fish I disembowelled was a child;
there is no Kaddish for aborted caviar.

Earth! Earth! is the bitch still green
liced with people and Aardvark powers?
And my shop on Baldwin street
does it stand? ... damp and sacred as the Wailing Wall

79

under the caterpillar'd canopy of God?
or has my neighbour swallowed up my Carp shrined enterprise
where I cradled images from Lake Genneserat
to fish fertiled ladies with halvah tongues
who shred my serpents into shrimp bread,
for fish food oscillates an old maid's chromosomes!
Carp, pickerel, transmogrified
where swimmers have been tranquilized
stomach's the body's palpitating madrigal.
God bless the primate's primeval stretch
but O to touch … touch …
a moon's vibration of a silver dollar
to see the fish scales rise and fall
before Lent's locust of Friday's carnivores.
Nephew, heaven is on Earth; above me
the sky is smiling like a White fish.
Its eyes are the moon and the sun.

ICHTHYCIDE

My uncle was Sabbath crazed
wouldn't flick a switch on Saturday
but on the caudal fin of Friday evening
he'd be cutting up Neptune's nudist colony
into mean kingdom cutlets.
On Friday, Uncle Nathan lowered a butterfly net
to catch an Alcatraz shadow
dreaming myriads of muscled minnows:
spice cuisines of Esther Williams — fish pornography.

Lips ellipsing; a spiny Baptist lay on newspaper
blue leviathan with chopped up vertebrae
fanned fins in vendor's prayer
while scaly fingers mummified the prophet
— a fish head conjured Salome in a basket —

I too have knifed the sacred fish
have carnivored to please my palate:
a bass from a Chinese steam bath
lay in a puddle of soya sauce.
This stranded swimmer on his oval casket
balanced death on optic centres;
animal penumbra expired for post mortem
I ghouled my way to the neck bone
then turned away from the Last Supper
for the eyes of Moby illuminated
or were they the fish eyes of Uncle Nathan?

Sleep Uncle Nathan, sexton in Narwhale's synagogue!

Ted Allan

LIES MY FATHER TOLD ME

My grandfather stood six feet three in his worn-out bedroom slippers. He had a long grey beard with streaks of white running through it. When he prayed, his voice boomed like a choir as he turned the pages of his prayer-book with one hand and stroked his beard with the other. His hands were bony and looked like tree-roots; they were powerful. My grandpa had been a farmer in the old country. In Montreal he conducted what he called "a second-hand business".

In his youth, I was told, Grandpa had been something of a wild man, drinking and playing with the village wenches until my grandmother took him in hand. In his old age, when I knew him, he had become a very religious man. He prayed three times a day on week-days and all day on Saturday. In between prayers he rode around on a wagon which, as I look back, rolled on despite all the laws of physics and mechanics. Its four wheels always seemed to be going in every direction but forwards. The horse that pulled the wagon was called Ferdeleh. He was my pet and it was only much later, when I had seen many other horses, that I realized that Ferdeleh was not everything a horse could have been. His belly hung very low, almost touching the street when he walked. His head went back and forth in jerky motions in complete disharmony with the rest of him. He moved slowly, almost painfully, apparently realizing that he was capable of only one speed and determined to go no faster or slower than the rate he had established some time back. Next to Grandpa I loved Ferdeleh best, with the possible exception of God, or my mother when she gave me candy.

On Sundays, when it didn't rain, Grandpa, Ferdeleh and myself would go riding through the back lanes of Montreal. The lanes then were not paved as they are now, and after a rainy Saturday, the mud would be inches deep and the wagon heaved and shook like a barge in a stormy sea. Ferdeleh's pace remained, as always, the same. He liked the mud. It was easy on his feet.

When the sun shone through my windows on Sunday morning I would jump out of bed, wash, dress, run into the kitchen where

Grandpa and I said our morning prayers, and then we'd both go to harness and feed Ferdeleh. On Sundays Ferdeleh would whinny like a happy child. He knew it was an extra special day for all of us. By the time he had finished his oats and hay Grandpa and I would be finished with our breakfast which Grandma and Mother had prepared for us.

Then we'd go through what Grandpa called "the women's Sunday song". It went like this: "Don't let him hold the reins crossing streets. Be sure to come back if it starts to rain. Be sure not to let him hold the reins crossing streets. Be sure to come back if it starts to rain." They would repeat this about three hundred times until Grandpa and I were weary from nodding our heads and saying, "Yes". We could hear it until we turned the corner and went up the lane of the next street.

Then began the most wonderful of days as we drove through the dirt lanes of Montreal, skirting the garbage cans, jolting and bouncing through the mud and dust, calling every cat by name and every cat meowing its hello, and Grandpa and I holding our hands to our ears and shouting at the top of our lungs, "Regs, cloze, botels! Regs, cloze, botels!"

What a wonderful game that was! I would run up the back stairs and return with all kinds of fascinating things, old dresses, suits, pants, rags, newspapers, all shapes of bottles, all shapes of trash, everything you can think of, until the wagon was filled.

Sometimes a woman would ask me to send Grandpa up to give her a price on what she had, and Grandpa would shout up from downstairs, "My feet ache. The boy will give you a price." I knew what he offered for an old suit, for an old dress, and I would shout down describing the items in question and the state of deterioration. For clothes that were nothing better than rags we offered a standard price, "Fifteen cents, take it or leave it." Clothes that might be repaired I would hold out for Grandpa to see and he'd appraise them. And so we'd go through the lanes of the city.

Sometimes the women would not be satisfied with the money Grandpa had given me for them. Grandpa would always say, "Eleshka, women always want more than they get. Remember that. Give them a finger and they want the whole hand."

My Sunday rides were the happiest times I spent. Sometimes Grandpa would let me wear his derby hat which came down over my ears, and people would look at me and laugh and I'd feel even happier feeling how happy everyone was on Sunday.

Sometimes strange, wonderful smells would come over the city, muffling the smell of the garbage cans. When this happened we would stop Ferdeleh and breathe deeply. It smelled of sea and of oak trees and flowers. Then we knew we were near the mountain in the centre of the city and that the wind from the river was bringing the perfume of the mountain and spraying it over the city. Often we would ride out of the back lanes and up the mountain road. We couldn't go too far up because it was a strain on Ferdeleh. As far as we went, surrounded on each side by tall poplars and evergreens, Grandpa would tell me about the old country, about the rivers and the farms, and sometimes he'd get off the wagon and pick up some earth in his hands. He'd squat, letting the earth fall between his fingers, and I'd squat beside him doing the same thing.

When we came to the mountain Grandpa's mood would change and he would talk to me of the great land that Canada was, and of the great things the young people growing up were going to do in this great land. Ferdeleh would walk to the edge of the road and eat the thick grass on the sides. Grandpa was at home among the trees and black earth and thick grass and on our way down the mountain road he would sing songs that weren't prayers, but happy songs in Russian. Sometimes he'd clap his hands to the song as I held the reins and Ferdeleh would look back at him and shake his head with pleasure.

One Sunday on our ride home through the mountain a group of young boys and girls threw stones at us and shouted in French: "Juif…. Juif …!" Grandpa held his strong arm around me, cursed back muttering "anti-Semites" under his breath. When I asked him what he said he answered, "It is something I hope you never learn." The boys and girls laughed and got tired of throwing stones. That was the last Sunday we went to the mountain.

If it rained on Sunday my mother wouldn't let me go out, so every Saturday evening I prayed for the sun to shine on Sunday. Once I almost lost faith in God and in the power of prayer but Grandpa fixed it. For three Sundays in succession it rained. In my desperation I took it out on God. What was the use of praying to Him if He didn't listen to you? I complained to Grandpa.

"Perhaps you don't pray right," he suggested.

"But I do. I say, Our God in heaven, hallowed be Thy name, Thy will on earth as it is in heaven. Please don't let it rain tomorrow."

"Ah! In English you pray?" my grandfather exclaimed triumphantly.

"Yes," I answered.

"But God only answers prayers in Hebrew. I will teach you how to say that prayer in Hebrew. And, if God doesn't answer, it's your own fault. He's angry because you didn't use the Holy Language." But God wasn't angry because next Sunday the sun shone its brightest and the three of us went for our Sunday ride.

On week-days, Grandpa and I rose early, a little after daybreak, and said our morning prayers. I would mimic his sing-song lamentations, sounding as if my heart were breaking and wondering why we both had to sound so sad. I must have put everything I had into it because Grandpa assured me that one day I would become a great cantor and a leader of the Hebrews. "You will sing so that the ocean will open up a path before you and you will lead our people to a new paradise."

I was six then and he was the only man I ever understood even when I didn't understand his words. I learned a lot from him. If he didn't learn a lot from me, he made me feel he did.

I remember once saying, "You know, sometimes I think I'm the son of God. Is it possible?"

"It is possible," he answered, "but don't rely on it. Many of us are sons of God. The important thing is not to rely too much upon it. The harder we work, the harder we study, the more we accomplish, the surer we are that we are sons of God."

At the synagogue on Saturday his old, white-bearded friends would surround me and ask me questions. Grandpa would stand by and burst with pride. I strutted like a peacock.

"Who is David?" the old men would ask me.

"He's the man with the beard, the man with the bearded words." And they laughed.

"And who is God?" they would ask me.

"King and Creator of the Universe, the All-Powerful One, the Almighty One, more powerful even than Grandpa." They laughed again and I thought I was pretty smart. So did Grandpa. So did my grandmother and my mother.

So did everyone, except my father. I didn't like my father. He said things to me like, "For God's sake, you're smart, but not as smart as you think. Nobody is that smart." He was jealous of me and he told me lies. He told me lies about Ferdeleh.

"Ferdeleh is one part horse, one part camel, and one part chicken," he told me. Grandpa told me that was a lie, Ferdeleh was all horse. "If he is part anything, he is part human," said Grandpa. I agreed with him. Ferdeleh understood everything we said to him. No matter what part of the city he was in, he could find his way home, even in the dark.

"Ferdeleh is going to collapse one day in one heap," my father said. "Ferdeleh is carrying twins." "Ferdeleh is going to keel over one day and die." "He should be shot now or he'll collapse under you one of these days," my father would say. Neither I nor Grandpa had much use for the opinions of my father.

On top of everything, my father had no beard, didn't pray, didn't go to the synagogue on the Sabbath, read English books and never read the prayer-books, played piano on the Sabbath and sometimes would draw my mother into his villainies by making her sing while he played. On the Sabbath this was an abomination to both Grandpa and me.

One day I told my father, "Papa, you have forsaken your fore-fathers." He burst out laughing and kissed me and then my mother kissed me, which infuriated me all the more.

I could forgive my father these indignities, his not treating me as an equal, but I couldn't forgive his telling lies about Ferdeleh. Once he said that Ferdeleh "smelled up" the whole house, and demanded that Grandpa move the stable. It was true that the kitchen, being next to the stable, which was in the back shed, did sometimes smell of hay and manure but, as Grandpa said, "What is wrong with such a smell? It is a good healthy smell."

It was a house divided, with my grandmother, mother and father on one side, and Grandpa, Ferdeleh and me on the other. One day a man came to the house and said he was from the Board of Health and that the neighbours had complained about the stable. Grandpa and I knew we were beaten then. You could get around the Board of Health, Grandpa informed me, if you could grease the palms of the officials. I suggested the obvious but Grandpa explained that this type of "grease" was made of gold. The stable would have to be moved. But where?

As it turned out, Grandpa didn't have to worry about it. The whole matter was taken out of his hands a few weeks later.

Next Sunday the sun shone brightly and I ran to the kitchen to say my prayers with Grandpa. But Grandpa wasn't there. I found my grandmother there instead — weeping. Grandpa was in his room ill. He had a sickness they called diabetes and at that time the only thing you could do about diabetes was weep. I fed Ferdeleh and soothed him because I knew how disappointed he was.

That week I was taken to an aunt of mine. There was no explanation given. My parents thought I was too young to need any explanations. On Saturday next I was brought home, too late to see Grandpa that evening, but I felt good knowing that I would spend the next day with him and Ferdeleh again.

When I came to the kitchen Sunday morning Grandpa was not there. Ferdeleh was not in the stable. I thought they were playing a joke on me so I rushed to the front of the house expecting to see Grandpa sitting atop the wagon waiting for me.

But there wasn't any wagon. My father came up behind me and put his hand on my head. I looked up questioningly and he said, "Grandpa and Ferdeleh have gone to heaven.... "

When he told me they were *never* coming back, I moved away from him and went to my room. I lay down on my bed and cried, not for Grandpa and Ferdeleh, because I knew they would never do such a thing to me, but about my father, because he had told me such a horrible lie.

Fredelle Bruser Maynard

JEWISH CHRISTMAS

Christmas, when I was young, was the season of bitterness. Lights beckoned and tinsel shone, store windows glowed with mysterious promise, but I knew the brilliance was not for me. Being Jewish, I had long grown accustomed to isolation and difference. Difference was in my bones and blood, and in the pattern of my separate life. My parents were conspicuously unlike other children's parents in our predominantly Norwegian community. Where my schoolmates were surrounded by blond giants appropriate to a village called Birch Hills, my family suggested still the Russian plains from which they had emigrated years before. My handsome father was a big man, but big without any suggestion of physical strength or agility; one could not imagine him at the wheel of a tractor. In a town that was all wheat and cattle, he seemed the one man wholly devoted to urban pursuits: he operated a general store. Instead of the native costume — overalls and mackinaws — he wore city suits and pearl-gray spats. In winter he was splendid in a plushy chinchilla coat with velvet collar, his black curly hair an extension of the high astrakhan hat which he had brought from the Ukraine. I was proud of his good looks, and yet uneasy about their distinctly oriental flavor.

My mother's difference was of another sort. Her beauty was not so much foreign as timeless. My friends had slender young Scandinavian mothers, light of foot and blue of eye; my mother was short and heavyset, but with a face of classic proportions. Years later I found her in the portraits of Ingres and Corot — face a delicate oval, brown velvet eyes, brown silk hair centrally parted and drawn back in a lustrous coil — but in those days I saw only that she too was different. As for my grandparents, they were utterly unlike the benevolent, apple-cheeked characters who presided over happy families in my favorite stories. (Evidently all those happy families were gentile.) My grandmother had no fringed shawl, no steel-rimmed glasses. (She read, if at all, with the help of a magnifying glass from Woolworth's.) Ignorant, apparently, of her natural role as gentle occupant of the rocking chair, she was ignorant too of the world outside her apartment in remote Winnipeg. She had brought Odessa with her, and — on my rare visits — she smiled lovingly, uncomprehendingly, across an ocean of time and space. Even more unreal was my grandfather, a black cap and a long beard bent over the Talmud. I felt for him a kind of amused tenderness, but I was glad that my schoolmates could not see him.

At home we spoke another language — Yiddish or Russian — and ate rich foods whose spicy odors bore no resemblance to the neighbor's cooking. We did not go to church or belong to clubs or, it seemed, take any meaningful part in the life of the town. Our social roots went, not down into the foreign soil on which fate had deposited us, but outwards, in delicate, sensitive connections, to other Jewish families in other lonely prairie towns. Sundays, they congregated around our table, these strangers who were brothers; I saw that they too ate knishes and spoke with faintly foreign voices, but I could not feel for them or for their silent swarthy children the kinship I knew I owed to all those who had been, like us, both chosen and abandoned.

All year I walked in the shadow of difference; but at Christmas above all, I tasted it sour on my tongue. There was no room at the tree. "You have Hanukkah," my father reminded me. "That is *our* holiday." I knew the story, of course — how, over two thousand years ago, my people had triumphed over the enemies of their faith, and how a single jar of holy oil had miraculously burned eight days and nights in the temple of the Lord. I thought of my father lighting each night another candle in the *menorah*, my mother and I beside him as he recited the ancient prayer: "Blessed art Thou, O Lord our God, ruler of the universe, who has sanctified us by thy commandments and commanded us to kindle the light of Hanukkah." Yes, we had our miracle too. But how could it stand against the glamor of Christmas? What was *gelt*, the traditional gift coins, to a sled packed with surprises? What was Judas Maccabaeus the liberator compared with the Christ child in the manger? To my sense of exclusion was added a sense of shame. "You *killed* Christ!" said the boys on the playground. "*You* killed him!" I knew none of the facts behind this awful accusation, but I was afraid to ask. I was even afraid to raise my voice in the chorus of "Come All Ye Faithful" lest I be struck down for my unfaithfulness by my own God, the wrathful Jehovah. With all the passion of my child's heart I longed for a younger, more compassionate deity with flowing robe and silken hair. Reluctant conscript to a doomed army, I longed to change sides. I longed for Christmas.

Although my father was in all things else the soul of indulgence, in this one matter he stood firm as Moses. "You cannot have a tree, *herzele*. You shouldn't even want to sing the carols. You are a Jew." I turned the words over in my mind and on my tongue. What was it, to be a Jew in Birch Hills, Saskatchewan? Though my father spoke of Jewishness as a special distinction, as far as I could see it was an inheritance without a kingdom, a check on a bank that had failed. Being Jewish was mostly not doing things other people did — not eating pork, not going to Sunday school, not entering, even playfully, into childhood romances, because the only boys around were *goyishe* boys. I remember, when I was five or six, falling in love with Edward, Prince of Wales. Of the many arguments with which Mama might have dampened my ardor, she chose surely the most extraordinary. "You can't marry him. He isn't Jewish." And of course, finally, definitely, most crushing of all, being Jewish meant not celebrating Christ's birth. My parents allowed me to attend Christmas parties, but they made it clear that I must receive no gifts. How I envied the white and gold Norwegians! Their Lutheran church was not glamorous, but it was less frighteningly strange than the synagogue I had visited in Winnipeg, and in the Lutheran church, each December, joy came upon the midnight clear.

It was the Lutheran church and its annual concert which brought me closest to Christmas. Here there was always a tree, a jolly Santa Claus, and a program of songs and recitations. As the town's most accomplished elocutionist, I was regularly invited to perform. Usually my offering was comic or purely secular — *Santa's Mistake*, *The Night Before Christmas*, a scene from *A Christmas Carol*. But I had also memorized for such occasions a sweetly pious narrative about the housewife who, blindly absorbed in cleaning her house for the Lord's arrival, turns away a beggar and finds she has rebuffed the Savior himself. Oddly enough, my recital of this vitally un-Jewish material gave my parents no pain. My father, indeed, kept in his safe-deposit box along with other valuables a letter in which the Lutheran minister spoke gratefully of my last Christmas performance. "Through her great gift, your little Freidele has led many to Jesus." Though Papa seemed untroubled by considerations of whether this was a proper role for a Jewish child, reciting *The Visit* made me profoundly uneasy. And I suppose it was this feeling, combined with a natural disinclination to stand unbidden at the feast, which led me, the year I was seven, to rebel.

We were baking in the steamy kitchen, my mother and I — or rather she was baking while I watched, fascinated as always, the miracle of the strudel. First, the warm ball of dough, no larger than my mother's hand. Slap, punch, bang — again and again she lifted the dough and smacked it down on the board. Then came the moment I loved. Over the kitchen table, obliterating its patterned oilcloth, came a damask cloth; and over this in turn a cloud of flour. Beside it stood my mother, her hair bound in muslin, her hands and arms powdered with flour. She paused a moment. Then, like a dancer about to execute a particularly difficult pirouette, she tossed the dough high in the air, catching it with a little stretching motion and tossing again until the ball was ball no longer but an almost transparent rectangle. The strudel was as large as the tablecloth now. *"Unter Freidele's vigele Ligt eyn groys veys tsigele,"* she sang. "Under Freidele's little bed A white goat lays his silken head." *"Tsigele iz geforen handlen Rozinkes mit mandlen...."* For some reason that song, with its gay fantastic images of the white goat shopping for raisins and almonds, always made me sad. But then my father swung open the storm door and stood, stamping and jingling his galoshes buckles, on the icy mat.

"Boris, look how you track in the snow!"

Already flakes and stars were turning into muddy puddles. Still booted and icy-cheeked he swept us up — a kiss on the back of Mama's neck, the only spot not dedicated to strudel, and a hug for me.

"You know what? I have just now seen the preacher. Reverend Pederson, he wants you should recite at the Christmas concert."

I bent over the bowl of almonds and snapped the nut-cracker.

"I should tell him it's all right, you'll speak a piece?"

No answer.

"Sweetheart — dear one — you'll do it?"

Suddenly the words burst out. "No, Papa! I don't want to!"

My father was astonished. "But why not? What is it with you?"

"I hate those concerts!" All at once my grievances swarmed up in an angry cloud. "I never have any fun! And everybody else gets presents and Santa Claus never calls out 'Freidele Bruser'! They all know I'm Jewish!"

Papa was incredulous. "But, little daughter, always you've had a good time! Presents! What presents? A bag of candy, an orange? Tell me, is there a child in town with such toys as you have? What should you want with Santa Claus?"

It was true. My friends had tin tea sets and dolls with sawdust bodies and crude celluloid smiles. I had an Eaton beauty with real hair and delicate jointed body, two French dolls with rosy bisque faces and — new this last Hanukkah — Rachel, my baby doll. She was the marvel of the town: exquisite china head, overlarge and shaped like a real infant's, tiny wrinkled hands, legs convincingly bowed. I had a lace and taffeta doll bassinet, a handmade cradle, a full set of rattan doll furniture, a teddy bear from Germany and real porcelain dishes from England. What *did* I want with Santa Claus? I didn't know. I burst into tears.

Papa was frantic now. What was fame and the applause of the Lutherans compared to his child's tears? Still bundled in his overcoat he knelt on the kitchen floor and hugged me to him, rocking and crooning. "Don't cry, my child, don't cry. You don't want to go, you don't have to. I tell them you have a sore throat, you can't come."

"Boris, wait. Listen to me." For the first time since my outburst, Mama spoke. She laid down the rolling pin, draped the strudel dough delicately over the table, and wiped her hands on her apron. "What kind of a fuss? You go or you don't go, it's not such a big thing. But so close to Christmas you shouldn't let them down. The one time we sit with them in the church and such joy you give them. Freidele, look at me.... " I snuffled loudly and obeyed, not without some satisfaction in the thought of the pathetic picture I made. "Go this one time, for my sake. You'll see, it won't be so bad. And if you don't like it — pffff, no more! All right? Now, come help with the raisins."

On the night of the concert we gathered in the kitchen again, this time for the ritual of the bath. Papa set up the big tin tub on chairs next to the black iron stove. Then, while he heated pails of water and sloshed them into the tub, Mama set out my clothes. Everything about this moment contrived to make me feel pampered, special. I was lifted in and out of the steamy water, patted dry with thick towels, powdered from neck to toes with Mama's best scented talcum. Then came my "reciting outfit". My friends in Birch Hills had party dresses mail-ordered from Eaton's — crackly taffeta or shiny rayon satin weighted with lace or flounces, and worn with long white stockings drawn up over long woolen underwear. My dress was Mama's own composition, a poem in palest peach crepe de chine created from remnants of her bridal trousseau. Simple and flounceless, it fell from my shoulders in a myriad of tiny pleats no wider than my thumbnail; on the low-slung sash hung a cluster of silk rosebuds. Regulation drop-seat underwear being unthinkable under such a costume, Mama had devised a snug little apricot chemise which made me, in a world of wool, feel excitingly naked.

When at last I stood on the church dais, the Christmas tree glittering and shimmering behind me, it was with the familiar feeling of strangeness. I looked out over the audience-congregation, grateful for the myopia that made faces indistinguishable, and began:

A letter came on Christmas morn
In which the Lord did say
"Behold my star shines in the east
And I shall come today.
Make bright thy hearth…. "

The words tripped on without thought or effort. I knew by heart every nuance and gesture, down to the modest curtsey and the properly solemn pace with which I returned to my seat. There I huddled into the lining of Papa's coat, hardly hearing the "Beautiful, beautiful!" which accompanied his hug. For this was the dreaded moment. All around me, children twitched and whispered. Santa had come.

"Olaf Swenson!" Olaf tripped over a row of booted feet, leapt down the aisle and embraced an enormous package. "Ellen Njaa! Fern Dahl! Peter Bjorkstrom!" There was a regular procession now, all jubilant. Everywhere in the hall children laughed, shouted, rejoiced with their friends. "What'd you get?" "Look at mine!" In the seat next to me, Gunnar Olsen ripped through layers of tissue: "I got it! I got it!" His little sister wrestled with the contents of a red net stocking. A tin whistle rolled to my feet and I turned away, ignoring her breathless efforts to retrieve it.

And then — suddenly, incredibly, the miracle came. "Freidele Bruser!" For me, too, the star had shone. I looked up at my mother. A mistake surely. But she smiled and urged me to my feet. "Go on, look, he calls you!" It was true. Santa was actually coming to meet me. My gift, I saw, was not wrapped — and it could be no mistake. It was a doll, a doll just like Rachel, but dressed in christening gown and cap. "Oh Mama, look! He's brought me a doll! A twin for Rachel! She's just the right size for Rachel's clothes. I can take them both for walks in the carriage. They can have matching outfits…. " I was in an ecstasy of plans.

Mama did not seem to be listening. She lifted the hem of the gown. "How do you like her dress? Look, see the petticoat?"

"They're beautiful!" I hugged the doll rapturously. "Oh, Mama, I *love* her! I'm going to call her Ingrid. Ingrid and Rachel.... "

During the long walk home Mama was strangely quiet. Usually I held my parents' hands and swung between them. But now I stepped carefully, clutching Ingrid.

"You had a good time, yes?" Papa's breath frosted the night.

"Mmmmmmm." I rubbed my warm cheek against Ingrid's cold one. "It was just like a real Christmas. I got the best present of anybody. Look, Papa — did you see Ingrid's funny little cross face? It's just like Rachel's. I can't wait to get her home and see them side by side in the crib."

In the front hall, I shook the snow from Ingrid's lace bonnet. "A hot cup of cocoa maybe?" Papa was already taking the milk from the icebox. "No, no, I want to get the twins ready for bed!" I broke from my mother's embrace. The stairs seemed longer than usual. In my arms Ingrid was cold and still, a snow princess. I could dress her in Rachel's flannel gown, that would be the thing.... The dolls and animals watched glassy-eyed as I knelt by the cradle. It rocked at my touch, oddly light. I flung back the blankets. Empty. Of course.

Sitting on the cold floor, the doll heavy in my lap, I wept for Christmas. Nothing had changed then, after all. For Jews there was no Santa Claus; I understood that. But my parents.... *Why* had they dressed Rachel?

From the kitchen below came the mingled aromas of hot chocolate and buttery popcorn. My mother called softly. "Let them call," I said to Ingrid-Rachel. "I don't care!" The face of the Christmas doll was round and blank under her cap; her dress was wet with my tears. Brushing them away, I heard my father enter the room. He made no move to touch me or lift me up. I turned and saw his face tender and sad like that of a Chagall violinist. "Mama worked every night on the clothes," he said. "Yesterday even, knitting booties."

Stiff-fingered, trembling, I plucked at the sleeve of the christening gown. It was indeed a miracle — a wisp of batiste but as richly overlaid with embroidery as a coronation robe. For the first time I examined Rachel's new clothes — the lace insets and lace overlays, the French knots and scalloped edges, the rows of hemstitching through which tiny ribbons ran like fairy silk. The petticoat was tucked and pleated. Even the little diaper showed an edge of hand crochet. There were booties and mittens and a ravishing cap.

"Freidele, dear one, my heart," my father whispered. "We did not think. We could not know. Mama dressed Rachel in the new clothes, you should be happy with the others. We so much love you."

Outside my window, where the Christmas snow lay deep and crisp and even, I heard the shouts of neighbors returning from the concert. "Joy to the world!" they sang,

> *Let earth receive her King!*
> *Let every heart prepare Him room*
> *And heaven and nature sing….*

It seemed to me, at that moment, that I too was a part of the song. I wrapped Rachel warmly in her shawl and took my father's hand.

Lela Parlow

DECEMBER: OUR STORE WINDOW

Ma tracks mountains and tunnels, plants
trees and flags (British and American, both came
with the set) you promise me the train.
She tinsels stations, hitches flatcars to
doll-faced coaches, sends cannonball into space
you promise me the train.

I wave to the flagman disappearing over
the hill/touch/the world's parts/one
finger/at a time/pull away/as the
engine approaches/pull away from/the steamy
other-child eyes pressing inward on
the window the train is mine.

Ma sells the train, we can't afford it
she says/you agree.
You give me a bride-doll for Hannukah.
She can't even walk.

A BASKET OF APPLES

This morning Pa had his operation. He said I was not to come for at least two or three days, but I slipped in anyway and took a look at him. He was asleep, and I was there only a minute before I was hustled out by a nurse.

"He looks terrible, nurse. Is he all right?"

She said he was fine. The operation was successful, there were no secondaries, instead of a bowel he would have a colostomy, and with care should last another ——

Colostomy. The word had set up such a drumming in my ears that I can't be sure now whether she said another few years or another five years. Let's say she said five years. If I go home and report this to Ma she'll fall down in a dead faint. She doesn't even know he's had an operation. She thinks he's in the hospital for a rest, a check-up. Nor did we know — my brother, my sister, and I — that he'd been having a series of x-rays.

"It looks like an obstruction in the lower bowel," he told us privately, "and I'll have to go in the hospital for a few days to find out what it's all about. Don't say anything to Ma."

"I have to go in the hospital," he announced to Ma the morning he was going in.

She screamed.

"Just for a little rest, a check-up," he went on, patient with her for once.

He's always hollering at her. He scolds her for a meal that isn't to his taste, finds fault with her housekeeping, gives her hell because her hair isn't combed in the morning and sends her back to the bedroom to tidy herself.

But Ma loves the old man. "Sooner a harsh word from Pa than a kind one from anyone else," she says.

"You're not to come and see me, you hear?" he cautioned her the morning he left for the hospital. "I'll phone you when I'm coming out."

I don't want to make out that my pa's a beast. He's not. True, he never speaks an endearing word to her, never praises her. He loses patience with her, flies off the handle and shouts. But Ma's content. Poor man works like a horse, she says, and what pleasures does he have. "So he hollers at me once in a while, I don't mind. God give him the strength to keep hollering at me, I won't repine."

Night after night he joins his buddies in the back room of an ice-cream parlor on Augusta Avenue for a glass of wine, a game of klaberjass, pinochle, dominoes: she's happy he's enjoying himself. She blesses him on his way out. "God keep you in good health and return you in good health."

But when he is home of an evening reading the newspaper and comes across an item that engages his interest, he lets her in on it too. He shows her a picture of the Dionne quintuplets and explains exactly what happened out there in Callander, Ontario. This is a golden moment for her — she and Pa sitting over a newspaper discussing world events. Another time he shows her a picture of the Irish Sweepstakes winner. He won a hundred and fifty thousand, he tells her. She's entranced. *Mmm-mm-mm!* What she couldn't do with that money. They'd fix up the bathroom, paint the kitchen, clean out the backyard. *Mmm-mm-mm!* Pa says if we had that kind of money we could afford to put a match to a hundred-dollar bill, set fire to the house and buy a new one. She laughs at his wit. He's so clever, Pa. Christmas morning King George VI is speaking on the radio. She's rattling around in the kitchen, Pa calls her to come and hear the King of England. She doesn't understand a word of English, but pulls up a chair and sits listening. "He stutters," says Pa. This she won't believe. A king? Stutters? But if Pa says so it must be true. She bends an ear to the radio. Next day she has something to report to Mrs. Oxenberg, our next-door neighbor.

I speak of Pa's impatience with her; I get impatient with her too. I'm always at her about one thing and another, chiefly about the weight she's putting on. Why doesn't she cut down on the bread, does she have to drink twenty glasses of tea a day? No wonder her feet are sore, carrying all that weight. (My ma's a short woman a little over five feet and weighs almost two hundred pounds.) "Go ahead, keep getting fatter," I tell her. "The way you're going you'll never be able to get into a decent dress again."

But it's Pa who finds a dress to fit her, a Martha Washington Cotton size 52, which but for the length is perfect for her. He finds a shoe she can wear, Romeo Slippers with elasticized sides. And it's Pa who gets her to soak her feet, then sits with them in his lap scraping away with a razor blade at the calluses and corns.

Ma is my father's second wife, and our stepmother. My father, now sixty-three, was widowed thirty years ago. My sister was six at the time, I was five, and my brother four when our mother died giving birth to a fourth child who lived only a few days. We were shunted around from one family to another who took us in out of compassion, till finally my father went to a marriage broker and put his case before him. He wanted a woman to make a home for his three orphans. An honest woman with a good heart, these were the two and only requirements. The marriage broker consulted his lists and said he thought he had two or three people who might fill the bill. Specifically, he had in mind a young woman from Russia, thirty years old, who was working without pay for relatives who had brought her over. She wasn't exactly an educated woman; in fact, she couldn't even read or write. As for honesty and heart, this he could vouch for. She was an orphan herself and as a child had been brought up in servitude.

Of the three women the marriage broker trotted out for him, my father chose Ma, and shortly afterward they were married.

A colostomy. So it is cancer....

As of the second day Pa was in hospital I had taken to dropping in on him on my way home from work. "Nothing yet," he kept saying, "maybe tomorrow they'll find out."

After each of these visits, four in all, I reported to Ma that I had seen Pa. "He looks fine. Best thing in the world for him, a rest in the hospital."

"Pa's not lonesome for me?" she asked me once, and laughing, turned her head aside to hide her foolishness from me.

Yesterday Pa said to me, "It looks a little more serious than I thought. I have to have an operation tomorrow. Don't say anything to Ma. And don't come here for at least two or three days."

I take my time getting home. I'm not too anxious to face Ma — grinning like a monkey and lying to her the way I have been doing the last four days. I step into a hospital telephone booth to call my married sister. She moans. "What are you going to say to Ma?" she asks.

I get home about half past six, and Ma's in the kitchen making a special treat for supper. A recipe given her by a neighbor and which she's recently put in her culinary inventory — pieces of cauliflower dipped in batter and fried in butter.

"I'm not hungry, Ma. I had something in the hospital cafeteria."

(We speak in Yiddish; as I mentioned before, Ma can't speak English.)

She continues scraping away at the cauliflower stuck to the bottom of the pan. (Anything she puts in a pan sticks.) "You saw Pa?" she asks without looking up. Suddenly she thrusts the pan aside. "The devil take it, I put in too much flour." She makes a pot of tea, and we sit at the kitchen table drinking it. To keep from facing her I drink mine leafing through a magazine. I can hear her sipping hers through a cube of sugar in her mouth. I can feel her eyes on me. Why doesn't she ask me, How's Pa? Why doesn't she speak? She never stops questioning me when I come from hospital, drives me crazy with the same questions again and again. I keep turning pages, she's still sucking away at that cube of sugar — a maddening habit of hers. I look up. Of course her eyes are fixed on me, probing, searching.

I lash out at her. "Why are you looking at me like that!"

Without answer she takes her tea and dashes it in the sink. She spits the cube of sugar from her mouth. (Thank God for that; she generally puts it back in the sugar bowl.) She resumes her place, puts her hands in her lap, and starts twirling her thumbs. No one in the world can twirl his thumbs as fast as Ma. When she gets them going they look like miniature windmills whirring around.

"She asks me why I'm looking at her like that," she says, addressing herself to the twirling thumbs in her lap. "I'm looking at her like that because I'm trying to read the expression in her face. She tells me Pa's fine, but my heart tells me different."

Suddenly she looks up, and thrusting her head forward, splays her hands out flat on the table. She has a dark-complexioned strong face, masculine almost, and eyes so black the pupil is indistinguishable from the iris.

"Do you know who Pa is!" she says. "Do you know who's lying in the hospital? I'll tell you who. The captain of our ship is lying in the hospital. The emperor of our domain. If the captain goes down, the ship goes with him. If the emperor leaves his throne, we can say good-bye to our domain. That's who's lying in the hospital. Now ask me why do I look at you like that."

She breaks my heart. I want to put my arms around her, but I can't do it. We're not a demonstrative family, we never kiss, we seldom show affection. We're always hollering at each other. Less than a month ago I hollered at Pa. He had taken to dosing himself. He was forever mixing something in a glass, and I became irritated at the powders, pills, and potions lying around in every corner of the house like mouse droppings.

"You're getting to be a hypochondriac!" I hollered at him, not knowing what trouble he was in.

I reach out and put my hand over hers. "I wouldn't lie to you, Ma. Pa's fine, honest to God."

She holds her hand still a few seconds, then eases it from under and puts it over mine. I can feel the weight of her hand pinioning mine to the table, and in an unaccustomed gesture of tenderness we sit a moment with locked hands.

"You know I had a dream about Pa last night?" she says. "I dreamt he came home with a basket of apples. I think that's a good dream?"

Ma's immigration to Canada had been sponsored by her Uncle Yankev. Yankev at the time he sent for his niece was in his mid-forties and had been settled a number of years in Toronto with his wife, Danyeh, and their six children. They made an odd pair, Yankev and Danyeh. He was a tall two-hundred-and-fifty-pound handsome man, and Danyeh, whom he detested, was a lackluster little woman with a pockmarked face, maybe weighing ninety pounds. Yankev was constantly abusing her. Old Devil, he called her to her face and in the presence of company.

Ma stayed three years with Yankev and his family, working like a skivvy for them and without pay. Why would Yankev pay his niece like a common servant? She was one of the family, she sat at table with them and ate as much as she wanted. She had a bed and even a room to herself, which she'd never had before. When Yankev took his family for a ride in the car to Sunnyside, she was included. When he bought ice-cream cones, he bought for all.

She came to Pa without a dime in her pocket.

Ma has a slew of relatives, most of them émigrés from a remote little village somewhere in the depths of Russia. They're a crude lot, loudmouthed and coarse, and my father (but for a few exceptions) had no use for any of them. The Russian Hordes, he called them. He was never rude; any time they came around to visit he simply made himself scarce.

One night I remember in particular; I must have been about seven. Ma was washing up after supper and Pa was reading a newspaper when Yankev arrived, with Danyeh trailing him. Pa folded his paper, excused himself, and was gone. The minute Pa was gone Yankev went to the stove and lifted the lids from the two pots. Just as he thought — *mamaliga* in one pot, in the other one beans, and in the frying pan a piece of meat their cat would turn its nose up at. He sat himself in the rocking chair he had given Ma as a wedding present, and rocking, proceeded to lecture her. He had warned her against the marriage, but if she was satisfied, he was content. One question and that's all. How had she bettered her lot? True, she was no longer an old maid. True, she was now mistress of her own home. He looked around him and snorted. A hovel. "*And* three snot-nose kids," he said, pointing to us.

Danyeh, hunched over in a kitchen chair, her feet barely reaching the floor, said something to him in Russian, cautioning him, I think. He told her to shut up, and in Yiddish continued his tirade against Ma. He had one word to say to her. To *watch* herself. Against his advice she had married this no-good Rumanian twister, this murderer. The story of how he had kept his first wife pregnant all the time was now well known. Also well known was the story of how she had died in her ninth month with a fourth child. Over an ironing board. Ironing his shirts while he was out playing cards with his Rumanian cronies and drinking wine. He had buried one wife, and now was after burying a second. So Ma had better *watch* herself, that's all.

Ma left her dishwashing and with dripping wet hands took hold of a chair and seated herself facing Yankev. She begged him not to say another word. "Not another word, Uncle Yankev, I beg you. Till the day I die I'll be grateful to you for bringing me over. I don't know how much money you laid out for my passage, but I tried my best to make up for it the three years I stayed with you, by helping out in the house. But maybe I'm still in your debt? Is this what gives you the right to talk against my husband?"

Yankev, rocking, turned up his eyes and groaned. "*You* speak to her," he said to Danyeh. "It's impossible for a *human being* to get through to her."

Danyeh knew better than to open her mouth.

"Uncle Yankev," Ma continued, "every word you speak against my husband is like a knife stab in my heart." She leaned forward, thumbs whirring away. "*Mamaliga?* Beans? A piece of meat your cat wouldn't eat? A crust of *bread* at his board, and I will still thank God every day of my life that he chose me from the other two the *shadchan* showed him."

102

In the beginning my father gave her a hard time. I remember his bursts of temper at her rough ways in the kitchen. She never opened a kitchen drawer without wrestling it — wrenching it open, slamming it shut. She never put a kettle on the stove without its running over at the boil. A pot never came to stove without its lid being inverted, and this for some reason maddened him. He'd right the lid, sometimes scalding his fingers — and all hell would break loose. We never sat down to a set or laid table. As she had been used to doing, so she continued; slamming a pot down on the table, scattering a handful of cutlery, dealing out assorted-size plates. More than once, with one swipe of his hand my father would send a few plates crashing to the floor, and stalk out. She'd sit a minute looking in our faces, one by one, then start twirling her thumbs and talking to herself. What had she done now?

"Eat!" she'd admonish us, and leaving table would go to the mirror over the kitchen sink and ask herself face to face, "What did I do now?" She would examine her face profile and front and then sit down to eat. After, she'd gather up the dishes, dump them in the sink, and running the water over them, would study herself in the mirror. "He'll be better," she'd tell herself, smiling. "He'll be soft as butter when he comes home. You'll see," she'd promise her image in the mirror.

Later in life, mellowed by the years perhaps (or just plain defeated — there was no changing her), he became more tolerant of her ways and was kinder to her. When it became difficult for her to get around because of her poor feet, he did her marketing. He attended to her feet, bought her the Martha Washingtons, the Romeo Slippers, and on a summer's evening on his way home from work, a brick of ice cream. She was very fond of it.

Three years ago he began promoting a plan, a plan to give Ma some pleasure. (This was during Exhibition time.) "You know," he said to me, "it would be very nice if Ma could see the fireworks at the Exhibition. She's never seen anything like that in her life. Why don't you take her?"

The idea of Ma going to the Ex for the fireworks was so preposterous, it made me laugh. She never went anywhere.

"Don't laugh," he said. "It wouldn't hurt you to give her a little pleasure once in a while."

He was quite keen that she should go, and the following year he canvassed the idea again. He put money on the table for taxi and grandstand seats. "Take her," he said.

"Why don't you take her?" I said. "She'll enjoy it more going with you."

"Me? What will I do at the Exhibition?"

As children, we were terrified of Pa's temper. Once in a while he'd belt us around, and we were scared that he might take the strap to Ma too. But before long we came to know that she was the only one of us not scared of Pa, when he got mad. Not even from the beginning when he used to let fly at her was she intimidated by him, not in the least, and in later years was even capable of getting her own back by taking a little dig at him now and then about the "aristocracy" — as she called my father's Rumanian connections.

Aside from his buddies in the back room of the ice-cream parlor on Augusta Avenue, my father also kept in touch with his Rumanian compatriots (all of whom had prospered), and would once in a while go to them for an evening. We were never invited, nor did they come to us. This may have been my father's doing, I don't know. I expect he was ashamed of his circumstances, possibly of Ma, and certainly of how we lived.

Once in a blue moon during Rosh Hashanah or Yom Kippur after shul, they would unexpectedly drop in on us. One time a group of four came to the house, and I remember Pa darting around like a gadfly, collecting glasses, wiping them, and pouring a glass of wine he'd made himself. Ma shook hands all around, then went to the kitchen to cut some slices of her honey cake, scraping off the burnt part. I was summoned to take the plate in to "Pa's gentlefolk." Pretending to be busy, she rattled around the kitchen a few seconds, then seated herself in the partially open door, inspecting them. Not till they were leaving did she come out again, to wish them a good year.

The minute they were gone, my father turned on her. "Russian peasant! Tartar savage, you! Sitting there with your eyes popping out. Do you think they couldn't see you?"

"What's the matter? Even a cat may look at a king?" she said blandly.

"Why didn't you come out instead of sitting there like a caged animal?"

"Because I didn't want to shame you," she said, twirling her thumbs and swaying back and forth in the chair Yankev had given her as a wedding present.

My father busied himself clearing table, and after a while he softened. But she wasn't through yet. "Which one was Falik's wife?" she asked in seeming innocence. "The one with the beard?"

This drew his fire again. "No!" he shouted.

"Oh, the other one. The pale one with the hump on her back," she said wickedly.

So ... notwithstanding the good dream Ma had of Pa coming home with a basket of apples, she never saw him again. He died six days after the operation.

It was a harrowing six days, dreadful. As Pa got weaker, the more disputatious we became — my brother, my sister, and I — arguing and snapping at each other outside his door, the point of contention being should Ma be told or not.

Nurse Brown, the special we'd put on duty, came out once to hush us. "You're not helping him by arguing like this. He can hear you."

"Is he conscious, nurse?"

"Of course he's conscious."

"Is there any hope?"

"There's always hope," she said. "I've been on cases like this before, and I've seen them rally."

We went our separate ways, clinging to the thread of hope she'd given us. The fifth day after the operation I had a call from Nurse Brown: "Your father wants to see you."

Nurse Brown left the room when I arrived, and my father motioned me to undo the zipper of his oxygen tent. "Ma's a good woman," he said, his voice so weak I had to lean close to hear him. "You'll look after her? Don't put her aside. Don't forget about her——"

"What are you talking about!" I said shrilly, then lowered my voice to a whisper. "The doctor told me you're getting better. Honest to God, Pa, I wouldn't lie to you," I whispered.

He went on as if I hadn't spoken. "Even a servant if you had her for thirty years, you wouldn't put aside because you don't need her any more——"

"Wait a minute," I said, and went to the corridor to fetch Nurse Brown. "Nurse Brown, will you tell my father what you told me yesterday. You remember? About being on cases like this before, and you've seen them rally. Will you tell that to my father, please. He talks as if he's——"

I ran from the room and stood outside the door, bawling. Nurse Brown opened the door a crack. "*Ssh!* You'd better go now; I'll call you if there's any change."

At five the next morning, my brother telephoned from hospital. Ma was sound asleep and didn't hear. "You'd better get down here," he said. "I think the old man's checking out. I've already phoned Gertie."

My sister and I arrived at the hospital within seconds of each other. My brother was just emerging from Pa's room. In the gesture of a baseball umpire he jerked a thumb over his shoulder, signifying OUT.

"Is he dead?" we asked our brother.

"Just this minute," he replied.

Like three dummies we paced the dimly lit corridor, not speaking to each other. In the end we were obliged to speak; we had to come to a decision about how to proceed next.

We taxied to the synagogue of which Pa was a member, and roused the shamus. "As soon as it's light I'll get the rabbi," he said. "He'll attend to everything. Meantime go home."

In silence we walked slowly home. Dawn was just breaking, and Ma, a habitually early riser, was bound to be up now and in the kitchen. Quietly we let ourselves in and passed through the hall leading to the kitchen. We were granted an unexpected respite; Ma was not up yet. We waited ten minutes for her, fifteen — an agonizing wait. We decided one of us had better go and wake her; what was the sense of prolonging it? The next minute we changed our minds. To awaken her with such tidings would be inhuman, a brutal thing to do.

"Let's stop whispering," my sister whispered. "Let's talk in normal tones, do something, make a noise, she'll hear us and come out."

In an access of activity we busied ourselves. My sister put the kettle on with a clatter; I took teaspoons from the drawer, clacking them like castanets. She was bound to hear, their bedroom was on the same floor at the front of the house — but five minutes elapsed and not a sound from the room.

"Go and see," my sister said, and I went and opened the door to that untidy bedroom Pa used to rail against.

Ma, her black eyes circled and her hair in disarray, was sitting up in bed. At sight of me she flopped back and pulled the feather tick over her head. I approached the bed and took the covers from her face. "Ma——"

She sat up. "You are guests in my house now?"

For the moment I didn't understand. I didn't know the meaning of her words. But the next minute the meaning of them was clear — with Pa dead, the link was broken. The bond, the tie that held us together. We were no longer her children. We were now guests in her house.

"When did Pa die?" she asked.

"How did you know?"

"My heart told me."

Barefooted, she followed me to the kitchen. My sister gave her a glass of tea, and we stood like mutes, watching her sipping it through a cube of sugar.

"You were all there when Pa died?"

"Just me, Ma," my brother said.

She nodded. "His kaddish. Good."

I took a chair beside her, and for once without constraint or self-consciousness, put my arm around her and kissed her on the cheek.

"Ma, the last words Pa spoke were about you. He said you were a good woman. 'Ma's a good woman,' that's what he said to me."

She put her tea down and looked me in the face.

"Pa said that? He said I was a good woman?" She clasped her hands. "May the light shine on him in paradise," she said, and wept silently, putting her head down to hide her tears.

Eight o'clock the rabbi telephoned. Pa was now at the funeral parlor on College near Augusta, and the funeral was to be at eleven o'clock. Ma went to ready herself, and in a few minutes called me to come and zip up her black crepe, the dress Pa had bought her six years ago for the Applebaum wedding.

The Applebaums, neighbors, had invited Ma and Pa to the wedding of their daugher, Lily. Right away Pa had declared he wouldn't go. Ma kept coaxing. How would it look? It would be construed as unfriendly, unneighborly. A few days before the wedding he gave in, and Ma began scratching through her wardrobe for something suitable to wear. Nothing she exhibited pleased him. He went downtown and came back with the black crepe and an outsize corset.

I dressed her for the wedding, combed her hair, and put some powder on her face. Pa became impatient; he had already called a cab. What was I doing? Getting her ready for a beauty contest? The taxi came, and as Pa held her coat he said to me in English, "You know, Ma's not a bad-looking woman?"

For weeks she talked about the good time she'd had at the Applebaum wedding, but chiefly about how Pa had attended her. Not for a minute had he left her side. Two hundred people at the wedding and not one woman among them had the attention from her husband that she had had from Pa. "Pa's a gentleman," she said to me, proud as proud.

Word of Pa's death got around quickly, and by nine in the morning people began trickling in. First arrivals were Yankev and Danyeh. Yankev, now in his seventies and white-haired, was still straight and handsome. The same Yankev except for the white hair and an asthmatic condition causing him to wheeze and gasp for breath. Danyeh was wizened and bent over, her hands hanging almost to her knees. They approached Ma, Danyeh trailing Yankev. Yankev held out a hand and with the other one thumped his chest, signifying he was too congested to speak. Danyeh gave her bony hand to Ma and muttered a condolence.

From then on there was a steady influx of people. Here was Chaim the schnorrer! We hadn't seen him in years. Chaim the schnorrer, stinking of fish and in leg wrappings as always, instead of socks. Rich as Croesus he was said to be, a fish-peddling miser who lived on soda crackers and milk and kept his money in his leg wrappings. Yankev, a minute ago too congested for speech, found words for Chaim. "How much money have you got in those *gutkess*? The truth, Chaim!"

Ma shook hands with all, acknowledged their sympathy, and to some she spoke a few words. I observed the Widow Spector, a gossip and trouble-maker, sidling through the crowd and easing her way toward Ma. "The Post" she was called by people on the street. No one had the time of day for her; even Ma used to hide from her.

I groaned at the sight of her. As if Ma didn't have enough to contend with. But no! here was Ma welcoming the Widow Spector, holding a hand out to her. "Give me your hand, Mrs. Spector. Shake hands, we're partners now. Now I know the taste, I'm a widow too." Ma patted the chair beside her. "Sit down, partner. Sit down."

At a quarter to eleven the house was clear of people. "Is it time?" Ma asked, and we answered, Yes, it was time to go. We were afraid this would be the breaking point for her, but she went calmly to the bedroom and took her coat from the peg on the door and came to the kitchen with it, requesting that it be brushed off.

The small funeral parlor was jammed to the doors, every seat taken but for four up front left vacant for us. On a trestle table directly in front of our seating was the coffin. A pine box draped in a black cloth, and in its center a white Star of David.

Ma left her place, approached the coffin, and as she stood before it with clasped hands I noticed the uneven hemline of her coat, hiked up in back by that mound of flesh on her shoulders. I observed that her lisle stockings were twisted at the ankles, and was embarrassed for her. She stood silently a moment, then began to speak. She called him her dove, her comrade, her friend.

"Life is a dream," she said. "You were my treasure. You were the light of my eyes. I thought to live my days out with you — and look what it has come to." (She swayed slightly, the black shawl slipping from her head — and I observed that could have done with a brushing too.) "If ever I offended you or caused you even a twinge of discomfort, forgive me for it. As your wife I lived like a queen. Look at me now. I'm nothing. You were my jewel, my crown. With you at its head my house was a palace. I return now to a hovel. Forgive me for everything, my dove. Forgive me."

("Russian peasant," Pa used to say to her in anger, "Tartar savage." If he could see her now as she stood before his bier mourning him. Mourning him like Hecuba mourning Priam and the fall of Troy. And I a minute ago was ashamed of her hiked-up coat, her twisted stockings and dusty shawl.)

People were weeping; Ma resumed her place dry-eyed, and the rabbi began the service.

It is now a year since Pa died, and as he had enjoined me to do, I am looking after Ma. I have not put her aside. I get cross and holler at her as I always have done, but she allows for my testiness and does not hold it against me. I'm a spinster, an old maid now approaching my thirty-seventh year, and she pities me for it. I get bored telling her again and again that Pa's last words were Ma's a good woman, and sometimes wish I'd never mentioned it. She cries a lot, and I get impatient with her tears. But I'm good to her.

This afternoon I called Moodey's, booked two seats for the grandstand, and tonight I'm taking her to the Ex and she'll see the fireworks.

Miriam Waddington

THE NINETEEN THIRTIES ARE OVER

The nineteen thirties
are over; we survived
the depression, the Sacco-
Vanzetti of childhood
saw Tom Mooney smiling
at us from photographs,
put a rose on the grave
of Eugene Debs, listened
to our father's stories
of the Winnipeg strike and
joined the study groups
of the OBU always keeping
one eye on the revolution.

Later we played records
with thorn needles, Josh
White's *Talking Union* and
Prokofief's *Lieutenant Kije*,
shuddered at the sound of
bells and all those wolves
whirling past us in snow
on the corner of Portage
and Main, but in my mind
summer never ended on the
shores of Gimli where we
looked across to an Icelandic
paradise we could never see
the other side of; and I
dreamed of Mexico and shining
birds who beckoned to me
from the gold-braided lianas
of my own wonder.

These days I step out
from the frame of my wind-
battered house into Toronto
city; somewhere I still
celebrate sunlight, touch
the rose on the grave of
Eugene Debs but I walk
carefully in this land
of sooty snow; I pass the
rich houses and double
garages and I am not really
this middle-aged professor
but someone from
Winnipeg whose bones ache
with the broken revolutions
of Europe, and even now
I am standing on the heaving
ploughed-up field
of my father's old war.

THE BOND

On Jarvis street the Jewish whore
smiles and stirs upon the bed,
sleep is the luxury of the poor
but sweeter sleep awaits the dead.

Sweeter sleep awaits the dead
than all the living who must rise
to join the march of hunger-fed
under the dawn of city skies.

Under the dawn of city skies
moves the sun in presaged course,
smoothing out the cunning lies
that hide the evil at the source.

I sense the evil at the source
now at this golden point of noon,
the misdirected social force
will grind me also, and too soon.

On Jarvis street the Jewish whore,
the Jewish me on Adelaide,
both of the nameless million poor
who wear no medals and no braid.

Oh woman you are kin to me,
your heart beats something like my own,
when idiot female ecstasy
transforms in love the flesh and bone;

And woman you are kin to me,
those tense moments first or last,
when men deride your ancestry;
whore, Jewess, you are twice outcast.

Whore, Jewess, I acknowledge you,
joint heirs to varied low estate,
no heroes will arise anew
avenging us twice isolate.

I who start from noonday sleep
to cry of triumph *aeroplane!*
hear nothing but the slippered creep
of famine through the surplus grain.

Exultant females shriek *parade!*
and crowd a hundred windows high,
from offices on Adelaide
they wave the khaki boys goodbye.

But heavy night is closing in,
signal omens everywhere,
you woman who have lived by sin,
and I who dwelt in office air,

Will share a common rendezvous
arranged by madness, crime, and race;
sister, my salute to you,
I will recognize your face.

WHY SHOULD I CARE
ABOUT THE WORLD

Gone is
the holiness
in where I
lived, my song.

Why should I care
what happens to
the world why
should I
broodingly
seek the cell of
holiness the
habit in where
I lived, my song?

(Your song
was only a few
ragged Scotsmen
in Kildonan, some
riff-raffy settlers,
half-breeds, Indians,
Galician labourers,
scraggly-ended
pee-smelling prairie
towns)

(it was a flat
stony mound
for a mountain
a silly tuft
of pine on
an island in
Lac du Bonnet,
berry-picking in a
buffalo summer

beside a wheat ocean
and jumping the
ditches brimming
with rain.)

Gone now; all
cracked open like
eggs at Easter
parted like three
feathers in a
bird's tail of wind.

And I can't even
go back to being
dirty Jew, to
hearing from the
conductor on the
Selkirk streetcar:
*your father is
a Bolshevik isn't
he little girl?*

This is a very
far very long
way to be away
from the holiness
in where I lived
my song.

Eli Mandel

ESTEVAN, 1934

remembering the family we
called breeds   the Roques
their house smelling of urine
my mother's prayers before
the dried fish she cursed
them for their dirtiness their
women I remember too
                  how
seldom they spoke and
they touched one another
even when the sun killed
cattle and rabbis
           even
in the poisoned slow air
like hunters
        like lizards
they touched   stone
they touched
          earth

NEAR HIRSCH A JEWISH CEMETERY

ann is taking pictures again
while I stand in the uncut grass
counting the graves: there are forty
I think
     the Hebrew puzzles me

the wind moving the grass
over the still houses of the dead

from the road a muffled occasional
roar   cars passing   no one there
casts a glance at the stone trees
the unliving forest of Hebrew graves

in the picture I stand arms outstretched
as if waiting for someone
                              I am
in front of the gates you can see
the wind here   the grass
always bending the stone unmoved

ON THE 25TH ANNIVERSARY OF THE LIBERATION OF AUSCHWITZ: MEMORIAL SERVICES, TORONTO, YMHA, BLOOR AND SPADINA, JANUARY 25, 1970

the name is hard
a German sound made out of
the gut guttural throat
y scream yell ing open
voice mouth growl
                    and sweat

"the only way out of Auschwitz
is through the chimneys"
                          of course
that's second hand   that's told
again   Sigmund   Sherwood   (Sobolewski)
twisting himself into that sentence
before us on the platform

                        the poem
shaping itself late in the after
noon later than it would be:

Penderecki's "Wrath of God"
moaning electronic Polish theatric
the screen silent
                        framed by the name
looking away from/pretending not there
no   name   no not   name   no

            Auschwitz
        in GOTHIC lettering
                            the hall
a parody a reminiscence a nasty memory
the Orpheum in Estevan before Buck Jones
the Capital in Regina before Tom Mix
waiting for the guns
waiting for the cowboy killers
one two three
                    Legionnaires
Polish ex-prisoners Association
Legions
            their medals their flags

so the procession, the poem gradually
insistent beginning to shape itself
with the others
                    walked with them
into the YMHA Bloor & Spadina
thinking apocalypse shame degradation
thinking bones and bodies melting
thickening thinning melting bones and bodies
thinking not mine/speak clearly
the poet's words/Yevtushenko at Babi Yar

there   this January   snow
heavy wet   the wind   heavy wet
the street grey white slush melted concrete
bones and bodies melting slush
                            saw

with the others
                the prisoner
in the YMHA hall Bloor & Spadina
arms wax stiff body stiff unnatural
coloured face blank eyes
                        walked
with the others toward the screen
toward the pictures
                SLIDES

        this is mother
        this is father
        this is
                the one who is
waving her arms like that
is the one who
                like
I mean running with her breasts bound
ing
        running
                with her hands here and there
with her here and
                        there
hands
        that   that is

the poem becoming the body
becoming the faint hunger
ing body
        prowling
                through
words the words words the words
opening   mouths   ovens
the generals smiling saluting
in their mythic uniforms god-like
generals uniforms with the black leather
with the straps and intricate leather
the phylacteries the prayer shawl
corsets and the boots and the leather straps
and the shining faces of the generals in their boots
and their stiff wax bodies their unnatural faces

and their blank eyes and their hands their stiff hands
and the generals in their straps and wax and stiff
staying standing
                melting bodies and thickening
                  quick flesh on flesh handling
                  hands

    the poem flickers, fades
the four Yarzeit candles guttering   one
    each four million lights dim
my words drift
              smoke from chimneys and ovens
      a bad picture, the power failing
    pianist clattering on and over and through
the long Saturday afternoon in the Orpheum
      while the whitehatted star spangled cowboys
        shot the dark men and shot the dark men
        and we threw popcorn balls and grabbed
    each other and cheered:
                      me jewboy yelling
for the shot town and the falling men
      and the lights come on
                and
    with the others
standing in silence

    the gothic word hangs
    over us on a shroud-white screen

and we drift away
      to ourselves
      to the late Sunday *Times*

        the wet snow
        the city

        a body melting

Eli Mandel

IN MY 57TH YEAR

This is the year my mother lay dying
knocked down by tiny strokes she claimed
never once hit her though when she lay
crib-like where they laid her there she wept
for shame to be confined so near her death.
This is the year the cancer inside my father's
groin began its growth to knock him down
strong as he was beside his stricken wife.
This is the year I grew, ignorant of politics,
specious with law, careless of poetry,
English anti-semitic poets, Hebrew myth.
There were no graves. The prairie rolled on
as if it were the sea. Today my children make
their way alone across those waves.
Do lines between us end as sharply
as lines our artists draw upon the plains?
I cry out. They keep their eye upon
their politics, their myths,
careful of lives as I was careless.

What shall I say? It is too late to tell again
tales we never knew. The legends of ourselves
spill into silence. All we never said, father
to daughter, son to unmanned man, we cannot say
to count the years.
        I no longer know time or age
thinking of parents, their time, their grave of names.
Telling the time, fiction consumes me.

Robert Currie

DIASPORA
LIPTON, SASK.

(for Eli Mandel)

I

The Jewish farmers wandered here from Russia
rode like dust upon the wind
they came for land and freedom
came to stay awhile   *Sammy Bateman*
                                        son of Markus
broke the land and worked the fields
                                        Israel Cohen
                                        Louis Reich
bent under the hot sun   *Mother Davidner*
over the hot stoves   *Grandmother Hannah Schwartz*
felt the land roll   a thousand miles from ocean
                         Max Silverman Born 1908
and when the wind blew their crops away
when the colony moved on   scattered
gone as many ways as wind
some of them stayed behind
                         Moses Swartz Died June 12, 1950
                         Jacob Baratz Died May 29, 1951
stayed beneath tin-plated roofs
safe in the line of final homes
that make a Main street
in the village of the dead

II

We stand in Lipton's Jewish cemetery
The first year   someone says
they lie with nothing
the wind alone to mark their graves
And now we cannot know the lives
of those beneath the worn and wooden signs
from which the dates have gone
the names have gone

no one alive to tell us
who is resting here
A few we can read

Mother Davidner
Died March 19, 1940

but her epitaph is Hebrew
her huge white stone water-stained
surrounded by a haze of purple thistle
brown-eyed Susans bending in the wind

III

The child passes through the leaning gate
her baseball cap a splash of blue
here where we expect to see
only muted tones   aged unpainted wood
She stops before the broken stone
where Israel Cohen lies
beneath a Star of David
beneath his own cracked photograph
She studies the man inside
the dark suit   the high white collar
His eyes are distant
as the look of death
She reaches for her father's hand
   Is he dead   Daddy?
    Everyone here is dead   Sara
    everyone but us

The wind is blowing
past the shattered stones
the shifted slabs
the wire fence humming
and they are moving
out through prairie grass
into wheat   green
and flowing
in the wind

Abraham Ram

MAMMA*

He awoke in the fuzzy half-dark of his room to muffled little noises. From the kitchen only a passage-width away came the clink and the scraping of a pot in the sink, the discreet slushing rise in pitch of the tap water filling the pot, the tempered shuffle and heel-click on the linoleum of his mother's moving about.

Up already, he thought. He listened hard for a moment.

Her voice, still as young and fresh as a spring (and she nearing seventy!) gurgled in an endless flow of Yiddish past his closed door and into his room, punctuated every now and then by an indignant "Ah!"

She was talking to herself. He couldn't hear what she was saying, but there was something wrong. He could tell.

He lay nude under the comforter, his right knee pulled up chest high, exploring a scab on his head with a gentle probing forefinger, letting her muttering sweep across him like a vindictive violin bow.

Inert under the cascading monologue, he thought: I'm still waking up to her voice as I used to when I was a boy and she would call me with that sharp urgency: Moe, it's time to get up, it's time to go to school....

And here he was, a middle-aging schoolteacher (part time, if you please!) ... still "among school children" (how the Yeatsian phrase stabbed: God, what hadn't Yeats accomplished at Moe's age ...!).

And he? A "public smiling man", that's what he was, hanging on to coat-tails ... a dime a dozen ... and run back home ("mamma *behalt mich* — mother, hide me!") ... run home like a kid to the parental nest ... denuded and cast down (Moses on the mount, ha!) ... sans wife, sans job, sans pride, sans everything, the sardonic thought came....

He sighed (yes ... those must be *smelts* sizzling and frying in the kitchen)....

*Chapter One of Abraham Ram's
 novel *The Noise of Singing*.

Where had those dreams come from?

He had been walking along a pavement in some dreary part of the city, and he had come upon a puddle of water inside which he noticed was an arm, a doll's arm.

When he reached down, he was surprised to find it so firm in his grasp. It was the arm of a girl who was floating head down, drowned. He pulled and she stepped out, very young, most enticing and wet, her dress clinging to her lithe body, her long hair straggling along her shoulders in strangely attractive fashion. He did not know her.

He looked around for a place to take her. Near the puddle was a door — dilapidated, brown, open. "Let's go in here," he said. They went inside, sat on the steps. A woman came out, surprising him as he sat with his arm around the young girl's shoulder. With an angry gesture, she commanded them to leave. He thought: Where to go?

The next part of the dream was vague. There were obstacles, he remembered — yes, all sorts of obstacles — cars, bridges, men working on construction projects. Suddenly, the girl said, "Let's go where I live — there." She pointed to a huge building. It was Notre Dame Cathedral.

"But —— " he began.

"Don't worry," she said, "I live there alone."

She embraced him. One hand tickled his palm. The other was hidden somewhere under the folds of her skirt. He could feel the secret promise as she pressed close to him.

"Do you want to?" he asked.

"Yes," she replied, and as she did so, he was suffused by a warm glow....

Suddenly the kitchen door opened. His mother padded quickly past his room. He lifted his head from the pillow to hear. There was a wet, harsh quality of hysteria in her voice.

Silence.

"*Nu,* why don't you answer!" she burst out. "Hear that? Not a word! Dumb! Deaf and dumb he's become! I talk to him, I get blue in the face talking and *he* doesn't answer! A person can go crazy, I tell you, crazy!"

"Tuh, tuh, tuh, tuh," came his father's voice from farther away, reedy with excitement. "Day and night! Talk, talk, talk! No end to it! Nothing stops her! Not fire, not water! A flood — with her tuh, tuh, tuh, tuh!"

"What then? Like you? Outside, in the restaurant, everywhere, he's everyone's good brother! The minute he steps into the house — finished! A mask on his face! I can explode talking and he sits there like a statue! A husband! Such a good year on my enemies, the kind of husband —— "

The cupboard door squeaked open.

"Where are you running? *In Gottin's villen,* the devil's running after you? Your breakfast's on the table — where are you running to all the black years!"

Farther and fainter, hoarse with rage, his father hurled at her, "Breakfast I need? I don't need you *with* your breakfast together! Poison! That's what you are to me — poison! Like poison I hate you! Like poison!"

A wail from her. "Look only! Listen only! The way a man talks! In God's name, what did I do you? I did you harm, maybe? Such an anger! Such hatred in him, I've never seen!"

"You make me crazy with your tuh, tuh, tuh! A dictator, a regular dictator over my head! A boss! Morning, noon and night. A boss!"

The door slammed.

Moe sat down on his bed, stared with distaste at the mess all around. Shoes, stockings, underwear, papers, books, magazines — all strewn on the pink carpet. Last night's apple core rotted under the lit lampbulb on his old writing desk.

He looked at his watch. He had forgotten to wind it.

"What time is it?" he called out. No answer. She was getting deaf.

He opened his door which gave on the passage. She was going to the kitchen, hunched up, muttering.

"What's all the noise about?" he grumbled sourly.

"Ask your nice father — such a luck on *him* and on *his* hands and feet!"

"What's wrong now?" he burst out with rancour.

"Sha, sha!" she waved at him with wet hands. "Can't you talk like a person? Like an angry bear only.... "

Sullenly he sat down to his two slices of buttered bread and his coffee.

"All right, all right," he said with great irritation, "so what happened?"

She wiped her hands on her apron, turned from the sink to face him.

"You hear? Yesterday he's sitting in the parlour looking out of the window. The way he always sits and looks out, the lazy good-for-nothing! To work he doesn't want to go!"

"Work! Again work!" muttered Moe.

"So listen, listen. I'm coming back from shopping...."

"So? So?"

"So let me speak out a word! So I'm carrying such heavy parcels — I almost fainted, you hear?"

"All right, all right! So?"

"So he's standing on the corner there, talking to one of his nice friends. And you know what he does?"

She spread her hands in an expressive, questioning gesture. He stole an oblique look at her wrinkled face.

He had to look away. It stabbed him. Worn ... anguished ... old....

"So he turns himself," she went on, "with his — you should excuse me — with his behind to me. You hear? *That fine* gentleman of the chickens! He makes out he doesn't see me across the street with all my parcels. *Such* a liar...."

She twisted her face into a grimace, her tone into a mockery. "So he takes himself — nice and fine! — a little stroll in the park with his no-good friends! *Nu* — I ask you! Is that the way? *That* way a person behaves? Such a *paskoodniak!*"

Scowling, Moe turned to her.

"Why don't you get the parcels delivered, for heaven's sake? I told you a million times! A business with parcels! Or leave them in the store and I'll pick them up!"

"And what's the matter with him, I'd like to know! He can't help me out? You hear! Such a nerve! Such *chutzpah*! *I* cook, *I* clean, *I* slave.... In God's name, what *don't* I do? And he? Such luck *he* should have, the kind of person *he* is.... *Gottinyu!*"

Moe got up.

"He's a sick man. Leave him alone, for heaven's sake!"

"Only with him, he sides — look at that! A sick man! As strong as a horse he is! Sick! If I wanted to be sick? How many times does he see me loaded down with parcels and he sits there, talking and joking? So many good years *I* should have! Sick? That's sick ...?"

"No," said Moe sarcastically, "he's *not* sick. *You* know everything! Everything *you* know...."

"What then? He is sick, you think? Such a good year on *me* how strong and healthy he is. I read it myself in the papers — written by a doctor, I should live so — it's no good to go around idle, doing nothing!"

He turned on his heel.

"Ah, what's the use of talking! The doctor says he's got diabetes. He takes pills. He's got high blood pressure. His heart's no good.... But to you, he's not sick. He's healthy. Ah, you make me sick!"

"So?" She held both hands out, questioning the wide world. "So thousands have diabetes and high blood pressure? A new craziness, a *meshugas*! What's the matter? He looks bad? People tell me how *good* he looks, I should only *live* so! Lazy! That's what he's become! Lazy as a lazy dog! He should go to work — that's where he should go!"

Furious, Moe turned on her.

"Work! He's worked since he's twelve. That's when he started to work. He's worked enough. Sixty years. What do you want from him? He's old, I tell you...."

She hunched her shoulders in indignant protest. "Old? That's old? Look at Mr. Kofsky. Eighty years he is — I should only live to see my great-grandchildren — and he's *glad* he's working! Did you ever hear such a thing! Old? He'd go crazy, Mr. Kofsky, if he didn't have something to do. *Crazy,* he should only be, your fine pa there!"

She bowed her head over her work.

"*Oi!* What's the use of talking?" Her voice had suddenly filled with tears. "Such a year on *him,* the life I've had.... Such a good year on all my enemies...."

Sullen, he went into the bathroom, began to shave. The phone rang. He listened.

"Doing?" he heard her say. "What should I be doing? I'm making meat.... Pa? Don't ask me about him, a fine father you have, Esther."

It was his sister.

"You hear? He's not talking to me already. Yeah — all day yesterday — since morning — and a whole last evening.... We're sitting and watching TV.... Not a word! Dumb! All evening.... Did you ever hear, a man should sit all evening and not say a word? You hear? Outside, he's everybody's good brother. In the house — a mask on his face! A regular mask! Mendel would also act this way to his Fannie — sure! Sure! And it comes nine o'clock, so what does he do? Goes to bed — with the chickens he goes to bed. So you hear? This morning I make him breakfast. Like it has to be. You know. Porridge the doctor told him to eat. And eggs and toast — everything! So listen. So he goes out angry and he doesn't eat! Such a thing"

A pause. Not for long.

"Why?" His mother burst out angrily. "All because I asked him to carry a parcel for me, that's why! Did you ever *hear* such a thing …? You hear? With my own eyes I saw him run and carry a parcel for the doctor's wife! I should only live to see your daughters married …! Only for others he's good. From me he runs away — he should only run, I don't want to say where! Tell me — I earned such respect from him? I ask you! A horse, that's what he is, a big oaf! A landlord he'd be if not for me? Sure, sure! And that's the thanks I get! Esther, you don't know your father. *Oi*, you'll never know him …. What I went through…. How I suffered…." Her voice sank. "What's the use of talking!"

Another pause.

"Yeah, yeah," she said, "I'm going right away to the butcher, I'll phone you later."

An instant later, she called Moe, "You're coming for dinner?"

"I'll phone," he said shortly.

"Such a good dinner I have, chops, potato latkes, a good barley soup…. "

"I said I'll phone." How she irritated him….

"All right, *nu*. Can't you talk like a person? Only angry. I'm going to the butcher to have something sent up to Esther's. Lock the door when you go."

It amazed him. Her voice was sunny and eager again. She hurried out.

"Boy, oh boy, oh boy, oh boy," he couldn't help muttering aloud. "Fighting again."

Just then his father slipped in, closed the door softly. How stooped he'd become….

"Where were you?" Moe asked brightly, watching the old man hang his coat in the hall cupboard, slowly, uncertainly.

"Eh? Nowhere."

His father blew his nose. There was a wild, drawn look in his eye.

"How's it outside?"

"Eh?"

"I said, how's the weather?"

"Eh? Oh, nice, nice — but not too warm."

His father sat down in his chair, stared blankly out the parlour window. Quickly Moe went and got a pair of his trousers out of the cupboard in his room.

"Look, pa," he said. "See these pants?" The cuffs were frayed. "I wanted to ask you — how about fixing them for me? They're going — see?"

The old man seized the pants with an erratic, jerky motion.

"Eh? Well, I dunno," he shrugged. "They're almost worn away." He turned them this way and that. "I can patch 'em up."

"No, I don't want patches, pa — they'll show. How about French cuffs?"

His father hunched his shoulders.

"Well, I dunno. There's not much cloth left.... How long you got this suit?"

"Long enough — it's not a new suit."

"Well, you see — it's old — and when it's old, all it's good for is to throw away. It don't last forever, you know."

Moe made no reply. Then he said, "O.K., pa. Do the best you can. Patch 'em up."

"O.K., O.K.," the old man said, with a pathetic attempt at business-like cheerfulness. "You don't need 'em right away, do you?"

"No, no, any time. What's the matter, pa, you didn't eat today?"

"Eh?" the old man said, hunched up, his face turned to the window so that Moe got a full look at the completely white, nearly bald head, the grizzled skin, the lost look.... "I went out," he said, shortly.

"Why?" asked Moe, more gently than usual.

"Why? Go ask her!" the old man exploded, gesticulating. "She doesn't even let me talk to my friends! Parcels she throws at me! What am I? Her servant?"

"So what? So what if you help her with a parcel once in a while?"

"Once in a while? Sure! A million times a day she goes looking for bargains! Rotten fruit half a cent cheaper! The storekeepers run when they see her coming!"

The phone rang. As Moe hurried out to answer, the old man was staring furiously out the window, his face red.

It was his sister again.

"Mamma back?" she asked.

Moe heard the door open. His father was leaving.

"Not yet," he said. The door closed.

"They're fighting again," he announced grimly.

"Yeah, she gave me an earful."

"I heard. Someone better tell her to lay off."

"He could be more co-operative! After all.... "

"Cat and dog, that's what it is!"

"Yeah. Now, when they should be at peace. I thought we'd invite them both to the club. But now —— "

The door opened again.

"Just a minute," he said, "here she is."

"Esther," his mother panted into the phone, "I told him to send you two *flanken*, but he's a regular *bandit*, that butcher! If the meat's no good, send them right back. You hear? And now I have to go to the hardware store. Everything *I* have to do! A landlord he is, your pa! Some landlord! A person has a house? So buy paint, hire a painter, fix the wall. But no! Everything has to be on *my* head!"

Moe was ready to leave. He paused in the hall before the picture of his mother as a girl of eighteen. How grave and placid and unlined her face was. How hopeful she must have been then — a lifetime ahead of her....

"And he, Esther?" he heard her say. "I have to sit here — but he?" With that ugly inflection, she mocked, "Only *dahn tahn* he goes — *dahn tahn*, that fine gentlemen of the chickens!"

Slowly Moe opened the door.

"Phone if you're coming for dinner!" she cried to him.

He did not answer, stood staring at himself in the full length mirror.

That look of disgust on his face. Those lines running down from nose to mouth. Those anguished, distorted eyes drowned beneath those thick lenses. Those puffy cheeks. Who are you, he asked himself, the question more a calcified bitterness than anything else.

He stepped outside into the raw wind, looked down the street. There was a storm blowing up.

He fancied he saw her, his mother, as he had seen her so many times, hunched up and shuffling down the street on scuffed heels, an old kerchief on her bowed head, her ancient mustard-coloured shapeless overcoat thrown about her, one hand at her coat collar, her precious parcels cradled....

But it was someone else. A trick of the imagination. He caught his bus at the corner.

Phyllis Gotlieb

THIS ONE'S ON ME

1. The lives and times of Oedipus and Elektra
   began with bloodgrim lust and dark carnality
   but I was born next to the Neilson's factory
   where every piece is different, and that's how I got
   my individuality.

2. I lived on Gladstone Avenue,
   2 locations on Kingston Rd.
   2 crescents, Tennis and Chaplin
   Xanadu, Timbuktu,
   Samarkand & Ampersand
   and many another exotic locality.

3. My grandparents came from the ghettos
   of Russia and Poland with no mementos
   one grandfather was a furrier, one a tailor,
   grey men in dark rooms tick tack to
   gether dry snuffy seams of fur and fibre
   my father managed a theatre

4. which one day (childhood reminiscence indicated) passing
   on a Sunday ride, we found
   the burglar alarm was ring
   alingaling
   out jumped my father and ran for the front door
   Uncle Louie ran for the back
   siren scream down the cartrack Danforth
   and churchbells ding dong ding
   (ting a ling)
   and brakescreech whooee
   six fat squadcars filled with the finest
   of the force of our fair city
   brass button boot refulgent
   and in their plainclothes too
   greysuit felthat and flat black footed
   and arrested Uncle Louie

Oh what a brannigan
what a brouhaha
while Mother and Aunt Gittel and me
sat in the car and shivered
delicious
ly

because a mouse bit through a wire.

5. For some the dance of the sugar-plum fairies
   means that.
   but the Gryphons and Gorgons of my dreams
   dance in the salon of Miss Peregrine Peers
   stony eyed, stone footed on Church Street
   up grey stairs
   where two doors down at Dr Weams I
   gnawed his smoky fingers and followed
   the convolutions of his twisted septum
   as he stretched and knotted little twines of silver
   on the rack of my oral cavity
   and all the while Miss Peregrine Peers
   tum tiddy tum tiddy TUM TUM TUM
   O Peregrine O Miss Peers
   I find you no longer in life's directories
   may you rest in peace
   and I do mean

6. Where, oh where are the lovely ladies who taught me
   to break the
   Hearts And trample the *Flowers* of the muses?

                                              Mrs Reeves
   gracile, a willow on a Chinese plate, who
   winced with an indrawn gasp when I struck a wrong
   note, or blew my nose in her handkerchief
   absentmindedly?
   Miss Marll, under whose tutelage icecubes
   popped from the pores of my arm
   pits and slid down to drop from my
   ELBOWS HELD HIGH FINGERS CURVED ON THE KEYS
   may you rot in hell
   subtly, Miss Marll.

7. O child of the thirties
   of stonewarm porches and spiraea snowfalls
   in print cotton dress with matching panties hanging well down
   (the faded snapshot says)
   hand on the fender of the Baby Austin
   (feel the heat and glare)
   gaptooth grin to be converted by braces
   myopic eyes fit for glasses
   and tin ears waiting to be bent
   by the patient inexorable piano teacher
   the postered car advertises in innocence:
   LADIES OF LEISURE
   See it at the Eastwood Theatre, friends,
   next time 1930 rolls around.

AMBIVALENCE

Yeshivah descants
the sweetness of Torah
to a quorum of brushcut
Sabras of distant
shores THEY SHALL INHERIT THE
paper-mills bowling alleys and bagel bakeries
OF THEIR FATHERS free-eyed
call teachers stormtroopers
joke at eternities of abomination
and dream rangeriders
cast off earthcoasts where

little bent men pore
on the Chumash, sidecurl
brushbleary page *oy
veh*, bim bam, the rabbi
spreads his handkerchief

Morley Torgov

THE MESSIAH
OF SECOND-HAND GOODS

Throughout his life my father was a missionary who combed the streets offering shelter and salvation to all sorts of world-weary goods — odd remnants of cloth, bent nails, used lumber, rusty tools. Over the years, the basement beneath his store became a hostel for a vast collection of castaway property. Each and every item in that collection he hoarded against the improbable day when it might come in handy.

During one of my last visits with him, my father confessed to me, in anguish, that the local fire department inspector had declared the place a hazard. Worse still, my father's insurance agent heartily endorsed the inspector's verdict.

"The bastards are in cahoots," he said bitterly.

"You mean, it's a conspiracy?" I asked, pretending to be horrified. "You think they really want all that stuff for themselves?"

"Why not? I bet between the two of them they haven't got a pot to piss in."

"They'll find one in your basement, that's for sure."

"If you're such a smart guy," my father said, sliding the phone book across his desk at me, "then call the sonsofbitches and tell 'em they can't force me to clear it all out."

"I can't do that," I protested. "At least, not until I've had a chance to study your insurance policy and the local fire regulations."

"I thought you're a lawyer —— "

"I am."

"Then how come you don't know these things?"

"I was absent from law school the day they took 'Junk Collections'. Just give me fifteen minutes please and I'll have some answers for you."

A half-hour later I was ready with my report. My father glanced impatiently at his watch. "What took so long, Lawyer? You're an hour late already."

"I read your policy and talked with the inspector —— "

"And?"

"And they're right. It is a hazard. You'll have to clear out the basement, that's all there is to it."

"For this I needed a lawyer in the family? I could've got better advice from a doctor."

I could feel my face reddening and suddenly my shirt-collar felt two sizes too small for my neck. "Let's not get into that lawyer-versus-doctor routine again. I'm thirty-seven years old and there's no way I'm going to medical school at this point in my life. It's about time you got used to the idea."

"With those hands," my father said, shaking his head sadly, "you would've made a brilliant surgeon."

"Don't change the subject. I'm a lawyer and I tell you the City is going to lay a charge against you under one of the bylaws. What's more, your insurance may be cancelled."

"I just don't understand it. Why all of a sudden now, after I've been in this place nearly thirty years?"

"Because last week — in case you didn't know it — was Fire Prevention Week."

"Fire Prevention Week?" My father was unimpressed. "That's for little kids, to teach them they shouldn't play with matches. What the hell has Fire Prevention Week got to do with me?"

"They're afraid you'll burn down the entire town. Like Mrs. O'Leary's cow."

"Mrs. O'Leary's cow took place in Chicago. This is Sault Ste. Marie."

"They claim you've got enough flammable material in the cellar to burn down Chicago too."

He refused to be convinced of the potential danger. Besides, he pointed out, he'd spent a lifetime accumulating the collection. "My God," he pleaded, "there's a goldmine down there, now."

To prove it, he conducted me on a tour of that dank subterranean space, and we squeezed ourselves along a narrow aisle that parted mountains of cardboard cartons, wooden boxes, and old steamer trunks. Spread out around me was a museum stuffed full of unremarkable objects, most of which should have been condemned to the rubbish heap years ago. I let out a low whistle of astonishment. "You sure don't believe in travelling light in this world," I commented.

He ignored me and gave his attention instead to a pile of round iron bars that lay on the floor near his feet, counting and re-counting them. "That's funny," he said, "there's only eleven and I could swear I had an even dozen."

"What're you planning to do with them?" I asked, picking up

one of the bars.

"I'm thinking of opening a jail, schmeckle," he answered, taking the bar from me and replacing it carefully on the pile.

I raised the lid on a large carton of men's rubber footwear. "What are you saving these for?"

"World War Three. They'll be worth a fortune. First thing that's short in a war is rubbers."

"How come they didn't sell in World War Two?"

"The sizes were too large."

"What makes you think they'll go over big in the next war?"

"People's feet are getting longer; it's a fact."

Crammed in a dark corner was an uncomfortable quartet of derelict female mannequins, their wigless heads almost touching the low joists overhead, their nude featureless bodies frozen into stiff unnatural poses. "And when do you expect to use *them* again?" I asked.

"Their time will come," he replied confidently.

"Do you really think women will ever look like that again? They haven't even got any nipples on their breasts."

"Nipples I can always buy in a drug store."

"Look," I said, "let's be serious."

"I am serious. You're the one who's treating this whole thing like a joke."

I tried to sound sympathetic. "I'm sure all this stuff means a great deal to you, and maybe some of it should be kept."

"Some of it!" he exploded. "You're all alike — you, the fire inspector, my wonderful insurance agent. Easy come, easy go; that's all you people know."

"Take it easy."

"Take it easy my ass! I'm not moving one stick, one nail, one piece of thread out of this basement. I'll set fire to it myself first."

After years of training, I had learned to walk away from the blowtorch of his temper. "You're crazy," I said quietly. And I turned and made my way through the narrow canyon that led out of the basement. I left him standing behind me in the aisle, in the company of the four hairless mannequins, calling after me, "I'm not crazy, the whole world's crazy; I'm the only one with any brains!"

All during the return flight from the Soo to Toronto I could think of nothing else but the man bellowing back there in that basement. How did he become the Messiah of Second-hand Goods?

How does anyone become a Messiah? Is it all in the way one is conceived?

My father was conceived on the rear platform of a horse-drawn cart, between bundles of clothing and an assortment of pots and pans, one black winter night while his parents were in full flight from a band of drunken Cossacks. It was the time of the annual pogrom, when Jews in that part of Russia were once again "in season" and were picked off in bunches, the way ripe strawberries are ravaged by hungry bears.

These were hours of frantic activity. Russian swords were swung and guns were fired. Jewish household goods were flung into wagons at midnight. Flames crackled in barns. Horses were whipped and cursed at to go faster along the back-country roads. In the midst of a frantic dash for the safety of the forests, my paternal grandfather — ever mindful of the uncertainties of tomorrow — entrusted his horses's reins to Fate, and there — in the back of their clattering cart — he and his wife pitched and rolled together, encouraged by sudden passion, and assisted by the rocky contour of the road.

Thus did my father come into being.

How do I know this?

I don't. There's nothing in the family records to bear witness — who would record such an act anyway? Certainly my father — gifted as he was with hindsight — remembered nothing of the precise circumstances, and if he did, he saw fit to disclose nothing. No matter. I have a photograph of my father's parents that tells all. There they stand, in their seventies, looking more like an old pair of boots than man and wife. There is snow on the ground and their faces are fierce and frostbitten. "Get on with it," they seem to be saying, "take the damn picture before we freeze to death here!" That they are being preserved on film for posterity is of little importance to them at this moment. Hurry up, get on with it. For today it's the winter that oppresses. And tomorrow it'll be the Russians again. And the day after — who knows?

Who knows?

There was another possible explanation for my father's nature: the devils in his life. Of them my father spoke frequently. Descendants of the demons that inhabited his boyhood home in Russia, these mid-twentieth-century devils were much more innovative and proficient than their European predecessors when it came to fouling things up. Applying contemporary techniques to ancient evils, they hovered over the stock market in his later years, casting sinister lights and shadows over his investments so that each speculation rose hopefully, plunged sharply, then levelled off many points below his aspirations. Sardonic memos in his diary summed up each day's luckless ventures: "Sold today 500 shares Consolidated Crap, bought 300 shares International Garbage." The same devils concocted overnight changes in the length of women's dresses so that yesterday's saleable garments became transformed into today's give-away rags. Like vampires, certain of the devils bled his cash register to pay income taxes, sales taxes, property taxes, and a hundred other levies imposed by other devils. Like masters of psychological warfare, they caused his love affairs to run aground on reefs of suspicion and jealousy. Like experts of chemical warfare, they poisoned old friendships and turned them sour.

Nature conspired against him. People could no longer be trusted. At this stage of his existence he believed in, and loved, only those things he could truly possess: land, buildings, chattels of every description. He loved things that could be spoken to and relied upon not to talk back, touched and relied upon not to bite; things that could be polished and were guaranteed to remain brilliant; that could be stored without aging and rotting; that could be nailed down, locked up, buried away from the sun in chests and closets without ever clamouring for freedom.

He loved equipment: tools, shovels, rakes, polishing cloths, paint brushes. He loved his sixteen-foot runabout with the silver-green outboard motor, and his fishing rods lined up absolutely parallel with each other.

He loved everything in its place. He loved horizontals and verticals, ninety-degree angles and perfect circles.

Whenever I brought my wife and children from Toronto to visit, he would greet us with wide-eyed enthusiasm, like a hermit happy to be discovered at last in his cave. But within twenty-four hours the smells of furniture wax and mothballs came between us and it was apparent that we were intruders in his world of order and timeliness. On the final day of our visit, he would begin to restore everything in the cave to its exact pre-arrival position, even before our bags were packed.

Whenever it came time to say goodbye to my father, we didn't depart — we checked out.

Six months after the local fire inspector ordered him to jettison all that excess cargo in the hold, my father learned from a chest specialist that he might also have to dispose of one of his lungs.

"I can never understand all that Latin baloney. What did the doctor call it again?" my father asked.

"He called it a slight irregularity, a minor tissue change." I tried to adopt the same casual manner displayed that morning by the doctor, tried to sound like a mechanic easing the mind of a Sunday driver whose engine had overheated. "On the x-ray it just shows as a tiny white spot."

'I didn't ask you to describe it in English. English I could understand. What did he call it in Latin?"

"I don't remember ——"

"I heard it before, once. Carson-something."

"I tell you I don't remember ——"

He snapped his fingers. "I remember. Carcinoma, that was it. What's it mean, exactly?"

"How should I know?"

"You're a lawyer aren't you? How come you don't know Latin?"

"I was away the day they took 'Carcinoma'."

"You must have been away a lot of days," he said, looking at me out of the corners of his eyes, shrewdly; he knew I was lying.

"Carcinoma happens to be a medical, not a legal, term."

He sighed. "You would know what it means if you had gone to medical school like I wanted."

"Okay, I'll make a deal with you," I said, inspired. "You submit to a biopsy, like the doctor recommended, and I'll apply for admission to any medical school you say. Is it a deal?"

"Are you crazy, or are you just out of your mind?" he retorted. "You really think I'm going to let those butchers play around with my insides?"

"I thought you worshipped doctors. Now all of a sudden they don't know what they're doing? You are incredible!"

"What's so incredible? You take Bill Lundy, the plumber. Looked like a million dollars. Went to the hospital for a hernia and never came out. Take for instance Tom McLatchey. Remember him? Strong like a bull; used to carry a tool box that weighed a ton. They found something in his stomach and he died right there on the operating table. And what about Milt Hershbaum, the traveller, wasn't he the picture of health? So what do you think happened to him? He went to some fancy clinic in Boston for a checkup — so help me God, a lousy checkup! — and they killed him and shipped his body home in a box."

"Alright, so Lundy and McLatchey and Milt whats-his-name had tough luck. What does that prove? Thousands upon thousands of people come out of hospitals cured. The exceptions are not the rule."

"It's always my luck to be an exception. Besides, I could tell from the way the doctor acted that I'm a goner. You and the doctor suppose maybe that I'm a yokel from Shtipovitz, don't you? Well I happen to have a damn good idea what Carcinoma means. It's a fifty-dollar word for cancer."

"Goddamit!" I yelled, furious. "Here I've been making an honest effort to keep the truth from you; the least you could have done was to make an honest effort to keep it from me. You're one helluva lousy sport!"

"I'm sorry. I never had cancer before. Nobody ever told me it's a game and I'm supposed to be a good sport."

"Listen to me," I said, calming down. "You're not a goner. The doctor says it's at an early stage and if you'd undergo this biopsy ——"

"Ach, what do doctors know? Look what they did to poor Sara Blackstein. Cut her up and sent her back to Sam in pieces. A real mess. Know what he told me confidentially? He says it's like sleeping with a jigsaw puzzle."

"But a biopsy is a fairly simple procedure."

"Alright, alright, I'll have the biopsy. Just leave me alone already."

"You will? When?"

"Soon."

"When?"

"When I'm ready."

"When will that be?"

"When I've looked after all my things. First things first."

"What things?"

"Everything. I want to check over everything, organize all my things, see they're stored properly."

"You can do all that when you get out of the hospital."

"And suppose I don't get out of the hospital? Don't forget what happened to Benny Koffman. I bet he wasn't a day over fifty when ——"

"Forget Benny Koffman, will you. There's no need for that now. Time is of the essence."

"Like I said before, first things first. I have to do what I have to do. That's my way."

"I'll stay here for a few days and look after your precious things."

"Like hell you will. The minute I'm out cold on the operating table you'll hire a couple of husky Talyainer and a truck and haul the whole kit and caboodle out of here. Just like you wanted to do when that low-life from Fire Prevention Week thought he discovered a volcano in my building."

"That low-life did you a favour."

"It's the other way around," my father said, slyly. "I did him a favour. I had him bring his wife into the store — you should have seen her — like a stray cat searching for milk, that's how she looked. But when she walked out of the store she looked like the Queen of Sheba. After that, I could've planted an atomic bomb down there and they would've given me a gold medal!"

"In other words, all that crap is still in the basement?"

"Every bit of it," he exulted.

"Look," I said, raising my right hand, "I solemnly promise not to touch one stick, one nail, one piece of thread down there. I'll put it in writing if you don't trust me. I'll even swear an affidavit."

Seizing my arm firmly, but smiling patiently, he said, "You don't understand. If you want me to save my life, that's very nice of you. I appreciate it and I thank you very much. But you've got to let me save it my way."

I tore my arm away. "I know what you're up to," I said, "but you're not going to pin this on me ——"

"Pin what? What're you talking about?"

"I'm wise to your little game. You want me to feel guilty about all this, don't you? Look at dear old Dad, everyone — standing there in that lousy basement gift-wrapping all those precious goodies for his little boy to inherit someday, and look at his little boy sitting in the meantime on his ass on the Riviera, sunning himself. I get the whole picture. It's the old Frederic Chopin routine again."

"Frederic who?"

"Chopin. In that movie *A Song to Remember.* He's supposed to be dying of TB but he insists on playing one last concert to raise money for Polish freedom. They even show him coughing blood all over the goddam keyboard. But good old Fred keeps right on playing to the very last drop, and at the end of the number — when he gets up from the piano — he makes a point of falling on his ass so the whole of Poland will feel good and guilty. And that's exactly what you're doing now — leaving me a basement full of guilt!"

"I thought you said a minute ago you weren't going to let me pin my sickness on you."

"That's right, I'm not going to accept any guilt in this matter."

"Then what the hell are you worried about?"

"I'm worried that you're going to die and neither of us will really have understood each other. Yes, I suppose that's it. I simply cannot understand any man whose priorities in this world are so screwed up."

"And I can't understand any man who doesn't have the slightest idea of what it means to have things, to own things, to start with nothing and end with something, to buy, pay off mortgages, to say this is mine and some day it'll be my son's. You don't understand me, and I don't understand you. But that's alright with me. You don't have to understand me. Just live your life and remember me. I don't give a damn how; you can light a candle once a year, blow your car horn, turn on the furnace, any way you want is okay by me. To remember is necessary; to understand isn't."

Later that day the plane carrying me back to Toronto flew along the shoreline of the St. Mary's River before veering south-east toward Lake Huron. In the distance to my left I could just barely make out the intersection of Queen and Bruce Streets and — a little to the east of it — my father's building. At that very moment I knew that he was in the bedroom I had occupied the night before. I saw him smoothing the creases in the bedspread, puffing the pillow where my head had left an indentation, picking up bits of lint from the rug where I had stood, running a finger along the bureau where I'd spilled some talc. Each lamp was being repositioned to within a fraction of an inch of where it had stood prior to my arrival. Each picture on the wall was rearranged dead level with the floor.

I had checked out of his house for the last time.

Within a year of the local fire inspector's report, my father was dead of cancer. And these are what he left me: a basement full of "things"; many puzzles (some of which I have managed to solve and some of which I haven't); and — every day, every night — car horns blowing, furnaces turning on, and candles burning in my mind.

Jerry Newman

AN ARAB UP NORTH

Enemies make me nervous; I can never tell what they may be about to involve me in. Friends, however, affect me in much the same way. The only people one can feel truly at ease with are those who are disinterested. Yet how can one be sure they are not merely *un*interested rather than disinterested? And if they are only uninterested then they may become interested at any time.

Take Mohammed Hassoun, for instance. He was an Arab; I am a Jew. When I was told that I was being sent to take charge of the Commissary and the kitchen staff at a DEW Line camp near the Canadian Arctic, I was given a list of the names of those I'd be responsible for. As soon as I looked at the list I spotted the name Hassoun and knew that I could not take the job. I turned to tell Derek that I would have to have another assignment.

Derek Maugham, my superior at Fox Base, who had handed me the list of names and the assignment that went with it, was another example of those who invariably cause me anxiety. An open-faced very handsome man in his early forties, with a forthright — an apparently forthright — manner and engaging cheer lines at the corner of his eyes, he was an ex-major in the British Army, a career man who, it was said, had been cashiered or rendered super-abundant, and he went about the camp with the sleeves of his khaki shirt rolled and an expression on his face that suggested that he was, reluctantly, just about to send a punitive expedition against some disorderly natives. His conduct toward the other men at the base — a uniformly low bunch — was, I thought, a model of enforced democratic adaptation. He treated them all as equals, both those whose jobs were ranked with his and those who were beneath him. I was the only one, however, because of my education, that he evidently felt close to. So he was a friend, technically. And it was in the friendliest manner that he had handed me the list and that he stood by as I read it and watched me go pale when I saw the name Hassoun.

"If you're worried about that Arab fellow," he said before I had a chance to say anything, "forget it. The way to handle this Arab fellow, and indeed any men who will ever serve under you, is to make absolutely clear to them from the start the limits you're prepared to tolerate in your relations with them. Let them know they're free to exploit those limits to the full, but one inch beyond that and they get the axe: the axe, absolutely."

If he had not regarded himself as my friend he would not have been moved to give me that advice, which I could no more apply than I could lie to people right to their faces the way Derek could and then dare them to contradict me. And if he had not given me that advice I could have asked to be relieved of the assignment, in favour of almost any other.

As it was I was left with no choice but to go.

With the company auditor who would supervise the handing-over of the inventory from the present clerk to me, I was flown in, a week later, on the DC3 that twice a month brought supplies, mail and new personnel to the auxiliary camps and took out those men who had served their contracts or were leaving on other grounds — sickness, compassionate leave and "nervous fatigue" were the most usual reasons men left before the end of their six-month contracts. There was good reason to serve out your contract; in addition to the relatively high rate of pay, those who completed their contracts got an extra $100 a month for every month they'd served; on the other hand, those who terminated their contracts for reasons not acceptable to the company not only lost out on the bonus, they were required to pay their air-fare to and from the camp — a substantial piece out of what they had earned, since the camp was just over two thousand miles from the nearest railhead. Still, many men failed to serve out their contracts. It was boring and maddeningly lonely in those camps, without women, with only the occasional movie or fight to break the routine of work seven days a week. Statistically, I would not need to feel too greatly dishonoured if I asked to be relieved before my time was up.

Before setting out in the plane I calculated what I had earned since coming to base camp two months before minus what it might cost me if I were to terminate my contract in, say, another month. Not very much would be left. However, set against four months in charge of twelve men who might all turn out to be difficult to manage (Mohammed Hassoun's contract, I had learned, had another three months to run), the balance of money that would be owing to me might not be so bad after all.

In addition to the unloading crew some two dozen men were on the landing strip when we touched down, as many as had been able to get off duty to see the plane arrive; it was one of the few diversions available at the camp. Before leaving the plane I looked out to see if I could spot a dark face among the group of men gathered about twenty or thirty feet away. I saw a couple of Negroes but, I thought, no Arabs. But it was the beginning of the Arctic Winter; and though we'd arrived in mid-afternoon it had already begun to grow dark. I came down from the plane and started walking after the auditor, alternately keeping close by his side and hanging back. The auditor and the clerk I was going to relieve, who had come forward to greet us, walked very briskly toward the snowmobile that would take us back to camp. They had about three hours before the plane took off again, to make the inventory and install me in charge. If they missed that plane they would have to wait at the camp with me for two weeks until the next regularly scheduled flight. That thought had occurred to me, so when I was not keeping close by their side in fear of being accosted by a silent figure in *keffiya* and *burnoose,* I hung back as much as I could to delay them. They talked quickly, briskly, as they walked, about the situation at camp and the procedures for carrying out the inventory, but now every now and then they looked back over their shoulders to see what was keeping me.

It was my right, if I chose, to insist that every sealed case in the stockroom be opened and its contents checked; clerks had been known to take over a site in good faith and then, on opening crates that had appeared to be sealed tight and that had been inventoried *in toto*, to find the contents half-removed. The danger existed in connection with every case of items intended for sale in the Commissary. At it was I merely asked for a sample crate to be opened here and there as a spot check. There was no call for the old clerk to give me dirty looks and to spit ostentatiously on the floor whenever I was about to walk in front of him. Or for the auditor, to whom it didn't much matter whether he spent the next two weeks at that camp or flying around between three or four others, to tell me, in a tone of exaggerated patience: "You know, if we don't get through with this very soon, there won't be time for John here to introduce you to all the staff. I'm sure he'd agree that it's important for you, get you off on the right foot, if he introduces you."

There was a grunt from John when the auditor looked at him for confirmation.

"Why?" I asked, welcoming this further delay but also eager for the information. "Are there any members of the staff I might have difficulty with?"

Of course I already knew the answer even before John said with malicious enthusiasm:

"There's one fellow in partick'ler. Arab lad. Nice enough lad but lazy as they come. And very good at getting 'round you. If you don't watch out, he'll be up to no work at all. There's a saying in the camp: 'If Mohammed won't come to the mountain it's prob'ly because he's asleep!' " The auditor let loose a couple of loud, knowing guffaws. "Arab fellow's name is Mohammed, you see," John said by way of explanation as he drove his crowbar hard into a crate that was alleged to contain a gross of Dubbin saddle-soap, and did.

For the next few days I was genuinely too busy to meet those members of my staff I did not come across in the course of my most pressing duties. I rearranged the Commissary stock to suit myself (John had let the little store, where the men came to buy toiletries, candy and the odd item of clothing and to gossip, fall into a comfortable mess), met with the cook to discuss the menu for the next several weeks, and inspected the sleeping quarters to see that my men were keeping them tidy. Hassoun worked nights in the kitchen, one of three men who served to feed the night shift. Hassoun was the dishwasher. The little I'd been able to learn about him back at base camp suggested he was capable of more responsible duties but that he preferred to work as a dishwasher and at night — when there was least supervision. I had decided without consulting anyone on the matter that unless there was very good reason to do otherwise, I would oblige him on all three counts, especially the part about minimal supervision. But after several more days the day cook told me that the night cook was beginning to feel slighted by my non-appearance, and what was more, that he had one or two problems he wanted to talk over with me. I had an uncomfortable feeling what these one or two problems might be. Okay, I said, tell the night cook to come and see me in my tent whenever he has a spare moment. The day cook looked at me in a curious way; that was perfectly all right with *him,* he said, but the *clerk* usually visited the *cook* on the latter's territory, and I *might* want to see for myself how the night crew was getting on.

That evening at ten I presented myself in the kitchen to the night cook and was introduced by him to the second cook, the only other man to be seen in the kitchen. The last of the labourers, foremen and engineers on night shift had had their breakfast — they came in for it at eight and were required to be through by nine; and the second cook was just then clearing the last of the dishes from the rows of trestle tables. This, I knew, was ordinarily the dishwasher's duty, and the second cook knew this too, as he intended me to understand from the dirty look he threw over his shoulder at the pile of dishes he'd stacked next to the sink before coming over to be introduced to me.

"Well," I said, "so you're the night crew."

"There's a dishwasher, too," the second said to me, looking again at the dishes.

"Yes. Well, he doesn't seem to be here...."

"He don't have to start same time as we do," the cook said. "The men don't come in to eat until eight, see, and the day crew sets the tables before they go. So the dishwasher don't come in until nine."

"Yes, but it's ...," I started to say as I looked over at the kitchen clock, falling neatly into his trap.

He followed my glance and said with a heavy air of surprise, "Why so it is — ten o'clock!"

Just then Mohammed Hassoun entered at the far end of the quonset dining-hall and walked with decisive but unhurried steps toward me.

I began to inspect the food that had been laid out to be cooked for dinner in two hours' time.

"Hassoun, Mohammed, reporting, sir," a deep, respectful voice said, not more than four feet away and more or less directly in front of me. I edged a little further away on the far side of the butcher's table where I had been examining the cuts of meat. Hassoun, Mohammed, dressed in the regulation DEW Line issue of baggy army trousers with pull-tight leg openings and thermo jacket (had I really expected him to appear in a *burnoose*?), moved after me, inclining a little in the friendliest possible manner across the table, on which there lay — as my nervous glance confirmed — several gleaming butcher's knives and one slightly bloody cleaver. I altered my position again, leaving him in possession of the knives and myself, I trusted, more handy to the cleaver.

Hassoun, I saw, had noted my glance at the table. A look of pained indignation passed quickly over his features (appropriately swarthy and pock-marked, with a strong hawk-like nose, a hairline moustache that was more than a little foolish on so young a face, and eyes of the most liquid brown) and then gave way to an expression of good-natured tolerance that said very clearly that he understood, he'd been the butt once again of the good old North American leg-pull. All the same he stepped back ostentatiously a foot or two from the table. I took advantage of this manoeuver on his part to dodge, as carefully as I could, around the table and out of the kitchen area altogether, to the far side of the counter that separated the kitchen from the dining room. Hassoun swivelled around after me but remained on the kitchen side of the counter.

"I understand, sir," he said when we had both come to rest, "that you and I have much in common?" He smiled at me with teeth that were much too large for my liking, healthy white teeth in a radiantly dark face. "Yes," he went on with easy, comfortable charm that soon began to make me feel quite ill, "I understand that you, too, have been to Palestine. So we have both had that honour; we have both been there — although, to be sure, at different ends of the political see-saw."

"No," I said. "Yes." How could he have found that out, I wondered bitterly. But in places such as the DEW Line, it seems, nothing that is to a man's discredit or that might conceivably cause him discomfort remains secret for very long. How could I have answered him truthfully? To admit that I had been to *Palestine* would mean renouncing a view of history I had been brought up to believe was sacred. But I might have renounced it all the same, for the sake of containing Middle-East tension in the Middle East, except that this might lead Hassoun to suppose I was his ally in other ways as well. While to insist that I had been, not to Palestine but to Israel, might be to invite him to open hostility. The image he had employed, of a political see-saw, made me altogether dizzy with its implications.

Behind Hassoun the second cook found a last dish he hadn't yet placed on the pile by the sink and proceeded to put it there with the maximum of noise. At almost the same time the cook brought his cleaver down on a joint with such violence that the severed halves leapt off their respective ends of the table. Hassoun ignored all this. He seemed to understand the predicament I was in and to be concerned only with putting me at my ease, for he smiled more broadly than ever and went on in an exceedingly kindly, laughing manner:

"Come, you must not think, because I am an Arab, that I am therefore anti-Semitic. That would be ridiculous, a logical impossibility." — Perhaps, but I believed that logic was as logic did — "And besides you must know that we Arabs have never been anything but hospitable to our Jewish cousins. Toward Zionists, our feelings are quite other. Surely to one of your subtle powers of discrimination such a distinction is not difficult to discern? One might be most passionately anti-Nazi and still find things to admire in the German character, history and culture. Don't you agree?"

"Perhaps," I thought, "perhaps." I couldn't help dwelling, however, on what seemed to me the excessively hypothetical nature of the words he'd used: "One might be. ..." Why hadn't he come right out and said, "*I am* most passionately anti-Nazi"? But perhaps, I thought with conscious charity, perhaps the difficulty lay with a faulty command of the English language. In answer to his question I confined myself to a non-committal, "Hmmm," adding, in case he should find this too curt, another "Hmmm."

"Well," Hassoun said, in effect dismissing me, "this has been a most stimulating discussion. There cannot be too many such exchanges of views, I think. But now, I'm afraid, I must get down to work." He gestured apologetically and in a wryly humorous way (a very *Semitically* humorous way, I thought inadvertently) in the direction of the huge pile of dishes.

Because the cook and the second cook had been listening to our "discussion" — and making no pretense about the fact — I thought I had better have the last word, and said firmly, "Now that you mention work, Mr. Hassoun, I wonder if the previous clerk may not have misinformed you about your actual hours. You start...."

"Oh no," Hassoun replied, "your predecessor had a number of faults — chief among them, in my view, that he was a decidedly unintellectual man — but he was very clear about the hours and duties of all of us. I am expected to start at *nine* o'clock. Only, you see, my back...."

"Your back?" I said. He nodded. "But you underwent a physical to get this job...."

He shrugged. "Five minutes with — please pardon my crudity — with one's pants down. Perhaps I should have volunteered the information about my back; but also perhaps Hassoun should have contented himself with the situation in which he was a poor student abroad, a hungry student, an *Arab* student: and therefore not precisely overwhelmed with offers of jobs."

"All the same ...," I said feebly.

"All the same," Hassoun said, smiling in the most understanding sort of way, "I must try to do a great deal better. Of course."

Of course he did no better than he had been doing, although I'm not prepared to say he didn't try. I get the uncomfortable impression, reading over what I've written so far, that Mohammed Hassoun emerges as an essentially droll person, almost a comic creation, hardly a real person at all. And I confess I do not know how to correct that impression. For if he *was* real, he was also decidedly unreal; he was in many ways a stereotype figure who had evidently chosen to play the part of the Arab as it is conceived by so many Westerners. Like a great many members of minority groups he had elected, for whatever reason, to play the part the majority had cast him for. Whether or not he believed in it, alone at night or with another Arab, I find it difficult to say. Or rather I think I can say that he did believe in it to some extent, it did correspond in some way to his own nature; but it was not the whole of him, and I find it hard to imagine what precisely he was like when he put off that role. But there was always a kind of leftover intensity in him that could not be encompassed by his role. He was like the comedian of very great comic powers whose comedy is in its own way every bit as profound and moving as tragedy, but who never ceases to dream of performing in a tragic part.

True to his word he came often to the Commissary when I was on duty and he was off, and to my hut when we were both off duty, and he would stay and become so caught up in our discussion — for it was always the same discussion that we carried on — that I would often have to remind him it was time for him to go to work. Then he would get up quietly, no matter what his state — and he was often in tears — and go off. He wept easily and copiously, and almost always at the same point in our discussion, at the question of the Arab refugees from Palestine. He described their situation most feelingly to me. He had visited a number of the refugee camps himself; it was a duty, he said, and he had cousins in several of them, cousins his own age who were entirely without education but who knew enough to say, when he begged them to leave the camps, "No, it is our destiny to suffer here. You may go and suffer for us in Cairo, in Damascus and in Amman, tell them of our suffering, remind them that we do not complain but that we count on their support and their brotherly tears. And if they weep, it must not be for us but for that portion of the Arab land it has been our misfortune to lose." At this Mohammed would almost always break down and cry, and sometimes I cried with him too, although more often I was merely made uncomfortable by his tears, feeling that they were somewhat too routine and operatic. At such times, I chided him gently for them. But I myself could almost always be sure of tears or the prelude to tears at reading or hearing any one of those names in that horrible litany of disaster, at Buchenwald or Auschwitz or Treblinka or Katowicz, and I would have turned with I cannot describe what vehemence upon anyone who had presumed to question my tears for the one-time residents of any of those synonyms of Hell. So I was always a little uneasy when we arrived late at the refugee question — and there was no way, I had soon learned, to defer that aspect of our discussion to another night — and I would have to dispatch Mohammed, the tears still fresh on his face, to his duties in the kitchen.

But the discussions we had gave me a better understanding of the Arab attitude to Israel and I believe Mohammed arrived at a better understanding of the Israeli view. We faltered only at the irreducible and mutually incompatible facts that had baffled, for the past nine and more years (for this took place in 1956), the two peoples whose views we represented. To the Arabs, Mohammed explained, Israel was a colonialist venture imposed upon the native people of Palestine by the guilt-ridden West, who had sought to atone for European persecution of the Jews at the expense of the Arabs, thereby displacing Jewish suffering onto the Arabs. For the Jews I argued that we *were* native people of Palestine despite our long, enforced absence from what we had never ceased to regard as our homeland; the whipped and beaten remnant of European Jewry had to have *some* place to go, nor could they have felt comfortable as the tolerated guests of another nation, even if there could have been found Western nations willing to put them up.

We were left, that is, Mohammed and I, with nothing more to be resolved between us than remained to be resolved between the Arabs and the Israelis themselves. In nothing did we evince more clearly that cousinhood of which Mohammed repeatedly spoke, than in our mutual obsession with the past, our utter inability to forget a single one of the wrongs or rights that history had dealt us.

And yet, through our growing respect and, yes, affection for one another we might yet have found the way to assert our respective rights without increasing the wrong done the other, had not the very conflict we were so near resolving just then refreshed itself.

For it was 1956, as I mentioned, and pressures were building up again in the Middle East. That great international lawyer and hell-fire preacher manqué, John Foster Dulles, had been instrumental in getting the United States to cut off its promised aid to Egypt's Aswan Dam project, because of the danger that U.S. money might soon be employed in a promiscuous way side by side with Russian money, and President Nasser of Egypt was threatening to nationalize the Suez Canal. Great Britain in turn threatened to retaliate on behalf of international freedom of passage through the Canal and of British stockholders in the Canal corporation. Israel, which for years had been sniped at and harassed by Arab terrorists on nearly every side and which now saw itself about to be permanently denied use of the Canal if Egypt nationalized it, Israel was reported to be deploying its troops on the borders of Sinai, and there was a corresponding Egyptian build-up.

Instead of carrying on with our usual discussion Mohammed and I took to spending the time together anxiously turning the dial of my short-wave radio, pulling in as many newscasts as we could. Yet, in a way, even here our debate continued. For even in the passive activity of listening to the news together we had had to negotiate a formal agreement; for every British or American broadcast we listened to, that is, we agreed to listen to one Russian English-language one. The Canadian point of view, I assured Mohammed, would be scrupulously neutral. Mohammed doubted this; towards Arab and Jew, he patiently reminded me as if he were my elder brother in suffering, there was no neutrality; only, in the very rare case, indifference. We compromised in this manner: we might listen to two Canadian newsbroadcasts in a row before searching out a Russian one.

Then one afternoon I could stand it no longer. Alone in the Commissary since morning except for the five or six men who came in to buy something (Mohammed, of course, slept during the day and almost never appeared before six o'clock, a few hours before he was due in the kitchen, or at eight in the morning when he quit work) I had been listening all day to the news — on the

Canadian Broadcasting Corporation almost exclusively, although once in a while I would turn with a guilty-obligatory feeling, and a morbid desire to hear what the other side was saying about me, to the Russian broadcasts. The news was as bad as it had been all month and perhaps a little worse; all the commentators now agreed that war was certain. At three o'clock I decided it was time that I personally did something. I had been going over in my mind for a long time just what it was I could do. Now I locked up the Commissary and walked over to the Marconi shack. There I gave the operator the message I had prepared. He looked it over quickly, then said: "You know I'm not supposed to send messages of a personal nature except in emergencies." "Send it anyway," I said. Everything operated in those camps on a barter system; almost everyone had a little power or authority or material to trade. My own position as Commissary clerk had provided me the means of storing up favours with most of the men. With this particular radio operator it was the yeast, the sugar and the apple juice I had slipped him from the kitchen stocks so that he could make the crude hard cider the men drank instead of the liquor they were forbidden to bring in. He sent my message. "Are you really going to go?" he asked. "If they send in a replacement for me," I said. "They'll never do it." "We'll see," I said. I was counting on ex-major Maugham's almost instinctive respect for anyone who evinced the wish to fight and preferably to die for his homeland. "I wonder what that Arab fellow would say if he knew what was in that message," the operator said.

I had been wondering and worrying about that myself. Of course, Mohammed need not know that a message had been sent at all until the plane was on the landing strip and I was ready to board it. The decent thing, however, the thing I owed him as a friend (you see what I mean about friends, as well as enemies, involving you in situations you would much rather not be involved in) was to have told him I was going to send the message and to have offered to request a replacement for him too. But that was just it; I had no intention of requesting a replacement for him. What would be the point of it? In the first place, if both of us requested replacements at once, neither of us would be likely to get one. But the second and more important point was that I wanted to go to Israel to help her win a war against a numerically superior army, and what was the sense in negating my enlistment on Israel's side by helping another man to join the Arab side?

Mohammed and I would only end up, as it were, killing each other, and the balance of forces would return to what they had been before we went there.

Of course, I could hardly expect Mohammed to see things this way, and I wondered whether I would have the courage to explain this to him before my replacement arrived.

As it happened I had no choice in the matter. Mohammed was waiting for me when I left the radio shack. He should still have been asleep at that hour and my first, illogical impulse was to scold him for affecting his health, and his efficiency as an employee, by doing without.

"You sent the message?" he said without preamble, falling in by my side as I resumed walking to the Commissary.

"I sent *a* message," I said. I had regularly to send messages to base-camp to advise them of some item that was in short supply or of a staff problem that had arisen. The occasion for sending messages was usually greatest a few days before the supply plane was due; as it was, just then, in three days' time.

Mohammed did not bother even to dismiss my attempted evasion.

"Do you think they will agree?" he asked eagerly.

"Agree to what?" I asked, increasing my pace in the hope of jogging his mind from the object it was fixed upon.

"To replace us," he said impatiently. "To let us go."

"Mohammed...."

"Yes, my friend?"

"Mohammed — I didn't ask for a replacement for you. If I had asked them to replace us both, chances are they wouldn't let either of us go. After I'm gone, if they let me go, you can...." But I realized that there was no longer anyone beside me to hear what I had to say. Mohammed had stopped in his tracks several paces back, when I had first confessed I hadn't asked for a replacement for him. I had to walk back to get him, though I'd much rather have continued on my own.

"You asked that only you be replaced?" he said very softly when I was in front of him. "That was not a very friendly thing to do, my friend."

"Not a friendly thing to do!" I exclaimed with desperate levity. "When it will result in saving you from the possibility of being killed?"

"That," he said, putting on, as it were, his comic-opera Arab regalia, "is not worthy of you. Not worthy of you at all. To suppose that I would value my life above this struggle."

"Come on, Mohammed — as if it will make the least bit of difference to what happens if either of us goes over."

"Then why do you wish to go?"

"Because I'm a Jew, Mohammed. Because my people have been pushed around for too long without being able to take a stand and without believing in the use of taking stands. It's just a gesture, really, on my part."

"And I wish to go because I am an Arab. I could repeat exactly your words in defence of my wish to go, and I would add: because people think the Arabs are fools, that they are capable *only* of gestures and are not to be taken seriously."

This was very close to the way I sometimes did think of Mohammed, and his putting it into words reinforced the feeling I already had that I had been unjust to him. Nevertheless I continued to argue. We argued all the way back to the Commissary and inside it. He pleaded with me first as a friend, and when that didn't work, as an enemy; and then, in what seemed to me an extraordinary feat of rhetoric, simultaneously as both friend and enemy. In the end he simply wore me down and I gave in through plain weariness.

"You will send the message? You'll send it now, right away?" he said in an eager, resonant voice. I nodded. "Very good," he said with intense but quiet emotion, and came over and embraced me. "I have always known in my heart that my Jewish cousin is of a most compassionate and generous nature."

"Oh sure," I thought. "We always go at least half-way to meet those who want to kill us." But when he had done embracing me and faced me at arms' length, his hands resting on my shoulders, I saw the emotion in his face and felt very close to tears myself. I couldn't say exactly what prompted his, but my own tears, I recall, were inspired by the spectacle of foolish earnestness he presented, and more, by the suspicion that Mohammed saw himself at that moment as if he stood fully and finally revealed with his arms held out to a mirror.

"I will go now," he said after a moment, "and rest, so that I may work well tonight. I have not slept since finishing work last night.

"But you will go directly to send the message? I will not accompany you myself to the radio shack but will trust you to send the message," he added — needlessly, in my opinion, if he really did trust me. But it wasn't in him not to dramatize every last one of his feelings.

Before he had closed the door behind him, with a last, solemn salute, a young French Canadian entered, another member of my staff, a thin young man of average height with cavernous cheeks that appeared to have been hollowed out to feed a great, thick, fleshy probe of a nose. As he came in he tipped his nose up and to one side, gesturing in that way after Mohammed.

"Won't be long now that fellow go for a walk in the snow," he said.

"What do you mean?" I snapped at him. I knew very well what he meant but didn't want to encourage him to think I shared his feelings toward Mohammed. I've mentioned that in order to quit a contract without having to pay one's air-fare to and from the camp, one of the things one could plead was "nervous fatigue". But of course it wasn't enough just to plead this; one had to be able to cite evidence, preferably with witnesses. This is how it worked: You decided one day that you had had enough of life in the camp and that you wanted to go for a walk in the snow. You then went on to announce this, before witnesses, with some such formula as: "Well, I guess I'll go on downtown now see what the girls are looking like." Whereupon you started off boldly in the direction of the outskirts of the camp; beyond which there was, literally, nothing but snow, nothing to be distinguished, nothing, that is, by which, once out of sight of the camp, you might find your way back. You did not, of course, get anywhere near the outskirts of the camp. As soon as you had made your announcement and had started walking briskly away, two of your friends leapt up to restrain you and drag you off to the Camp Superintendent's office to report that you had been just about to walk off in the snow. The Superintendent would grunt and agree to send immediately for a replacement for you. You would then go directly back to work since there was nothing else to do in camp, even for a victim of "nervous fatigue", and a few days alone in your hut or merely walking about the camp might really induce you to go for a walk in the snow.

Although I had known what the young French Canadian meant when he said that Mohammed might soon be going for a walk in the snow, I hadn't wanted to acknowledge the remark because I didn't much care for the man who had made it. He was one of those who had made insulting jokes about Mohammed one day when the latter was with me in the Commissary. Just before this French-Canadian fellow and his friends had come in I had been asking Mohammed why he chose to continue working as a dish-washer. The clerk before me had reported that, although decidedly lazy, Mohammed was probably capable of carrying responsibility, and I, too, thought that he might be put in charge of the crew that cleaned the huts or might be sent back to base camp to be trained as a clerk. When the men who had been making fun of him left, Mohammed said to me: "Now do you see why I prefer working as the lowest of the low? Can you imagine that fellow or others like him taking orders from me?"

The evening of the day I sent the messages to base camp requesting replacements for Mohammed and me, I went to the kitchen to tell Mohammed that I had carried out my promise. Again he embraced me, before the suspicious glances of the cook and second cook. Eager and conspiratorial, Mohammed leaned toward me to discuss the message and its likely consequences. You would have thought, from the warmth of his manner, that he and I were about to go off side by side on some peaceful adventure instead of to fight each other. He asked me to tell him with "utmost candour" whether I thought base camp would send in our replacements on the next plane.

"No," I said.

His eyebrows shot up, his eyes grew wide, displaying an inordinate amount of white, miming surprise in so broad a manner that a blind man would have known what he intended. "No?" I shook my head. "But they cannot do otherwise than send in replacements for us. We have said that we will go. They cannot doubt our intentions. They must send in replacements."

"Mohammed," I said in an exaggeratedly weary voice — I was suddenly resentful of his habitual assumption of the role of devil-may-care, incautious, damn-the-consequences romantic — a sort of Arab T.E. Lawrence — obliging me to play the part of a crimping pragmatist, "I did not tell them that we *would* go, but that we'd like to. They may not see things exactly our way. In fact I very much doubt if the rest of the world takes our quarrel with the seriousness that you — that we do."

"But we will go whether they send replacements for us or not," he said. He started out saying it with great firmness but somehow his voice betrayed him at the end, rising to a question. "You *will* go? You *will* go? You must go!"

"Maybe they won't let either of us go, Mohammed. Then things will be balanced out and...."

He raised his hand into the air between us, palm out, to stop me, turned and walked away with great dignity. The whole of this gesture had the effect of saying that if I were willing to demean myself, so be it, but my friend who knew my heart refused to stay and watch me do it. I shook my head in wonder and went back to my hut to wait.

We waited for the plane and for the cabled reply to the two messages I had sent. As the time for the plane to arrive drew near, and no cable arrived, it seemed obvious to me that we were going to be turned down. If they intended to replace us they would surely have advised us to be ready to fly out when the plane came; they'd have advised me at least to prepare for an inventory. Not necessarily, Mohammed argued, when I told him what I thought; if, from my cable, Major Maugham (Mohammed had taken, the last few days, to restoring Derek Maugham's rank to him, as if from a sense of professional camaraderie), if Major Maugham assumed from my cable that I was *determined* to leave he would also assume that I was going ahead with preparations for an inventory — as indeed I was, but without hope. As to his own case, Mohammed continued, everyone knew that an Arab was ready to strike his tent and move on at a moment's notice; and he *was* packed.

But when the plane arrived there was no auditor on it and no replacement for me or for Mohammed: only a letter for me in Derek Maugham's plain, strong handwriting. " ... Understand your concern ... admire your impulse to go and stand with your people," I read. "However ... can assure you ... absolutely no need for concern. Best military estimates" — meaning, of course, his own — "indicate Jews will soundly rout Arab forces. And as for that Arab fellow," the letter finished off with hardly disguised contempt, "tell him he'd best save his skin by sticking where he is." I burned with humiliation at what I took to be Maugham's friendly conde-scension toward me, and even more at his offhand dismissal of Mohammed; no mention of *his* admirable impulse to stand with his people.

I turned to share my bitterness with Mohammed, but he had gone. I thought I'd find him in the despatcher's hut at the end of the airstrip — he hated standing around in the cold — but he wasn't there either. I took the first lift I could get back to camp, looked for Mohammed in his hut and then in the kitchen, and when I couldn't find him I concluded he must be off somewhere sulking in private. I was a little worried about him but decided there was nothing I could do until he came around to see me.

Two hours later a messenger arrived at the Commissary from the Camp Superintendent. The Superintendent had had a telephone call from the airstrip: one of my men had been caught trying to stow away on the plane. He'd been discovered just as the plane was about to take off and was being returned to camp in the snowmobile — under guard; it seemed he had put up a struggle when told to leave the plane and had had to be forced off. A few minutes later I heard the snowmobile pull up outside the Commissary and I went out to meet Mohammed.

Even though I had expected his presence to be infused with the drama of the occasion, I was very much taken aback — and moved to protest — at the sight of him. He stood at an erect military posture behind the snowmobile between the men who'd brought him. The two men, wrapped to their ears against the sub-zero temperature, seemed to be terribly embarrassed, for Mohammed was dressed in full Arab regalia — *keffiya*, *burnoose*, sash and sandals — and held himself as if before a firing squad.

"Mohammed! What the hell's the meaning of all this?"

"Sir?" Mohammed replied with iron neutrality.

"I guess we can go now, eh boss?" one of the two guards said to me. "We were told just to bring him to you and now here he is." Having formalized his part in the occasion with these words, the man scampered off backwards with his mate and into the snowmobile. They drove away with their heads turned right around, staring back at us. Mohammed had not wavered an inch where he stood.

"Come into the Commissary, Mohammed," I said as gently as I could. I was tempted to laugh but, somehow, could not.

"Sir. I prefer to stay out here."

"But you'll freeze. In those clothes."

"These clothes are my national costume," he said with very precise dignity.

"But you're not in your native land!" I found, suddenly, that I was shouting.

"Through no choice of my own."

"All right. So they wouldn't let us go. But what are you going to do now?"

For a moment Mohammed lowered his head and appeared to

be looking at the toe of his sandal where it protruded below the hem of his *burnoose*. Then he raised his head and looked directly at me.

"Since you would not go, and I was not able to," he said this last with light but very distinct stress, "we must fight here."

"Fight?"

"Yes. You may have your choice of weapons."

"What weapons?"

"We can get knives from the kitchen," he said. "Or" — he looked around in the dusk at the buildings nearest us; next to one of them a D-8 stood, a number of tools scattered around the floor of the cab — "we can take some of those tools. Whatever you prefer," he concluded carelessly.

"This is crazy, Mohammed, and you know it. Whatever goes on over there, you and I are friends."

"We must fight," he said. "Here."

"It's against the rules to fight here!"

"Then we will go outside the camp," he said, and swung his arm — the gesture amplified by his loose, hanging sleeve — in a magnificent sweep that lay the desert before me where I had been accustomed to seeing only huts, machinery and snow.

"No."

"You will not fight?"

"No! Of course not."

He gave me a very melancholy look, bowed his head a moment, then raised it and started walking away. "So be it then," he said.

"Where are you going?" I called after him.

He gestured again in the direction of the dark that lay beyond the perimeter of the camp.

"I will walk in the direction of base camp. If they want to send a small plane after me, to fly me out, I will be walking in that direction." He stopped beside the D-8 and picked up a large wrench. "Do not come after me unless you are prepared to fight."

"Why should I come after you?" I shouted. "You damned fool! You're out of your mind! And you wonder why people think Arabs are foolish! Do you realize how foolish you're being? You'll freeze! You'll be the laughing-stock of the camp! You'll freeze to death! You fool! You fool, you fool!"

But he continued on his way. With his legs concealed beneath the *burnoose* he appeared to be gliding across the snow as if it were the warm, rolling desert sands. The white *burnoose* remained visible for several moments after the rest of him — eloquent dark hands, dark face, and even his gleaming white teeth — disappeared into the dark. Just before the *burnoose*, too, faded out, I heard him call, from a darker patch above his shoulders, in a lonely, pleading voice: "Come fight. Come fight. Come fight." Then he disappeared altogether.

I ran as fast as I could to tell the Camp Superintendent that someone had at last genuinely gone "for a walk in the snow."

But the Superintendent was not in his office–living-quarters and it was close to half an hour before I found him playing poker in another hut with some friends of his. He resented the interruption. Ordinarily, none of the men undertook to go for a walk in the snow except during daylight hours. But as soon as I mentioned the name Hassoun in connection with the word "snow" the Superintendent was on his feet arranging for every available vehicle and portable light to be brought to the place where I had seen Mohammed disappear.

For all the Superintendent's efficiency, it took a further half-hour before the search was fully organized and ready to get under way. During that time I waited some thirty yards from the Commissary at the spot where I had last seen Mohammed. As I waited I called into the dark that was by now, beyond the camp, absolute: "Mohammed! Mohammed! Where are you?" Once or twice, after looking around to be sure nobody was there yet to hear me, I added, feeling extremely foolish: "I want to fight with you! Mohammed, I want to fight! Do you hear me? I am ready to fight! We must fight, I insist on it!" There was no reply.

Then the search began. It consisted of about a dozen vehicles — the snowmobile, the Superintendent's jeep, a one-ton truck, three D-8's and a number of smaller tractors, all fitted with the extra lights that were necessary for night work — strung out in parallel formation about eight feet apart and proceeding in line against the massed Arctic darkness. Behind us an emergency crew fixed spotlights around the perimeter of the camp, facing off into the invisible snow-covered plains. I rode with the Superintendent in his jeep, the middle vehicle in the line, and listened to him call through a portable loudspeaker: "Hassoun! Hassoun! This is the Superintendent calling! Come back! Do you hear me? Come back!" But beyond the noise of the machines on either side of us I heard, as if in my heart, only the Arctic silence, which had been appropriated by Mohammed. Once, the Superintendent turned to me, and handing me the loudspeaker, said: "Look, there was something between you guys. I don't know what it was, but I hope to hell it wasn't responsible for this obscene stupidity. You try to call him. Maybe he'll answer to you." Hopelessly I took the loudspeaker, and trembling with cold and with embarrassment at what the Super might think, I called again: "Mohammed! Mohammed! It's me! I want to fight with you! Do you hear? I insist on fighting with you! Come back! We must settle this business once and for all!" But all the answer we got was Mohammed's foolish and determined silence.

So it went all through the night. We proceeded for about thirty minutes at a speed of about ten miles an hour, then all the vehicles stopped, made a right turn where they were and followed across each other's tracks until the leftmost vehicle was in the place previously occupied by the vehicle that had been at the extreme right of the line. Then we made another right turn and headed back to camp, going at a faster rate and calling as we went. At the camp's perimeter we checked with one of the men who were posted all around the camp to watch for Mohammed if he returned. Then the line of vehicles moved along to cover the next sector of the perimeter and we moved off again into the dark. On the second trip out we went at the same rate of speed but to a slightly longer distance, increasing the distance we penetrated with each fresh sector we covered, to allow for the extra distance Mohammed might have gone. Now and then we had to wait at the camp while the vehicles were refueled; we would jump up and down then to get the bitter cold out of us, and smack our hands together. I had instructed the kitchen night shift to keep a supply of hot coffee on hand and to make sandwiches. These, with several layers of the warmest clothing each of us had and the special heaters in every vehicle, helped us a little to bear the temperature that kept dropping and dropping. A wind had begun blowing up, however, and as the night wore on and our bodies grew tired, the cold got more and more into our systems until it seemed that the worst of the cold was inside us. I trembled to think how Mohammed was doing, alone and without any of these aids against the cold. Once, when we had stopped to refuel, I heard some of the men standing near me speculate on this same question, and heard one of them joke that perhaps "the Arab" had special means of dealing with cold and hunger, "just like them camels of his." Feeling, an instant, total rage I would have gone over to give that man the fight to the death that I had denied Mohammed, but the Superintendent, who had also overheard the remark, restrained me. His manner seemed to imply that it wasn't, after all, the man's compassion we needed at the moment but his simple mechanical ability to propel a vehicle back and forth over the snow. All the same, I made a note of the man's face and swore I'd find a way of fixing him later. I remember thinking that Mohammed would have approved and understood my resolution — and the futility of it.

We didn't find Mohammed that night. In the morning the Superintendent and I went to the Marconi shack to send out a request for an RCMP search plane. ("*One* plane, for Chrissake!" I protested. The Super shrugged. "It's probably all they have available, and if they had more, it's probably all they would consider necessary." He might as well have said explicitly that Mohammed, if he were to be found at all, would be just as frozen three days hence as he almost certainly was at that moment.) As we were leaving the shack, one of the men came running up to us, shouting.

"They found the Arab! They found the Arab!" In answer to the reluctant question on our faces, he said, "Yeh, he's dead. Froze stiff. Only maybe he kilt himself first when he fell down."

With the Superintendent I followed the man across camp to the back of the garage. There, face down on a pile of discarded and rusting machine parts, Mohammed lay. As the man who had brought the news to us had said, Mohammed was frozen, but a great deal of blood showed on the side of his face that we could see, and there was blood on various pieces of machinery beneath his head. It didn't seem hard to reconstruct what had happened. Either Mohammed had decided to return, or in the near total darkness that had fallen beyond the camp, before the emergency lights and the lights in every hut had been turned on, he had unwittingly re-entered the camp, stumbled over the pile of junk, and in falling, had struck himself a blow that had killed him — or knocked him unconscious long enough for the cold to kill him. In the dark he had come full circle, as men do wandering in the featureless desert wastes of snow or sand; the same thing might have happened to Mohammed, I reflected, if he had set out alone into the desert beyond Alexandria, for he had been born and raised there and knew nothing of the desert, despite the costume he affected.

The thought gave me a curious kind of comfort, as if I had

thereby rationalized his death. He looked terribly pathetic lying there, his useless *burnoose* frozen stiff around him, the wrench he'd picked up the afternoon before, in case I decided to come after him, still clutched in his right hand: pathetic and in need of some kind of rationale.

The Superintendent may have felt the same need to provide himself some kind of meaningful explanation for Mohammed's death, for he turned away from the junk heap on which Mohammed lay and shouted at the garage foreman: "How many obscenity-ing times have I told you I want this obscenity-ing junk pile cleared away? You'll go down in my report for this: you'll answer for it!"

The thought of writing a report seemed to lure him away with the promise of purposeful, useful activity. I had no such lure, however, and suddenly nothing at all to do but say a silent farewell to my late enemy and friend — to whom I had been, in the end, neither good friend nor good enemy — and go back alone to my hut.

Three days later, on November the 25th, the day of the combined Israeli, British and French attack on Egypt, I too went for a walk in the snow, but in a daylight hour. Although I did not tell anyone I was going, I was seen to go off, brought back and reported to the Superintendent. A replacement for me arrived on the very next plane.

Norman Levine

IN QUEBEC CITY

In the winter of 1944 when I was twenty and in the RCAF I was stationed for seven weeks in Quebec City. Fifty newly commissioned pilot officers were billeted in an old building right opposite a cigarette factory. It used to be a children's school. The wooden steps were wide and worn in the middle but they rose only a few inches at a time.

We were sent here to kill time and to learn how to behave like officers. Some of the earlier Canadian Air Force officers who were sent to England lacked the social graces. So they had us play games. We took turns pretending we were orderly officers, putting men on charge; being entertainment officers, providing the escort for a military funeral. We were instructed how to use knives and forks. How to make a toast. How to eat and drink properly. It was like going to a finishing school.

To keep fit we were taken on early morning route marches. We walked and ran through frozen side-streets then across a bridge to Lévis. And came back tired but with rosy cheeks. Evenings and weekends were free. We would get into taxis and drive to the top to the restaurants, have a steak and French fries, see a movie. On Sunday we behaved like tourists. Took pictures of Champlain, Bishop Laval, The Golden Dog, the Château Frontenac, the wall around the city, the steps to Lower Town. There was not much else to do.

On the Monday of the second week Gordie Greenway, who was make-believe orderly officer for the day, came up to me during lunch.

"Someone rang asking for you."

"Who?" I asked. I didn't know anyone in Quebec.

"They didn't give their name," he said and continued his tour of inspection.

Next morning I received this letter.

Quebec, 15 January.

Dear Pilot Officer Jimmy Ross,

We would be honoured if you could come to dinner this Friday.

It would give me and my wife much pleasure to meet you. If I don't hear from you I'll take it that we'll see you on Friday at 8.

> Yours sincerely,
> Mendel Rubin.

Out of curiosity I decided to go. The taxi driver drove to the most expensive part, just off Grande Allée, and stopped at the base of a horseshoe drive in front of a square stone building with large windows set in the stone.

I rang the bell.

A maid in black and white uniform opened the door. She said with a French accent, "Come in, sir."

I came inside. A short man in a grey suit came quickly up to me, hand outstretched. He wore rimless glasses and had neat waves in his dark hair.

"I'm so glad you could come," he said smiling. "My name is Mendel Rubin. Let me have your coat and hat. You didn't have any trouble getting here?"

"No," I said.

He led me into the living-room. And introduced his wife, Frieda. She was taller than he was, an attractive dark-haired woman. Then to their daughter, Constance. She was around seventeen or eighteen, like her mother, but not as pretty.

"It's nice of you to ask me over," I said.

"Our pleasure," Mendel said. "Now, what will you drink. Gin? Scotch? Sherry?"

"Gin is fine," I said.

He went to a cupboard at the far end of the room.

"Where are you from?" Frieda asked.

"Ottawa."

"I've been there a few times," she said. "But I don't know it well. Mendel knows it better."

He came back with drinks on a tray.

"Do you know the Raports?" he asked. "The Coopers? The Sugarmans?"

"I went to school with some of the kids," I said.

"Where do you live?"

"On Chapel Street — in Sandy Hill."

"It's a part of Ottawa I don't know too well," he said. "What does your father do?"

"He's a teacher."

The maid came in to announce that dinner was ready. And we walked towards the dining-room.

"I bet it's a while since you have had a Jewish meal," he said.

"Yes," I said, "it is."

"Every time a new draft comes in I find out if there are any Jewish officers. Then we have them up. It's nice to be with your own kind — you can take certain things for granted. Come, sit down here." And he put me in a chair opposite Constance.

While Mendel talked I had a chance to glance around the room. The walls were covered with some kind of creeper. The green leaves, like ivy leaves, clung to the walls on the trellis-work and to the frames of oil paintings. The paintings looked amateurish, as if they had been painted by numbers.

"Do you like the pictures?" Mendel asked. "My wife painted them."

"They're very good," I said.

Mendel did most of the talking during the meal. He said they were a tiny community. They had to get their rye bread, their kosher meat, flown in from Montreal.

"We're so few that the butcher is only a butcher in the back of the shop. In the front he sells antiques."

After the meal we returned to the other room. It was dimly lit. The chandelier looked pretty but did not give much light and there were small lights underneath more of Frieda's pictures on the walls. The far wall was one large slab of glass. It had now become a mirror. And I could see ourselves in this room, in the dark glass, as something remote.

Mendel went to a cupboard and brought back vodka, brandy, whisky, liqueurs. He gave me a large cigar.

"You know what I feel like after a meal like that? How about we all go to the theatre?"

"But it's half past nine," Constance said.

"How time goes when you're enjoying yourself," Mendel said. Then he glanced at his wrist. "I think we'll still catch it."

He walked to the far cupboard and turned on a radio. A Strauss waltz was being played. It stopped. And a commercial came on. A sepulchral voice boomed *Rubins.* And then *bins ... bins ...* echoed down long corridors. Then another voice spoke rapidly in French And again *Rubins* and the echoing *bins....*

He switched the radio off.

"I have a store in Lower Town. We carry quality goods and some cheap lines. Sometime I'll show you around, Jimmy. But what can we do *now*?"

"Mummy can play the piano," Constance said. "She plays very well."

"I don't," Frieda protested.

"Play us something," Mendel said.

Frieda went to the piano and played "Für Elise", some Chopin, while we drank brandy and coffee and smoked cigars.

At eleven he was driving me back to the children's school.

"Do you know the one about the two Anglican ministers?"

"No," I said.

"There were these two Anglican ministers," Mendel said. "One had seven children. The other had none. The one with the seven children asked the other. "How do you do it?"

"I use the safe period," the other minister said.

"What is that?"

"When *you* go out of the house — *I* come in. It's safe then." And Mendel laughed.

"Here's another one. There was this Jewish tailor. He had an audience with the Pope. When he got back to Montreal they asked him — How was the Pope? A nice-looking man, the Jewish tailor said. 36 chest, 32 waist, 28 inside leg...."

"Are you taking out Constance tomorrow night?"

"Yes," I said.

I took her to a movie. We got on fine. On Sunday we went out in the country to ski. We skied for miles. We both seemed to have so much energy. We came to a hill. I went down first. She followed and fell at the bottom. I picked her up and we kissed.

"My father is worried that I'll be an old maid," she said laughing.

I didn't think he needed to have any worries about that.

"He only lets me go out with Jewish boys."

We kissed again.

"Am I going to have a baby?"

"You don't have babies that way," I said.

"I know. But I have a girlfriend in Montreal. She told me that if you let a boy kiss you like that you can become pregnant."

Although I was being thrown together with Constance (we went out often for meals, saw movies, had romantic night-rides in a sleigh, wrapped in fur skins, behind the swaying rump of a horse) and Mendel took me to several hockey games, it was Frieda who interested me. But so far I didn't have a chance to be alone with her. If Mendel was there, he didn't let anyone else talk. If Constance was there, I was expected to be with her.

I managed to get away from the children's school early one Wednesday and drove up to the house to find that Mendel and Constance had driven to his branch store in Three Rivers.

"I was just reading," Frieda said when I came into the living-room.

She got me a drink. We stood by the glass wall looking out. It's a nice time, in winter, just before it gets dark. When the snow on the ground has some blue in it, so has the sky. She told me she came from Saint John, New Brunswick. Her father was a doctor. At seventeen her parents sent her to Montreal. "Just the way we worry about Constance." She met Mendel. He was working for his father who founded Rubins Department Store in Quebec. She was eighteen when they married and Constance came along when she was nineteen.

"After she grew up I found I had nothing to do with my time. And when I tried things — I found that I can't do anything well. That's my trouble."

"You had Constance," I said.

"Anybody can do that," she said contemptuously.

"I tried to paint — I have all these nice pictures in my head — but look how they come out. I tried writing — but it was the same. Sometimes when I'm walking through the streets or in a restaurant I see something. It excites me. But what can I do with it? There's no one I can even tell it to. I hardly go out of the house now. I feel trapped."

"Can't you leave Quebec City," I asked, "for a short——"

"I don't mean by this place," she interrupted. "I mean by life."

This conversation was out of my depth. I didn't know what she wanted. But her presence excited me far more than did Constance.

"I taught myself French," she said, "so I could read Colette in the original. And I have my flowers. Do you like flowers?"

"Yes," I said. "I like the colours."

She led me to her conservatory. It was full of orchids: yellows, purples, oranges, pinks, browns. There were other exotic flowers. I didn't know their names. There were several creepers overhead. And a smell of jasmine from the one in a corner. But it was mostly orchids, and in different stages. Some were only beginning to grow. They seemed to be growing out of stuck-together clusters of grotesque gooseberries. While outside the glass of the conservatory the thick snow had a frozen crust. It glittered underneath the street light.

She showed me a striped orchid on the table in the hall. Yellow with delicate brown stripes. It was open and curved in such a way that you could see deep inside the flower.

"Do you know how Colette describes an orchid?"

"No," I said.

"Like a female genital organ — I have shocked you," she said with a smile. "I would be promiscuous if I was a man. I know it. I wouldn't be like my husband. He's so old-fashioned — telling jokes. But I can't do anything like that here. If I step out of line——"

She broke off again. She would talk, follow a thought then, unable to see it through, break into something else.

"Poor Mendel. He desperately gets in touch with every Jewish officer who comes to Quebec. Throws them together with Constance as much as he can. Then they go overseas. They promise to write. But they never do."

I heard a car drive up. Mendel and Constance came through the door.

"Hello Jimmy," he said, "boy, it's a cold night."

The other officers complained about the deadness of the place. They thought I was lucky. Some met girls through a church dance or YMCA do. A few could speak French. Most tried to pick something up.

Tucker and Fleming got into trouble accused of raping a waitress. But nothing came of the charge, except they were confined for three days to a make-believe cell in the children's school.

I tried to get Frieda alone again. The only time I did she was upset. The boiler for the conservatory had broken down.

"You must get a plumber," she appealed to me. "If I can't get a plumber the orchids will die."

I got a taxi into Lower Town. Half an hour later I came back with a French Canadian plumber.

Our time was up. To see how we finally passed, the Air Force organized a ball at the Château Frontenac and all the eligible debutantes from Quebec and district were invited to be escorted by the officers. I took Constance. She looked very nice in a long white gown. We danced, made small talk, ate, passed the carafe of wine around. The dance band played.

> *To you he might be just another guy*
> *To me he means a million other things.*
> *An ordinary fellow with his heart up in the sky,*
> *He wears a pair of silver wings.*

Air Marshals made speeches calling us "Knights of the Air", "Captains of the Clouds".

At half past two we left the Château Frontenac. In the taxi, driving back, she pressed against my side.

"Don't you love me a bit, Jimmy?" she said softly.

"I'll be gone in a few days," I said.

She took my hand.

"Would you like to come up to my room? You'll have to be very quiet going up the stairs. I'll set the alarm for six. You'll have to be out by then."

I wondered how many times this had happened before.

"Is this the first time?" I asked.

"No," she said. "There have been other officers passing through." She squeezed my hand. "I didn't like them as much as you."

"How many others?"

"Four. This will be my fifth time."

She spoke too soon. After we went up the stairs, closed the door of her room, undressed, got into bed, turned out the light, I found I couldn't do a thing. And she didn't know how to help things along.

"Let's have a cigarette," I said, "and relax for a while."

I lit one for her and one for me. We lay on our backs, the cigarette ends glowing in the dark.

I was wondering what to do when I heard a door open. Then footsteps. Someone was walking in the corridor. The footsteps stopped by the door.

"Con, are you awake?"

It was Frieda on the other side.

We both stopped breathing. I was aware of Constance's body becoming tense with fear.

"Con — you awake?"

She was lying beside me, not moving, breathing deeply and rapidly.

I waited for the steps to go away, the sound of a far door closing. I put out our cigarettes. And took her easily.

"That was the best yet," she said softly. "Goodnight darling. Wake me before you go."

She lay on her side, away from me, asleep. And I lay on my back, wide awake. I listened to the ticking clock, her regular breathing, and thought of Frieda.

Just after five I got out of bed, dressed, disconnected the alarm, straightened the covers on Constance. And went out of the room, down the stairs, and out.

It was snowing. Everything was white and quiet. It felt marvellous walking, flakes slant, very fine. I didn't feel at all tired. I heard a church bell strike and somewhere further the sound of a train whistle, the two notes like the bass part of a mouth organ. The light changed to the dull grey of early morning and the darker shapes of a church, a convent, came in and out of the falling snow.

Next day we were confined to barracks and told to pack. That afternoon we boarded a train for Halifax. And at Halifax we walked from the train onto the waiting troopship. Two weeks later we docked at Liverpool.

Those first few months in England were exciting. I moved around a lot. A week in Bournemouth in the Majestic Hotel. Ten days leave in London. Then a small station, in Scotland, for advanced flying on Ansons. Then operational training near Leamington on Wellingtons. Before I was posted to a Lancaster Squadron in Yorkshire.

Perhaps it was this moving around? Perhaps it was being twenty, away from Canada for the first time, spring, meeting new people, new situations? The uniform was open sesame to all sorts of places. And there were plenty of girls around. I had forgotten about the Rubins except to send them a postcard from London.

In the middle of May I had an air-letter, re-directed twice, from Constance.

Dear Jimmy,

I hope this will reach you soon. Probably you are having all kinds of exciting things happen to you … meeting new people … doing things … and you have long forgotten me and the time we had together. I hope not.

Now my news. We're just getting over winter. It's been a long one, cold and lots of snow. The next lot of officers after you was a complete washout. But the one now has three Jewish officers. Shatsky and Dworkin from Montreal. And Lubell from Winnipeg. None of them are as nice as you ... but I like Shatsky best ... he's fun.

Don't forget to write when you can and take care. Mummy and Daddy send their regards. We all miss you.

Love,
Constance.

Two months later I received a carton of *Macdonald* cigarettes from Mendel. I bet he sent them to all the boys he had up at the house.

When the war was over I went back to Ottawa and to the job I had in the Government with the construction department. In my absence I was promoted. Now I'm assistant to the Head.

I have not married. Nor have I been to Quebec City, until this winter when I had to go to New Brunswick to see about a proposed dam that the Federal Government was thinking of putting some money in. The plane stopped at Quebec longer than the usual stop to let off and pick up passengers. A blizzard was blowing. Flying was off. A limousine brought us from the snow fields of the airport to the Château Frontenac. We were told the next weather inspection would take place at three.

I took a taxi to Lower Town. Down St Jean. Down the slope. Passed the cheap stores, the narrow pokey side streets, horses pulled milk sleighs, the bargain clothes hung out, the drab restaurants. An alligator of schoolgirls went by along the sidewalk with two nuns behind. Even with the snow falling men doffed their hats to priests.

I found Mendel standing in the furniture department. He looked much older and fatter in the face, the skin under the jaw sagged, and the small neat waves of hair were thin and grey.

"Hullo Mendel," I said.

He didn't recognize me.

"I'm Jimmy Ross," I said. "Remember during the war?"

"Of course," he said becoming animated. "When did you get in?"

"Just now. The plane couldn't go on to Fredericton because of the snowstorm."

"Let's go and have some coffee next door," he said. "It's been snowing like this all morning."

We went to the Honey Dew and had coffee. The piped-in music played old tunes. And bundled-up people with faces down went by the plate-glass window.

"I wish Constance were here," he said." I know she would be glad to see you."

"How is Constance?"

"She's living in Detroit. Married. He came over from Germany after the war. His name is Freddie. He's an accountant. They're doing well. They have four kids. And she's expecting another. How about you?"

I told him briefly what I had done.

"There were some good times during the war——" he said.

"How is Frieda?"

"She died a year and half ago. I married again. Why don't you come up to the house and meet Dorothy."

"I'd like to," I said. "But I don't want to miss the plane."

"They won't take off in this weather," he said. "But here I am telling *you* about airplanes."

"That was twenty-two years ago," I said. "I couldn't fly the airplanes today."

We got into his black Cadillac with black leather seats. He drove through all-white streets, the windshield wipers going steadily, to the house.

Dorothy was the same size as Mendel, plump, a widow, very cheerful.

"This is Jimmy Ross," Mendel said. "He was a young Air Force officer here during the war. He used to be much handsomer." He went to the far cupboard to get some drinks.

The oil paintings, the creepers, the flowers, were gone. A rubber plant stood by the plate-glass wall. Its bottom leaves shrivelled and brown.

"Would you like some sponge cake?" Dorothy asked.

"She makes an excellent sponge," Mendel assured me.

"I had lunch on the plane," I said. "I can't stay very long."

It had almost stopped snowing. Only the wind, in gusts, blew the loose snow up from the ground and down from the roofs.

"Where are you from Mr. Ross?" Dorothy asked.

"Ottawa," I said.

I felt awkward. It was a mistake to have come.

Mendel drove me to the Château Frontenac.

"Don't forget," he said. "Next time you're here let me know in advance. We'll have you up for dinner."

"You used to tell me jokes, Mendel," I said. "Where did they come from?"

"From the commercial travellers. They come to see me all the time. All of them have jokes. I had one in this morning. What is at the bottom of the sea and shakes?"

"I don't know," I said.

"A nervous wreck," he said and smiled. "Here is another. Why do cows wear bells around their necks?"

I said nothing.

"Because their horns don't work."

He stopped the car outside the entrance of the Château Frontenac.

"When I write to Constance I'll tell her I saw you——"

An hour later I was back in the Viscount taking off from a windswept runway.

Leonard Cohen

THE DANCE HALL*

Suspended from the centre of the ceiling a revolving mirrored sphere cast a rage of pockmarks from wall to wall of the huge Palais D'Or on lower Stanley Street.

Each wall looked like an enormous decayed Swiss cheese on the march.

On the raised platform a band of shiny-haired musicians sat behind heavy red and white music stands and blew the standard arrangements.

> *There's but one place for me*
> *Near you.*
> *It's like heaven to be*
> *Near you*

echoed coldly over the sparse dancers. Breavman and Krantz had got there too early. There was not much hope for magic.

"Wrong dance-hall, Breavman."

By ten o'clock the floor was jammed with sharply dressed couples, and, seen from the upstairs balcony, their swaying and jolting seemed to be nourished directly by the pulsing music, and they muffled it like shock absorbers. The bass and piano and steady brush-drum passed almost silently into their bodies where it was preserved as motion.

Only the tilt-backed trumpeter, arching away from the mike and pointing his horn at the revolving mirrored sphere, could put a lingering sharp cry in the smoky air, coiling like a rope of rescue above the bobbing figures. It disappeared as the chorus renewed itself.

"Right dance-hall, Krantz."

They scorned many public demonstrations in those prowling days but they didn't scorn the Palais D'Or. It was too big. There was nothing superficial about a thousand people deeply engaged in the courting ritual, the swinging fragments of reflected light sweeping across their immobile eye-closed faces, amber, green, violet. They couldn't help being impressed, fascinated by the channelled violence and the voluntary organization.

*Chapter Twenty-five of Leonard Cohen's
  novel *The Favourite Game*.

Why are they dancing to the music, Breavman wondered from the balcony, submitting to its dictation?

At the beginning of a tune they arranged themselves on the floor, obeyed the tempo, fast or slow, and when the tune was done they disintegrated into disorder again, like a battalion scattered by a land mine.

"What makes them listen, Krantz? Why don't they rip the platform to pieces?"

"Let's go down and get some women."

"Soon."

"What are you staring at?"

"I'm planning a catastrophe."

They watched the dancers silently and they heard their parents talking.

The dancers were Catholics, French-Canadian, anti-Semitic, anti-Anglais, belligerent. They told the priest everything, they were scared by the Church, they knelt in wax-smelling musty shrines hung with abandoned dirty crutches and braces. Everyone of them worked for a Jewish manufacturer whom he hated and waited for revenge. They had bad teeth because they lived on Pepsi-Cola and Mae West chocolate cakes. The girls were either maids or factory help. Their dresses were too bright and you could see bra straps through the flimsy material. Frizzy hair and cheap perfume. They screwed like jack rabbits and at confession the priest forgave them. They were the mob. Give them a chance and they'd burn down the synagogue. Pepsies. Frogs. Fransoyzen.

Breavman and Krantz knew their parents were bigots so they attempted to reverse all their opinions. They did not quite succeed. They wanted to participate in the vitality but they felt there was something vaguely unclean in their fun, the pawing of girls, the guffaws, the goosing.

The girls might be beautiful but they all had false teeth.

"Krantz, I believe we're the only two Jews in the place."

"No, I saw some BTOs on the make a couple of minutes ago."

"Well, we're the only Westmount Jews around."

"Bernie's here."

"O.K. Krantz, I'm the only Jew from Wellgreen Avenue. Do something with that."

"O.K. Breavman, you're the only Jew from Wellgreen Avenue at the Palais D'Or."

"Distinctions are important."

"Let's get some women."

At one of the doors in the main hall there was a knot of young people. They argued jovially in French, pushing one another, slapping back-sides, squirting Coke bottles.

The hunters approached the group and instantly modified its hilarity. The French boys stepped back slightly and Krantz and Breavman invited the girls they'd chosen. They spoke in French, fooling no one. The girls exchanged glances with each other and members of the party. One of the French boys magnanimously put his arm around the shoulder of the girl Breavman had asked and swept her to him, clapping Breavman on the back at the same time.

They danced stiffly. Her mouth was full of fillings. He knew he'd be able to smell her all night.

"Do you come here often, Yvette?"

"You know, once in a while, for fun."

"Me too. *Moi aussi*."

He told her he was in high school, that he didn't work.

"You are Italian?"

"No"

"English?"

"I'm Jewish."

He didn't tell her he was the only one from Wellgreen Avenue.

"My brothers work for Jew people."

"Oh?"

"They are good to work for."

The dance was unsatisfying. She was not attractive, but her racial mystery challenged investigation. He returned her to her friends. Krantz had finished his dance, too.

"What was she like, Krantz?"

"Don't know. She couldn't speak English."

They hung around for a little while longer, drinking Orange Crush, leaning on the balcony rail to comment on the swaying mob below. The air was dense with smoke now. The band played either frantic jitterbug or slow fox trot, nothing between. After each dance the crowd hovered impatiently for the next one to begin.

It was late now. The wallflowers and the stag-line expected no miracles any more. They were lined along three walls watching the packed charged dancers with indifferent fixed stares. Some of the girls were collecting their coats and going home.

"Their new blouses were useless, Krantz."

Seen from above, the movement on the floor had taken on a frantic quality. Soon the trumpeter would aim his horn into the smoke and give the last of Hoagy Carmichael and it would be all over. Every throb of the band had to be hoarded now against the end of the evening and the silence. Soak it through pressed cheeks and closed eyes in the dreamy tunes. In the boogie-woogie gather the nourishment like manna and knead it between the bodies drawing away and towards each other.

"Let's get one more dance in, Breavman?"

"Same girls?"

"Might as well."

Breavman leaned over the rail one more second and wished he were delivering a hysterical speech to the thick mob below.

... and you must listen, friends, strangers, I am binding the generations one to another, o, little people of numberless streets, bark, bark, hoot, blood, your long stairways are curling around my heart like a vine....

They went downstairs and found the girls with the same group. It was a mistake, they knew instantly. Yvette stepped forward as if to tell Breavman something but one of the boys pulled her back.

"You like the girls, eh?" he said, the swaggerer of the party. His smile was triumphant rather than friendly.

"Sure we like them. Anything wrong with that?"

"Where you live, you?"

Breavman and Krantz knew what they wanted to hear. Westmount is a collection of large stone houses and lush trees arranged on the top of the mountain especially to humiliate the underprivileged.

"Westmount," they said with one voice.

"You have not the girls at Westmount, you?"

They had no chance to answer him. In the very last second before they fell backwards over the kneeling accomplices stationed behind them they detected a signalling of eyes. The ringleader and a buddy stepped forward and shoved them. Breavman lost his balance and as he fell the stoolie behind him raised himself up to turn the fall into a flip. Breavman landed hard in a belly-flop, a couple of girls that he had crashed into squealing above him. He looked up to see Krantz on his feet, his left fist in someone's face and his right cocked back ready to fly. He was about to get up when a fat boy decided he shouldn't and dived at him.

"Reste là, maudit juif!"

Breavman struggled under the blankets of flesh, not trying to defeat the fat boy but merely to get out from under him so he could do battle from a more honourable upright position. He managed to squeeze away. Where was Krantz?

There must have been twenty people fighting. Here and there he could see girls on their tiptoes as though in fear of mice, while boys wrestled on the floor between them.

He wheeled around, expecting an attack. The fat boy was smothering someone else. He threw his fist at a stranger. He was a drop in the wave of history, anonymous, exhilarated, free.

"O, little friends, hoot, blooey, dark fighters, shazam, bloop!" he shouted in his happiness.

Racing down the stairs were three bouncers of the management's and what they feared most began to happen. The fighting spread to the dance floor. The band was blowing a loud dreamy tune but a disorganized noise could already be heard in opposition to the music.

Breavman waved his fist at everyone, hitting very few. The bouncers were in his immediate area, breaking up individual fights. At the far side of the hall the couples still danced closely and peacefully, but on Breavman's side their rhythm was disintegrating into flailing arms, blind punches, lunges, and female squeals.

The bouncers pursued the disruption like compulsive house-keepers after an enormous spreading stain, jerking fighters apart by their collars and sweeping them aside as they followed the struggle deeper into the dance floor.

A man rushed onto the bandstand and shouted something to the bandleader, who looked around and shrugged his shoulders. The bright lights went on and the curious coloured walls disappeared. The music stopped.

Everyone woke up. A noise like a wail of national mourning rose up and at the same time fighting swept over the hall like released entropic molecules. To see the mass of dancers change to a mass of fighters was like watching a huge highly organized animal succumb to muscular convulsions.

Krantz grabbed Breavman.

"Mr. Breavman?"

"Krantzstone, I presume."

They headed for the front exit, which was already jammed with refugees. No one cared about his coat.

"Don't say it, Breavman."

"O.K. I won't say it, Krantz."

They got out just as the police arrived, about twenty of them in cars and the Black Maria. They entered with miraculous ease.

The boys waited in the front seat of the Lincoln. Krantz's jacket was missing a lapel. The Palais D'Or began to empty of its victims.

"Pity the guys in there, Breavman — and don't say it," he added quickly when he saw Breavman put on his mystical face.

"I won't say it, Krantz, I won't even whisper that I planned the whole thing from the balcony and executed it by the simple means of mass hypnosis."

"You had to say it, eh?"

"We were mocked, Krantz. We seized the pillars and brought down the temple of the Philistines."

Krantz shifted into second with exaggerated weariness.

"Go on, Breavman. You have to say it."

THE GENIUS

For you
I will be a ghetto jew
and dance
and put white stockings
on my twisted limbs
and poison wells
across the town

For you
I will be an apostate jew
and tell the Spanish priest
of the blood vow
in the Talmud
and where the bones
of the child are hid

For you
I will be a banker jew
and bring to ruin
a proud old hunting king
and end his line

For you
I will be a Broadway jew
and cry in theatres
for my mother
and sell bargain goods
beneath the counter

For you
I will be a doctor jew
and search
in all the garbage cans
for foreskins
to sew back on again

For you
I will be a Dachau jew
and lie down in lime
with twisted limbs
and bloated pain
no mind can understand

LOVERS

During the first pogrom they
Met behind the ruins of their homes —
Sweet merchants trading: her love
For a history-full of poems.

And at the hot ovens they
Cunningly managed a brief
Kiss before the soldier came
To knock out her golden teeth.

And in the furnace itself
As the flames flamed higher,
He tried to kiss her burning breasts
As she burned in the fire.

Later he often wondered:
Was their barter completed?
While men around him plundered
And knew he had been cheated.

I HAVE NOT LINGERED IN EUROPEAN MONASTERIES

I have not lingered in European monasteries
and discovered among the tall grasses tombs of knights
who fell as beautifully as their ballads tell;

I have not parted the grasses
or purposefully left them thatched.

I have not released my mind to wander and wait
in those great distances
between the snowy mountains and the fishermen,
like a moon,
or a shell beneath the moving water.

I have not held my breath
so that I might hear the breathing of God,
or tamed my heartbeat with an exercise,
or starved for visions.
Although I have watched him often
I have not become the heron,
leaving my body on the shore,
and I have not become the luminous trout,
leaving my body in the air.

I have not worshipped wounds and relics,
or combs of iron,
or bodies wrapped and burnt in scrolls.

I have not been unhappy for ten thousand years.
During the day I laugh and during the night I sleep.
My favourite cooks prepare my meals,
my body cleans and repairs itself,
and all my work goes well.

LAST DANCE AT THE FOUR PENNY

Layton, when we dance our freilach
under the ghostly handkerchief,
the miracle rabbis of Prague and Vilna
resume their sawdust thrones,
and angels and men, asleep so long
in the cold palaces of disbelief,
gather in sausage-hung kitchens
to quarrel deliciously and debate
the sounds of the Ineffable Name.

Layton, my friend Lazarovitch,
no Jew was ever lost
while we two dance joyously
in this French province,
cold and oceans west of the temple,
the snow canyoned on the twigs
like forbidden Sabbath manna;
I say no Jew was ever lost
while we weave and billow the handkerchief
into a burning cloud,
measuring all of heaven
with our stitching thumbs.

Reb Israel Lazarovitch,
you no-good Romanian, you're right!
Who cares whether or not
the Messiah is a Litvak?
As for the cynical,
such as we were yesterday,
let them step with us or rot
in their logical shrouds.
We've raised a bright white flag,
and here's our battered fathers' cup of wine,
and now is music
until morning and the morning prayers
lay us down again,
we who dance so beautifully
though we know that freilachs end.

Irving Layton

FOR MY BROTHER JESUS

My father had terrible words for you
— whoreson, bastard, *meshumad*;
and my mother loosed Yiddish curses
on your name and the devil's spawn
on their way to church
that scraped the frosted horsebuns
from the wintry Montreal street
to fling clattering into our passageway

Did you ever hear an angered
Jewish woman curse? Never mind the words:
at the intonations alone, Jesus,
the rusted nails would drop out
from your pierced hands and feet
and scatter to the four ends of earth

Luckless man, at least
that much you were spared

In my family you
were a *mamzer*, a *yoshke pondrick*
and main reason for their affliction and pain.
Even now I see the contemptuous curl
on my gentle father's lips;
my mother's never-ending singsong curses
still ring in my ears more loud
than the bells I heard each Sunday morning,
their clappers darkening the outside air

Priests and nuns
were black blots on the snow
— forbidding birds, crows

Up there
up there beside the Good Old Man
we invented and the lyring angels
do you get the picture, my hapless brother:

deserted daily, hourly
by the Philistines you hoped to save
and the murdering heathens,
your own victimized kin hating and despising
you?

       O crucified poet
your agonized face haunts me
as it did when I was a boy;
I follow your strange figure
through all the crooked passageways
of history, the walls reverberating
with ironic whisperings and cries,
the unending sound of cannonfire
and rending groans, the clatter
of bloodsoaked swords falling
on armour and stone
to lose you finally among your excited brethren
haranguing and haloing them
with your words of love,
your voice gentle as my father's

THE BLACK HUNTSMEN

Before ever I knew men were hunting me
I knew delight as water in a glass in a pool;
The childish heart then
Was ears nose eyes twiceten fingers,
And the torpid slum street, in summer,
A cut vein of the sun
That shed goldmotes by the million
Against a boy's bare toe foot ankle knee.

Then when the old year fell out of the window
To break into snowflakes on the cold stones of City Hall
I discovered Tennyson in a secondhand bookstore;
He put his bugle for me to his bearded mouth,
And down his Aquitaine nose a diminutive King Arthur
Rode out of our grocery shop bowing to left and to right,
Bearing my mother's *sheitel* with him;
And for a whole week after that
I called my cat Launcelot.

Now I look out for the evil retinue
Making their sortie out of a forest of gold;
Afterwards their dames shall weave my *tzitzith*
Into a tapestry,
Though for myself I had preferred
A death by water or sky.

THE SEARCH

My father's name was Moses; his beard was black
and black the eyes that beheld God's light;
they never looked upon me but they saw
a crazy imp dropt somehow from the sky
and then I knew from his holy stare
I had disgraced the Prophets and the Law.

Nor was I my mother's prayer;
she who all day railed at a religious indolence
that kept her man warm under his prayershawl
while her reaching arm froze with each customer
who brought a needed penny to her store;
added to another it paid the food and rent.

An ill-matched pair they were. My father
thought he saw Jehovah everywhere,
entertaining his messengers every day
though visible to him alone in that room
where making his fastidious cheese
he dreamt of living in Zion at his ease.

My mother: unpoetical as a pot of clay,
with as much mysticism in her as a banker
or a steward; lamenting God's will for her
yet blessing it with each Friday's candles.
But O her sturdy mind has served me well
who see how humans forge with lies their lonely hell.

Alien and bitter the road my forbears knew:
fugitives forever eating unleavened bread
and hated pariahs because of that one Jew
who taught the tenderest Christian how to hate
and harry them to whatever holes they sped.
Times there were the living envied the dead.

Iconoclasts, dreamers, men who stood alone:
Freud and Marx, the great Maimonides
and Spinoza who defied even his own.
In my veins runs their rebellious blood.
I tread with them the selfsame antique road
and seek everywhere the faintest scent of God.

ISRAELIS

It is themselves they trust and no one else;
Their fighter planes that screech across the sky,
Real, visible as the glorious sun;
Riflesmoke, gunshine, and rumble of tanks.

Man is a fanged wolf, without compassion
Or ruth: Assyrians, Medes, Greeks, Romans,
And devout pagans in Spain and Russia
— Allah's children, most merciful of all.

Where is the Almighty if murder thrives?
He's dead as mutton and they buried him
Decades ago, covered him with their own
Limp bodies in Belsen and Babi Yar.

Let the strong compose hymns and canticles,
Live with the Lord's radiance in their hard skulls
Or make known his great benevolences;
Stare at the heavens and feel glorified

Or humbled and awestruck buckle their knees:
They are done with him now and forever.
Without a whimper from him they returned,
A sign like an open hand in the sky.

The pillar of fire: Their flesh made it;
It burned briefly and died — you all know where.
Now in their own blood they temper the steel,
God being dead and their enemies not.

Jack Ludwig

A WOMAN OF HER AGE

Once a week, even now, Mrs. Goffman makes that chauffeur drive her slowly down from the mountain, back to St. Lawrence Boulevard and Rachel Street; she doesn't want any old cronies who might still be alive spotting her in that hearse of a limousine, so she gets out a couple of blocks from the Market and walks the rest of the way, not in her Persian lamb or her warm beaver, but in that worn cloth coat she bought at Eaton's Basement years ago, the black one. Long, gaunt as a late afternoon shadow, Mrs. Goffman concentrates on smiling. Otherwise she looks like a spook. At seventy-five you can feel warm, sweet, girlish even, but an old, old face has trouble expressing soft feelings. Those reddish-brown eyebrows that didn't turn white with the rest of her hair, they're to blame, so bushy, so fierce, with an ironic twist that was snappy when she was a hot young Radical, but now, when she's old enough to be a great-grandmother, who needs it?

"Wordsworth," her son Jimmy used to call her. In a drugstore window she sees reflected Wordsworth's broad forehead, deep-set eyes, small mouth, short chin. By God, she tells herself, this is a darned good face. Jimmy had this face. Her father had it too — who knows how far back these purplish lips go, or the dark rings under eyes, or the pale olive complexion? Moses might have had similar colouring. Her nose gives a sly twitch to call attention to itself; Wordsworth's large humped nose she has too, and it deserves the dominant spot it earned for itself on Mrs. Goffman's face. She judges everything by its smell. That's why the Ambassador's mansion she lives in flunks so badly — it's not only quiet as a church, it smells like a church. Six days a week her nose puts up with that dry lonely quiet smell, does what a nose is supposed to do in Westmount, breathe a little. On St. Lawrence Boulevard a nose is for smelling, and Mrs. Goffman doesn't miss a sniff. Families are getting ready for sabbath.

Doba, catch that goose roasting, her nose seems to say. Hey, poppyseed cookies! *Real* stuffed fish! St. Lawrence Boulevard, I love you!

2

Mitchell the "Kosher Butcher" nodded his usual pitying nod as she walked past his full window — fresh-killed ducks and chickens hanging by their feet, cows' brains in pools, tongues like holsters, calves' feet signed by the Rabbi's indelible pencil. Mrs. Goffman nodded her black-turbaned head at Mitchell but he'd already given *his* nod, and only stared back, open-mouthed, his hands pressed against his slaughterhouse-looking apron. Naturally Mitchell has her pegged: doesn't he know this shopping trip is a fake, that Mrs. Grosney, the cook, does Mrs. Goffman's buying and cooking? Mitchell knows about the Persian lamb coat she doesn't wear to Market. Mitchell knew her dead husband well. Mitchell, like all of Montreal, knows the story of her dead son Jimmy.

When Simon-may-he-rest-in-peace was still alive the Goffmans lived down here, among people, in life. Now life was a novelty to Mrs. Goffman. Six days to Westmount, one to St. Lawrence and Rachel Street, what idiotic arrangement was that? Some day she'd get real tough with her son Sidney. Marry him off. Make him sell the Ambassador's mansion and lead a normal life.

Her eyebrows went into their ironic arch. You, Doba, they seemed to mock her, when could you get your kids to do anything?

3

In front of Bernstein's Kiddies' Korner a young girl pressed her lovely dark face against the window, her hand nervously rocking a baby carriage. Black hair, heavy lips, nursing breasts, what a beauty of a mother, Mrs. Goffman thought; she could double for Jimmy's Shirley! By rights Mrs. Goffman should have a granddaughter this girl's age. One? A dozen!

What would it hurt if she *pretended* she had come to Kiddies' Korner to buy something or other for her granddaughter and great-grandchild? The thought made her feel wonderful.

"Dear," she said, "good morning, dear. How's baby?"

The girl nodded absently. She had eyes only for a white bunting in the window. If she wanted pink or blue I'd know at least if my great-grandchild was a boy or girl, Mrs. Goffman thought. In her low Russian-sounding voice she cooed at the baby, tried to make her granddaughter look at her.

"Dear," she tried again, "what do you think is nice, eh dear?"

"That bunting," the girl said, still not looking at her grandmother, "but what a high price!"

"Twenty-five bucks! Highway robbery," Mrs Goffman said in a loud voice, thinking she'd better not ham it up too much. Her purse was lined with dough — a few fifties, four or five twenties, a dozen tens, fives, ones, even a two — Mrs. Goffman was never too neat about money. Every handbag was loaded this way, and what Montreal bank didn't have Doba Goffman as an account? Money to her was like a big soup: you cooked it in a vat but then came the problem of how to store it. You pour in one jar, then another, then another — except that with Sidney and Jimmy there was no end to what she had to put in jars. The faster she stored money away the faster they brought her more. No matter what she did to get rid of it — charities, trips to New York every week to see shows, an opera, flights to Israel, Hawaii, buying those bozos Sulka ties at fifty bucks a crack — no matter how fast she gave it, they stuffed her accounts, lined handbags, papered the walls, those successes of hers, those imbeciles!

Bernstein's clerk poked his head out the door.

"Highway robbery, is that what you call it, *babbe*?" he said in a hurt voice. "Come inside. I'll show you my cost."

Years ago Mrs. Goffman felt offended when people called her *babbe*, grandmother, but not now. She turned her head and gave the man a mirthless smile.

"Honey," he said to the girl, "let your *babbe* stay out here with the baby. You come in. I've got a real bargain for the kid."

The girl didn't seem to hear.

"Go 'head, dear," Mrs. Goffman said warmly. "I'll rock the baby."

The girl wheeled the carriage around and hurried toward the Market. Mrs. Goffman followed quickly.

4

At the corner of Rachel and St. Lawrence Mrs. Goffman stopped to let a horse-drawn waggon go by. What a wonderful stink an old nag gave off! Wheels creaking was a melody to her deafish ears. Across the way was Simon's old store, the "upstairs" they used to live in. Dimly, like an imagination, Mrs. Goffman made out the *S. Goffman and Sons* which *J. Olin and Brother* had been painted over. Her nose sniffed at the rubber and leather smell coming from the old store. Those French perfumes Sidney gives her should only smell so nice!

Crossing the street she hurried after her granddaughter, but, suddenly, without warning, tears gushed from Mrs. Goffman's eyes, biting, salty tears mixed in with the heady fish fragrance around the Rachel Street Market stalls. Stop it, old fool, she told herself, but the tears kept running.

She pretended she was buying, dropped her eyes, rubbed a cold slimy fish with her manicured fingernails, poked open a carp's small-toothed mouth, combed its stiff freezing fins with her wrinkled hand. Next to Simon's gold wedding band was the hideous ruby Sidney gave her for her birthday last year; above them both was Jimmy's gift, a diamond-studded watch.

"*Babbe, babbe*," a gentle voice said to her, "why are you crying?"

She didn't have to open her eyes to know the man was new on the job: everybody on Rachel Street knew why Mrs. Goffman cried.

"A cold," she said.

"In the eyes?" the voice said skeptically. "Then maybe you shouldn't handle my fish?"

"Listen," Mrs. Goffman said wildly, "give me two large carp and three nice whitefish!"

"There's an order!" the man clapped his hands together. "Only your generation, eh *babbe*? Big families need a full table!"

The girl with the baby wheeled up beside Mrs. Goffman, hefted a small pike, looked wistful. Mrs. Goffman moved over to give her granddaughter more room.

"Mister," she said to the fishman, "I've got lots of time. Look after the mother with the baby first."

The girl had turned around and was poking at the baby's blankets. The fishman grabbed at a floppy-tailed carp beating its fins on the damp wood stall.

"Today's girl," he laughed, "can wait longer than you, *babbe*. Your generation grinds, stuffs, cooks — just like my ma-may-she-rest-in-peace — two dozen people at *shabbes* table wasn't too much. But these kids?" He pointed at Mrs. Goffman's granddaughter. "She'll toss a pike in a frying-pan and one, two, it's *shabbes*."

A second carp, big as a shark, fell with a splat against the first; three dancing whitefish got buried in a wad of newspaper.

"Dear," Mrs. Goffman said sweetly, "he's ready to take your order."

Again she didn't look up. Mrs. Goffman wanted to holler — *Hey sleeping beauty, can't you even answer when your* babbe *talks to you?*

"*Babbe*," the fishman said, "this parcel's too heavy. You live right around here somewheres? St. Dominique maybe? I'll deliver you the fish myself."

"I'm a strong woman," Mrs. Goffman said, holding out her arms.

"I can see, *babbe*. I only wish I should be in your shape at your age," the man said enthusiastically. "Have a good sabbath. Enjoy the kiddies. You deserve the best. I can tell!"

"Goodbye, dear," Mrs. Goffman said to her granddaughter.

"Goodbye, goodbye," the fishman answered, clapping his hands together. "Next."

5

The moment the fish touched her arms they seemed to revive and start swimming — twenty, thirty pounds writhing in her helpless arms! Fish? Who needed fish? When did she cook fish last? That last batch stunk up Sidney's limousine so badly he had to sell it for next to nothing!

The newspaper parcel was leaking all over her coat. Let it bust and she'd be chased by every cat in Montreal! Was she out of her mind? Seventy-five years in this world and still not able to resist the most foolish impulse!

Her arms hurt, her face turned red, her heart beat crazily. Leave it to an old Radical to act like a nut! Two blocks away is that healthy horse of a chauffeur sitting on his fanny and sunning himself. Two blocks? She'd never make it. But where could you dump this useless stuff? In the empty baby carriages scattered around St. Lawrence Boulevard? She thought of letting it fall casually on the sidewalk, like a lost handkerchief. Maybe she could slip it into the empty moving-van she saw across the street. Who but a woman loaded with money could afford such grandstand plays?

Fish water soaked her gloves, dribbled down her coat front: a bit of fin slipped through the dissolving newspaper, a sappy fish-eye made peek-a-boo. In a shop window Mrs. Goffman caught sight of herself — a black streak, a bundle, eyebrows. Get sloppy sentimental and this is the result!

Triminiuk's. She suddenly came up with a brainwave: Captain Triminiuk would save her! Giggling, panting, giddy, red-faced, she staggered across the street and into Triminiuk's Delicatessen.

The fish hit the counter like an explosion; the whitefish, wild as Cossacks, danced out of their covering.

"Come save an old sap, Gershon," Mrs. Goffman called to the back of the store. "I overstocked myself with fish."

She wiped her coat with orange wrappers, fell back, laughing helplessly, into one of Gershon's old chairs. Only Captain Triminiuk's Delicatessen still had these small round marble-top tables with wire legs and matching chairs with backs like wire carpet-beaters. The air inside was like a home-made mist — garlic pickles, pastrami, salami, sauerkraut, fresh rye bread, Triminiuk himself, who smelled like a real smokehouse.

Marching — he never walked — one-eyed Triminiuk came toward her, disapproving, as usual, everything about her. He stood at attention, his black cuff-guards up to his armpits, tieless collar buttoned at the neck, vest unbuttoned, also part of his pants. One of his eyes was almost closed, the other bright as turquoise, his moustache bristly, yellowed with tobacco.

Forty years ago, when she and Simon first met the old bluffer, he was just out of the Russian army, a cook who lost an eye from splattering fat. Since then Triminiuk, in recognition of himself, every ten years or so gave himself a promotion. Now he was a captain. Now the missing eye was a result of a sabre in the Russo-Japanese War.

"Fish?" he sniffed.

"Be a pal. Take it off my hands, Gershon," she said flirtatiously.

"I need charity, Doba?"

"Don't play poor mouth with me, you bandit," she laughed. "You want to be independent, give me a tea with lemon."

He didn't budge. Long ago she had given up trying to explain things to a stubborn old bluffer like Triminiuk. All he saw was that Doba Goffman, the hot-headed young Radical, became Mrs. S. Goffman, prominent member of an Orthodox synagogue, patroness of the foolishness her sons' success brought her. Try to convince Gershon that she'd joined the Orthodoxes in protest against her sons' becoming Anglican-like Reform Jews? If those characters had stayed on St. Lawrence Boulevard, she would never have set foot in a synagogue. But when they climbed Westmount, bought that enormous mansion from the Ambassador, bragged about looking out on Nun's Island, took her to Temple where the Rabbi pursed his lips in such a way that everybody should know he learned Hebrew not at home but in a University, then she, in protest, became again a Jew! Gershon should have seen the lousy Jewish-style cooking she, a Radical who had nothing to do with kitchens, forced her big-shot sons to eat — he should only know she got her Jewish recipes from *Better Homes and Gardens*!

Gershon accepted no explanations. He considered her a traitor. Worse. Maybe even a Zionist!

"My tea, Captain," Mrs. Goffman said.

Triminiuk looked toward the door.

A fat woman, hair messy, hands dug deep in the ripped pockets of an old, flowered housecoat, drove several kids into the store in front of her, stood for a second sighing, muttering, scratching herself under the pockets. Corns stuck out of her pink-and-aqua wedgies.

"Captain," she said in a high nasal whine, "my kids came to eat me up alive again. Let a mouse try to find a crumb by me, let. Herbie's wetters, Gertie's soilers, four five already, and Gertie's carrying again, you've heard about such misfortunes? They act like Westmount millionaires. You can't afford kids, don't have, I keep telling."

Triminiuk, Mrs. Goffman saw, was trying to shut the woman up.

"Lady," he said in his military voice, "what can I get for you?"

One of the children, about seven, a girl with black hair, black eyes, front teeth out, stared at Mrs. Goffman.

"Ma," Mrs. Goffman's deafish ears heard her whisper, "why's the old lady all in black?"

"Gimme a couple rye loaves to stop up the mouths quickly," the woman said shrilly, "a salami, a few slices lox...."

"Ma," the little girl stole behind her mother's housecoat and peeked at Mrs. Goffman, "is it a witch?"

"Tammy, stop botherin'," the woman said absently, fingering the fish on the counter. "Captain, how can you make today's kid stop carrying? It's living here with the French that makes 'em like this, hah?"

"Lady," Triminiuk snapped, "is this everything?"

"Ma," the little girl tugged at her mother's sleeve, "I'm afraid of her...."

"Let me be," the woman whined, shoving the child at Mrs. Goffman. Hard as Mrs. Goffman's old face tried, it couldn't come up with a look to reassure the child.

"You're very sweet, dear," she said softly.

The child seemed to shudder.

"What did you say?" the woman mumbled.

"She's a very sweet little girl," Mrs. Goffman said.

"Listen, you want her? She's yours, the pest. You can have these others in the bargain," the woman said without a smile.

"$2.05," Triminiuk all but shouted.

"What's he getting sore for? Don't I pay in time? Here," she threw down a dollar bill, "payday I'll give the rest."

"Gramma," the smallest kid in the store said quietly, "can each of us have a sucker?"

"I got no money for suckers," the woman said nastily, missing with a slap she'd aimed at the kid. Tammy, the little girl, frightened, jumped toward Mrs. Goffman, grew more frightened, jumped back, catching her mother's corns with her shoe.

"For godsake, pests!" the woman shouted, slapping Tammy across the cheek. "Get out of this store!"

"Don't cry, dear," Mrs. Goffman tried to make Tammy hear.

"I'm sorry these crazy kids bothered you, lady," the woman said as she shooed them out the door. "With these pests gone you can have peace."

6

Triminiuk went to get her her tea.

That kid Tammy was right, Mrs. Goffman thought as she caught sight of herself in Triminiuk's small calendar mirror. A witch. Black. What sentimental soft-headedness made her dress this way? What right did she have to dump her mourning on St. Lawrence Boulevard? In her old age she was becoming a professional widow, a dopey eccentric? Tomorrow she'd go down to one of those fancy French shops on Sherbrooke and get gussied up in pink, violet, maybe even yellow.

Sentimentality, respectability, a tough old Radical like Mrs. Goffman had been had, by America. How else did a revolutionary become a quiet-spoken tea-sipper dumb with good taste? By God, an old-fashioned St. Dominique Street ma would have chased her kids out of the house with a broom, made their lives so miserable they would *have* to marry, in self-defence. And when Simon died, what stopped her from marrying again? Loyalty. Love. Now, when the time for praying was past and with the lock on the synagogue door, now she realized that love too was smaller than life. A stepfather would have been another way of getting her boys into life on their own. Jimmy had been a bachelor till forty-five, just a year before his death. Poor Sidney, still unmarried, fifty-three, a pill-swallower, complained his way from hotel to hotel across three continents.

Waste, Mrs. Goffman thought with a sinking feeling, waste is the law of America — too much money, too much talent, even too much fish. Getting stuck with something useless like money and fish was judgement against her and her sons.

Triminiuk came shuffling toward her, balancing a cup of tea in one hand, a glass in the other. Should she say something? I've done too much damage with silence, Mrs. Goffman thought.

"Listen here, Capatanchik," she said nastily, "what's the big idea bringing me tea in a cup and yourself in a glass?"

"Westmount ladies drink from china cups," the old bluffer said without batting an eye.

"Turn right around, you pirate, and get me a glass," Mrs. Goffman said, hitting her palm against the marble top. "To hell with Westmount!"

"I got only one glass," Triminiuk came back.

"Then it's for me," Mrs. Goffman said in triumph. "Hand it over."

To show he was the winner, Triminiuk poured his tea into a saucer and sipped noisily, like a roughneck.

"How's the rich son?" he asked. She couldn't tell for sure if he was being nasty.

"Sidney's fine," she lied. One thing Sidney never was was fine, especially since without Jimmy he was a total loss in the world. He hadn't been with a woman in over a year. Women weren't Sidney's line — his hair was red and thin, his face chubby and round, his eyes watery and always blinking, his lower lip ready to blubber.

But Jimmy!

Elegant, taller than his tall mother, with her face, her colouring, dressed like a British diplomat, smooth with continental manners, chased by every woman in Montreal, and for what, what for? "Fun," he called it, and what came of his fun? Ashes, dust. The dopiest kid on St. Dominique Street had more claim on life than her handsome Jimmy. He drove a Bentley, wore a white leather raincoat, a British vest with brass buttons, a Parisian necktie — what he wore Montreal copied, the gals he took out were immediately stamped with approval. "Lover boy" the high school yearbook nicknamed him. "Lover man" was what they called him at McGill, and "Don Giovanni". Women, women, hundreds upon hundreds of women, affairs without number, and what came of it all? "Listen to me, bozos," she had said years ago, when they'd first moved to the Ambassador's mansion, "let's get down to life now, eh? At sixty I'm *entitled* to grandchildren. Who'll mourn me when I'm dead, our bankers?"

Mrs. Goffman's eyes filled, blood rushed to her face, in anger and despair she beat her ringed hand against the marble table. Jimmy, that poor fool Jimmy, marrying at forty-five, and how, with a nineteen-year-old who'd been living with another man since sixteen!

Triminiuk put his hand on her shoulder.

"What are you aggravating yourself for?" His blind eye looked like the dead fish's.

"Gershon, the worst thing is for people to die out of their own generation."

"If people died neatly," Triminiuk said, raising his face from the tilted saucer, "we'd both be long buried by now."

A little French girl barged into the store, wiggling her hips, pushing out her breasts. Her hair was tight with nasty bobby-pin curls that gave Mrs. Goffman the pip, her skin was broken out, badly powdered and rouged. She chewed gum with an open mouth. Her arms, though, were lovely and slim, and her legs were shapely. Even you, you tramp, Mrs. Goffman thought as she watched Triminiuk give the girl a package of Sweet Caporal, even a gum-chewing slut like you I would have taken for a daughter-in-law at the end, when I saw what the score was.

"Bye, Cap," the girl said with a wink. Triminiuk dismissed her with a wave.

"What were we saying, Doba?"

"I was being depressed," she reminded him with a smile, "and you were trying to snap me out of it."

"Why should you be depressed?" Triminiuk said after a long slurp. "The boy died a big success. It should happen to all my grandchildren, such a success."

All his grandchildren — Gershon, big-shot atheist, lived by "increase and multiply" the Bible's way. He *was* a success. Eight or nine kids, twenty-five or thirty grandchildren. Jimmy and Sidney took "increase and multiply" to mean mergers, expansion, deals, transactions. Hundreds of thousands Jimmy left his mother, and bonds, and buildings, and tracts of land — ashes, dust, because neither his loins nor Sidney's produced a child.

She felt the blood rush to her face again. Imbecility, America's imbecility, Jimmy galloping after success while life runs off right under his feet. Mocking, teasing. His Shirley was a born mother, gorgeous, built to bear children. Not Jimmy's though. On Jimmy's money Shirley, the most beautiful widow in Montreal, married that childhood sweetheart of hers. For him Shirley became a mother.

"Your tea's cold, I betcha," she heard Triminiuk's voice say gruffly.

"I'll be your guest," said Mrs. Goffman. Triminiuk gave her a searching look, nodded briskly, shuffled with a military swagger to the back of the store.

He understood everything. Sitting with Gershon was comfortable, even in silence. Their conversations were one-quarter open, three-quarters between the lines, as it used to be with Simon. But the other kind of silence, the silence that buzzed in her deafish ears in the Ambassador's mansion, that kind Mrs. Goffman couldn't stand. That silence frightened her more than the loudest noise. That silence was the noise of death.

"Gershon!" she called out in spite of herself.

"Look how a madamchikeh can't wait for a glass of tea," the old man scolded, but she noticed he was coming back in a big hurry.

"Gershon," she said as he sat down, "if we're lucky in life we *see*, if only for a split second. Life *or* death, there's no other issue, Gershon. Jimmy learned it too late. Not till the end could he stop for life, but he had to stop for death."

"Doba," Triminiuk said bluntly, "you're beginning to sound religious."

"What religious, when religious?" she cried out. "In those clear moments blindness drops from us, we see and know everything!"

Twice I knew, she thought: once when Shirley's lover turned up at Jimmy's funeral in Jimmy's clothes. The other time too was at a funeral.

"So cut away my blindness," Triminiuk said gently, poking at his inert gluey eye.

"*Touché*," she said, hiding her face behind the tea glass. Triminiuk didn't press his advantage.

She glanced quickly at him and imagined him naked. She flushed. His face was weather-beaten, sketched over with tiny red-and-blue blood vessels, but his body would be blue-and-white, his back rounded, his rib cage prominent as a starving man's. Mrs. Goffman grew conscious of her own body — so long, so gaunt, so like a stranger's now the skin was dry and criss-crossed, now her breasts were flat with colour faded out of the nipples. Her nails didn't grow much, or her hair. Whatever was shrivelled in a man like Gershon was spent, whatever shrivelled on her was wasted.

Wisdom was overrated. It had little to do with life. She was wise, but powerless. When she had power she must have been stupid. Pride, shyness, loyalty to Simon's memory seemed so important years ago. Now Mrs. Goffman knew she should have married even a gargoyle of a man, and had more children. But by the time she caught on to what Jimmy's and Sydney's fate was, it was too late for her to do anything for them, or herself. "Fun," Jimmy said, relying on his mother's Radical tolerance, sneaking beauty after beauty into the house and his bed — for what, what for? All those gorgeous Rachels, but never a fruitful Leah.

"Gershon," Mrs. Goffman suddenly said, "blaming is for innocents. I don't blame Shirley. I don't even blame Doba Goffman."

Shirley dressed like a Hollywood star for the funeral — a large black picture-hat, dark glasses, elbow-length black gloves, a clinging sheath dress so open down the front the grave-diggers scattered dirt in all directions trying to stay in position to stare at her. Her lover wore Jimmy's black Italian suit. They whispered together. Shirley didn't pretend to cry. She didn't even carry a handkerchief.

Sidney, for once in his tired life, got hot, wanted to throw himself at the two of them. Mrs. Goffman wouldn't let him. What was Shirley's lower-animal foolishness compared to the horrible truth — Jimmy in the ground without a child to mourn for him! Who was left, Mrs. Goffman, an old woman with teeth falling out of her head?

"I get such a cold feeling," she whispered to Triminiuk. "We threw life aside like a rag. When we die it's an end — papa's line, Simon's line — a crime, Gershon, a crime against the whole human race."

Triminiuk nodded stiffly, like an officer commending a subordinate.

It *was* a crime against the whole human race. Life wasn't something to be kicked aside just because you happened to have it. In crowds, on the street, Mrs. Goffman felt the difference bitterly — not she alone, not Sidney alone, a whole strain in the human race was dying in them! Simon's stubborn look was finished! Her pa's bass voice. Jimmy's way of greeting you — a *hello*, his arm thrown in front of his eyes as if you were the sun and so brilliant he couldn't absorb you. Jimmy made you feel that you were morning. Even Sidney had qualities the race shouldn't lose. Character, size, shape, all human magnificence, all possibility dying, dying, dying.

Mrs. Goffman thought she would pass out.

"Doba, Doba," Triminiuk's voice sounded urgent in her ear, "stop aggravating, I said. Look on St. Lawrence. The kids are coming home from school."

He steered her into the doorway, made her look out on the boulevard. Dabs and specks of red, green, blue danced in the distance, faint squeals and shrieks washed terror of silence away from her ears. Gershon knew his onions. Bending down — Triminiuk was the same size as Simon, a peanut — she kissed him on his wrinkled forehead. He shook her off, stood rigid at attention, nodded her away.

"Thanks for taking the fish off my hands," she said.

"Don't do it again," he answered gruffly.

7

Mrs. Goffman concluded she would have to change her life, and immediately. She ordered her chauffeur to drive her to Fifi's, Shmifi's — a fancy French place for clothes horses. It would be a double victory — she'd get spiffed up and stop scaring kids, she'd unload most of the money choking her handbag.

Not all the perfumes of Paris could overcome the fish smell as Mrs. Goffman entered the shop. Only her liveried chauffeur and that funeral car parked in front saved her from being tossed out on her ear. She gave the salesgirls, who sniffed usually just from snobbery, something real to sniff about!

"That coat!" she said, in a voice as military as Triminiuk's.

A salesgirl hid her nose in a useless frilly hankie and came at Mrs. Goffman sideways. The coat was a Marlene Dietrich type — magenta. Mrs. Goffman made a trade. The girl almost passed out.

"A Gloria Swanson hat — burn the coat, dollie, don't cling to the rag," Mrs. Goffman dismissed the salesgirl who was greenish and crampy-looking from the fish smell. "Get me a flapper number. And a handbag too." With one motion she dumped all her money on the counter. The salesgirl's eyes, sick as they had been, bugged with the proper respect money always got.

"I look like a big popsicle, eh Josef?" Mrs. Goffman said to her chauffeur. If kids didn't get scared to death by this number, they were still in danger of laughing themselves to death looking at her.

"Take, take," Mrs. Goffman waved the girl onward to the pile of bills on the counter. "Put what's left in my new bag, dollie."

Without bitterness Mrs. Goffman reflected how easy it was in America to buy everything you don't want.

She left the store, salespeople bowing to her right and to her left as if she were Queen Mary, gave them a queenly wave while her nose triumphantly recorded that in the air, wistful, fleeting, elusive as Chanel Number Five, was Rachel Street Fish.

8

Josef put down her armrest, adjusted a small reading-light over her newspaper — Sidney's style. Headlines shimmered in front of her eyes, and the usual faces — Khrushchev the hearty liar, Dulles' sour face set permanently in a "no", Eisenhower with that puzzled look which meant if his press secretary didn't say something fast he was a goner. What was it Jimmy said? Everybody in Eisenhower's cabinet was a millionaire except for Martin Durkin and God Almighty. The headlines recorded imbecile explosions, tests in Siberia, Nevada. Sincere falseness in Ottawa, Washington, false sincerity in Moscow. Idiots! Suckers! At least Jimmy at the end *knew*; these crumbs would never know!

"Josef, go home the long way," she said gently. Those French put their cemeteries right in the middle of the city — grey crosses stamped on the sky, cold stone saints, wreaths of dark artificial flowers. Silence was loudest near cemeteries.

What the heck was she doing going back up there anyways? Rachel Street was like a wonderful party she couldn't stand to see end. Six more days of nothing was coming.

"Josef, drive your slowest," she requested.

Every stage in her kids' success mocked her on these trips home. Goffman buildings, Goffman businesses. The banks their money was in. The houses they'd lived in during their climb to the top of Westmount and the Ambassador's mansion. I dragged my feet, Mrs. Goffman remembered with sadness, but I didn't interfere. A young Radical became an old dishrag! Good taste left a bad taste in her mouth.

In her small vanity mirror she made a John Foster Dulles face and laughed herself back into a better humour.

9

The limousine passed the Mount Royal Hotel. Cabs lined up, people were running, some school kids tumbled out of a car and skipped giggling toward St. Catherine Street. Mrs. Goffman wanted to try her new outfit on a kid and see what the reaction would be. She still felt bad about frightening that young girl Tammy.

Brighten up, sister, she told herself, but the Mount Royal had done its damage already. Jimmy first saw Shirley at a Mount Royal New Year's Eve Frolic — he loved to tell about it, to begin with.

The Mount Royal was Jimmy's home ground, a perfect setting for his style. He had Sally Rossen with him that night — a Toronto deb-type, gorgeous, crazy for Jimmy, hot and burning. They danced every dance, drank champagne, moved arm-in-arm through the ballroom, visiting parties in different rooms, Jimmy in terrific shape, gay, gallant, witty, full of life. Then he saw Shirley. Sally was out.

How his eyes lighted up when he talked about Shirley — her hair he said was like a quiet waterfall in total darkness; her black eyes with that heavy fringe of eyelashes skimmed over Jimmy; she was in white, bare-shouldered, proud of her beautiful young full breasts, her sexy body, her slow, slow walk. Elegant Jimmy lost his manners. Clumsy as an ox he bumped his way across the floor, leaving Sally standing all alone. Up went Jimmy's arm in that gesture all Montreal knew — Shirley's beauty was blinding, he couldn't look.

Shirley cut him dead.

Sucker! He should have quit! Shirley's lover said something nasty — Jimmy heard — about "old enough to be your father." Shirley giggled, leaned on her boy Maxie, and left Jimmy standing just as he had left Sally! Don Giovanni, huh? Mrs. Goffman thought in her agitation. Big-shot-lover? He couldn't quit.

"My dance, beautiful," he said, almost chasing after her through the crowd. He gave the old flourish, poured on the charm.

"My card is filled," Shirley said coldly; they had him.

Like a crack had appeared in a great building. He didn't fall apart then and there, where Westmount society surrounded him, where he was familiar, where his ways could get a gentle response. Later it started, at home, when she caught him in front of the mirror.

"Since when did you pull out grey hair, Jimmy?" she had asked. Jimmy didn't answer.

"Grey hair makes you look distinguished."

"Distinguished and old," Jimmy said with a wink.

Lines on his face from laughing, character lines which made Jimmy the handsome guy he was, he couldn't stand them now. He wanted to rub everything out, be as young-looking as that pimply-faced Maxie who had the only woman who had ever denied Jimmy anything at all. Didn't his mother see Jimmy's reaction? He started to take out younger and younger girls — one was seventeen, not even out of high school! A photographer told him his left side was more handsome than his right, so the dope sat with his right side hidden, as if it had been burned! He sent Shirley flowers, pins, necklaces, phoned her, wired her — what a set-up for those two kids! Jimmy would spend a fortune on Shirley, but Maxie would spend the night!

Mrs. Goffman smiled to herself: in a way — if Jimmy's end wasn't so horrible — there was justice in it. The most brilliant lawyer and financier in Montreal getting trimmed down to his BVDs by a couple of snot-nosed kids! Shirley had been sleeping with Maxie for four or five years, but not till her eighth date with Jimmy did she let him so much as peck her on the cheek. Don Giovanni?

Late one night Mrs. Goffman had overheard a conversation that made her want to ring bells and blow whistles.

"Jimmy, you, getting married?" Sidney had said. He couldn't have been more shocked if Jimmy had grown sidecurls and turned Hassidic.

"I can't get it from her any way else," Don Giovanni admitted.

Didn't she know he was going to get trimmed? But what did she care about money by that time? Life — a child — that was at stake, not Jimmy's lousy fortune. Marry even a prostitute for all Mrs. Goffman cared by then, but get married. Why, when Marie, the upstairs maid, got pregnant, didn't Mrs. Goffman hope one of her boys had done it? To hell with Westmount's ways! She knew. She had seen the truth by then. So who has to be the knocker-up, this chauffeur Josef!

"Drive more slowly," she said savagely, thinking how many snot-nosed kids this overgrown squash of a driver must have already brought into the world.

Josef looked back at her, startled.

"Please, I mean," she added.

A child — she was a lunatic on the subject. After the wedding she nagged, coaxed, threatened, whined. "Kids, go home early." "Shirley, maybe you're late this month, eh, dollie?" Vulgar and rude and coarse — her father's line, Simon's, that's what the stakes were! Sidney was past praying for, she herself couldn't have kids. Everything was up to Jimmy. And he wanted a child too — that was the heartbreaking thing! Jimmy knew, saw, understood everything.

Mrs. Goffman felt herself suffocating in the closed car. Her ears pulsed, her heart beat fast, she felt cold all over. Weakly, falteringly, she rolled down the window.

If only a child *had* come out of that marriage. Suffering was a man's lot in life. Everybody suffered, but not senselessly, like Jimmy. His suffering did nothing, made nothing, was worse than death. Noises made him jump. Coffee made him nervous. He began gobbling Sidney's pills. How could a hot-looking girl turn out so cold? He was repulsive, old, a mark, a fool — his nerves went.

Every bourgeois cliché that she as a Radical had scoffed at came thudding home — *you only live once*, what was more ghastly than that realization? *You're not getting any younger*, how that mocked Jimmy! What good was Mrs. Goffman to her suffering son? Could she reverse her campaign to make him want a child? Could she destroy what he felt for Shirley just by telling him exactly what he knew anyway — that he was a cinch, a target, a bankroll, but feeling his age, and growing helpless?

Mrs. Goffman began to cough, gasp, and with a great effort pushed her face close to the open window.

"Madam, what is it?" Josef said, slowing down.

"I'm all right," she lied, "don't stop."

It was all as if life and time couldn't hold back their revenge. Shirley sneaked ties to Maxie, money, let him put things on Jimmy's charge accounts. Flagrant, open, Jimmy was Montreal's parlour-car joke. And Mrs. Doba Goffman watched and waited, hoping hoping hoping.

Shirley never did bear Jimmy a child.

10

The limousine made a sudden swoop, a turn, a halt, then began its progress up the hill. Mrs. Goffman craned her head, trying to get a last look at what wasn't Westmount. Her nose behaved like a pair of opera glasses after the opera, folding itself up, awaiting the next liberation. Streets were empty, windows heavily draped so you couldn't see a sign of movement. Closer to the Ambassador's house there were no sidewalks, black limousines sped out of hidden driveways. Like the one, Mrs. Goffman thought, sickening.

What a terrible death! Her confident Jimmy, worrying about flat tires all the time, stopping the car a dozen times to make Josef check, or getting out himself. Nothing was ever wrong, only Jimmy's shot nerves — he was half-destroyed when he stepped into the fog on Summit Circle. A limousine crushed him against his rear bumper and finished the job! Upstairs in the Ambassador's mansion Mrs. Goffman heard the smash and Jimmy's screams — horrible, horrible!

Mrs. Goffman writhed, pinned her new hat against her ears, tears streaming from her eyes. Like a tiny boy Jimmy shrieked for her, screaming, screaming, and she ran into the cold dark mist, barefoot, in her nightgown, seeing nothing, hearing nothing but silence. That silence. Death's.

She'd screamed too — slapped at Josef, called him pig, ingrate, block, crook, shirker — why didn't he get out of the car instead of Jimmy? But now, when everything was past blaming, Mrs. Goffman conceded the truth: Josef had more claim to life than Jimmy, much as she loved her son, great as his success had been.

She pulled wet terrified eyes away from the limousine floor and looked out at the houses on Summit Circle.

Right here! On this spot! She closed her eyes again and waited.

11

You fake, she chided herself. A real Radical would never cry. What a way to louse up this new magenta outfit — streaming eyes, a shiny shnozzola! You'd think she'd spent her afternoon at a Yiddish tear-jerker.

As Josef turned into the driveway Mrs. Goffman touched her

sulking nose with a powder puff, dried her eyes, made her old face smile. When there was hope it was okay to despair, but now hope was gone, what was the point of it? She winked at herself.

Sidney's worried face peeked out from her heavy drapes, his wristwatch close to his bad eyes. Why depress Sidney? She'd jolly him up a little, tell him how ridiculous she looked carrying the fish, how she stunk up that ritzy dress shop good.

She shielded her eyes, sighed, smiled more broadly, seeing past Josef's shoulder Nuns' Island. It was for sale. A million bucks they wanted.

By rights, Mrs. Goffman thought as she looked toward her door, they shouldn't sell it. Nuns should stay on an island.

Mordecai Richler

MORTIMER GRIFFIN, SHALINSKY
AND HOW THEY SETTLED
THE JEWISH QUESTION

I was, at the time, beginning my first scholastic year as a lecturer in English literature at Wellington College in Montreal. You've probably never heard of Wellington. It's a modest institution with a small student body. There's the Day College, composed, for the most part, of students who couldn't get into McGill, and the Evening College, made up of adults, most of them working at full-time jobs and trying to get a college education after hours. I was responsible for two Evening College courses, English 112 (Shakespeare) and English 129 (The Modern Novel). Shalinsky registered for both of them.

Until my fourth lecture I was only aware of Shalinsky as a ponderous presence in the third row. My fourth lecture dealt with Franz Kafka, and naturally I made several allusions to the distinctively Jewish roots of his work. Afterwards, as I was gathering my notes together, Shalinsky approached me for the first time.

"I want to tell you, Professor Griffin, how much intellectual nourishment I got out of your lecture tonight."

"I'm glad you enjoyed it."

I'm afraid I was in a hurry to get away that night. I was going to pick up Joyce at the Rosens'. But Shalinsky still stood before my desk.

His wisps of grey curly hair uncut and uncombed, Shalinsky was a small, round-shouldered man with horn-rimmed spectacles, baleful black eyes, and a hanging lower lip. His shiny, pin-striped grey suit was salted with dandruff round the shoulders. A hand-rolled cigarette drooped from his mouth, his eyes half-shut against the smoke and the ashes spilling unregarded to his vest.

"Why did you change your name?" he asked.

"I beg your pardon. Did you ask me why I changed my name?"

Shalinsky nodded.

"But I haven't. My name is Griffin. It always has been."

"You're a Jew."

"You're mistaken."

Shalinsky smiled faintly.

"Really," I began, "what made you think——"

"All right. I'm mistaken. I made a mistake. No harm done."

"Look here, if I were a Jew I wouldn't try to conceal it for a moment."

Still smiling, blinking his eyes, Shalinsky said: "There's no need to lose your temper, Professor *Griffin*. I made a mistake, that's all. If that's the way you want it."

"And I'm not a professor, either. *Mr*. Griffin will do."

"A man of your talents will be famous one day. Like ... like I.M. Sinclair. A scholar renowned wherever the intelligentsia meet. Thanks once more for tonight's intellectual feast. Good night, Mr. Griffin."

In retrospect, on the bus ride out to Hy and Eva Rosen's house, I found the incident so outlandishly amusing that I laughed aloud twice.

Joyce had eaten with the Rosens, and Eva, remembering how much I liked chopped liver, had saved me an enormous helping. I told them about Shalinsky, concluding with " ... and where he ever got the idea that I was Jewish I'll never know." I had anticipated plenty of laughter. A witty remark from Hy, perhaps. Instead, there was silence. Nervously, I added: "Look, I don't mean that I'd be ashamed ... or that I was insulted that someone would think I was — Christ, you know what I mean, Hy."

"Yes," Hy said sharply. "Of course."

We left for home earlier than usual.

"Boy," Joyce said, "you certainly have a gift. I mean once you *have* put your foot in it you certainly know how to make matters worse."

"I thought they'd laugh. God, I've known Hy for years. He's one of my best friends. He——"

"*Was*," Joyce said.

"Look here," I said, "you don't seriously think that Hy thinks I'm an anti-Semite?"

Joyce raised one eyebrow slightly — an annoying college-girl habit that has lingered.

"Don't be ridiculous," I said. "Tomorrow, the day after, the whole thing will be forgotten, or Hy will make a joke of it."

"*They* have an excellent sense of humour," Joyce said, "haven't they? There's Jack Benny and Phil Silvers and——"

"Oh, for Christ's sake!"

Two days later a copy of a magazine called *Jewish Thought* came in the mail. Attached was a printed note. WITH THE COMPLIMENTS OF THE EDITOR, and underneath, penned with a lavish hand, *Respect-fully, J. Shalinsky*. It took me a moment or two to connect Shalinsky, the editor, with Shalinsky, my student. I began to flip through the pages of the little magazine.

The editorial, by J. Shalinsky, dealt at length with the dilemma of Jewish artists in a philistine community. The lead article, by Lionel Gould, B.COMM (McGill), was titled "On Being a Jew in Montreal West". Another article by I.M. Sinclair, M.D., was titled "The Anti-Semite as an Intellectual: A Study of the Novels of Graham Greene". There were numerous book reviews, two senti-mental poems translated from the Yiddish, a rather maudlin Israeli short story, and, surprisingly, "Stefan Zweig and J. Shalinsky: A Previously Unpublished Correspondence".

That night, as soon as my Eng. 112 lecture was finished, Shalin-sky loomed smiling over my desk. "You got the magazine?" he asked.

"I haven't had time to read it yet."

"If you don't like it, all you have to do is tell me why. No evasions, please. Don't beat around the bush." Shalinsky broke off and smiled. "I have something for you," he said.

I watched while he unwrapped a large, awkward parcel. The string he rolled into a ball and dropped into his pocket. The brown wrapping paper, already worn and wrinkled, he folded into eight and put into another pocket. Revealed was an extremely expensive edition of colour plates by Marc Chagall.

"It occurred to me," he said, "that a man so interested in Kafka might also find beauty in the art of Marc Chagall."

"I don't understand."

"Would you be willing," Shalinsky said, "to write me a review, a little appreciation, of this book for the next issue of *Jewish Thought?*"

I hesitated.

"We pay our contributors, of course. Not much, but ——"

"That's not the point."

"And the book, it goes without saying, would be yours."

"All right, Mr. Shalinsky. I'll do it."

"There's something else. You have no lectures next Wednesday night. You are free, so to speak. Am I right?"

"Yes, but ——"

"Next Wednesday night, Mr. Griffin, the Jewish Thought Liter-ary Society will be meeting at my house. It is a custom, at these meetings, that we are addressed by a distinguished guest. I was hoping——"

"What would you like me to talk about?" I asked wearily.

"Kafka," he said. "Kafka and Cabbalism. Refreshments will be served."

The address Shalinsky had given me was on St. Urbain Street. His house smelled of home-baked bread and spices. The living-room, almost a hall once the double doors had been opened, was filled with folding chairs, all of them vindictively directed at the speaker's table. The walls were laden with enormous photographs of literary giants protected by glass and encased in varnished wooden frames. Tolstoy, a bearded scarecrow on horseback, glared at the refreshments table. Dostoyevsky and Turgenev, their quarrels forgotten, stood side by side. Opposite, Marcel Proust smiled enigmatically.

At dinner I was introduced to Shalinsky's wife and daughter. Mrs. Shalinsky was a round rosy-cheeked figure with a double chin. The daughter — plump, plum-cheeked Gitel Shalinsky — wore a peasant blouse laced tightly over a tray of milky bosom, and a billowy green skirt. Her thick black hair she wore in an up-sweep; glittering glass ear-rings dripped from her cup-shaped ears. A wooden clasp, GRETA, rode one breast, and a rose the other. Throughout dinner Gitel never said a word.

I handed Shalinsky my twelve-hundred-word article on Chagall, titled — rather brightly, I thought — "The Myopic Mystic". My editor pondered the piece in silence, waving his hand impatiently whenever his wife interrupted him, a frequent occurrence, with remarks like, "Chew your meat, Jake," and, in an aside to me, "If I gave him absorbent cotton to eat, you think he'd know the difference?" and again, baring her teeth in a parody of mastication, "Chew, Jake. *Digest*."

Shalinsky read my article unsmilingly and folded it neatly in four.

"Is there anything the matter?" I asked.

"As an intellectual exercise your article is A-1, but——"

"You don't have to print it if you don't want to."

"Did I say I wouldn't print it? No. But, if you'll let me finish, I had hoped it would be a little more from the soul. Take the title, for instance. 'The Myopic Mystic'," he said with distaste. "Clever. Clever, Mr. Griffin. But no heart. Still, this is a fine article. I wouldn't change a word. Not for the world."

The first of Shalinsky's guests arrived and he went into the living-room with him. Mrs. Shalinsky excused herself, too, and so I was left alone with Gitel. "Your father," I said, "is quite an extraordinary man. I mean at his age to take university courses and edit a magazine ——"

"*The Ladies' Home Journal*," Gitel said. "*There's* a magazine for you. But *Jewish Thought*. An eight-hundred-and-forty-two circulation, counting give-aways — that's no magazine."

"Your father tells me he's printed work by S.M. Geiger. He's a very promising poet, I think."

"Some poet. He comes up to here by me. Alan Ladd — there's another twerp. How long are you going to speak tonight?"

"I'm not sure."

"Make it short, Morty. The blabbers never get invited back."

Three-quarters of an hour after my lecture was supposed to have started, only twelve people, all middle-aged men, had turned up, though many more had been prepared for. "It's the rain," Shalinsky said. A half-hour later six more people had drifted into the living-room: eight, if you counted the woman with the baby in her arms. Her name was Mrs. Korber. She lived upstairs and, in passing, I overheard her say to Mrs. Shalinsky, "Tell Mr. Shalinsky it's no trouble. Harry and the boy will be here the minute *Dragnet* is finished."

At that moment my jacket was given a fierce tug from behind. Whirling around, I was confronted by a small, wizened man with rimless glasses. "I am I.M. Sinclair," he said.

Retreating, I said: "You're a doctor, I believe."

"Like Chekhov."

"Oh. Oh, I see."

"I'm the only poet in Canada. Go ahead, laugh." Then, as though he were composing on the spot, I.M. Sinclair said: "I am an old man ... an old man in a dry month ... waiting for rain."

"You ought to write that down," I said.

"I have burned better lines. We have a lot to talk about, Griffin. The moment in the draughty synagogue at smokefall...."

I broke away just in time to see Harry and the boy arrive. Shalinsky quickly called the meeting to order. There were three of us at the speaker's table — Shalinsky, myself, and a thin man with a fat ledger open before him. Shalinsky gave me a fulsome introduction, and Harry's boy — a fourteen-year-old with a running nose — poked two grimy fingers into his mouth and whistled. The others applauded politely. Then, as Mrs. Korber fed her baby with a bottle, I began.

"Louder," barked a voice from the back row.

So I spoke louder, elaborating on Kafka's difficulties with his father.

"What does he say?" somebody shouted. I waited while the man next to him translated what I had said into Yiddish. "Nonsense," his neighbour said. "A Jewish education never harmed anybody."

I rushed through the rest of my lecture, omitting half of it. A short question period was to follow. A Mr. Gordon was first.

"Mr. Griffin, my son is studying at McGill and he wishes to become a professor too. Now my question is as follows. How much can my Lionel expect to earn after five years?"

I had barely answered Mr. Gordon's question when a man in the back row began to wave his arm frantically.

"Yes," Shalinsky said. "What is it, Kaplan?"

Kaplan shot up from his seat. "I move a vote of thanks to Mr. Griffin for his excellent speech. I also move no more questions. It's nearly a quarter to eleven."

"Second both motions," cried a little man with thick glasses. "Segal. S,E, — no I — G,A,L. Get that in the minutes, Daniels."

A moment later Shalinsky and I were abandoned on one side of the room. Everyone else crowded round the refreshments table. I asked for my coat. At the door, Shalinsky thanked me profusely for coming.

"It's you I ought to thank," I said. "I enjoyed myself immensely."

"You see," Shalinsky said, "it's good to be with your own some-times."

"Just what do you mean by that?"

Shalinsky smiled faintly.

"Look, will you please get it through your head that I'm not Jewish."

"All right, all right. I'm mistaken."

"Good night," I said, banging the door after me.

Joyce was waiting up for me in bed. "Well," she asked, "how did it go?"

"Skip it."

"What's wrong?"

"I don't want to talk about it, that's all."

"I don't see why you can't tell me about it."

I didn't answer.

"I mean you don't have to bite my head off just because I'm curious."

"There's nothing to tell."

"You've left a cigarette burning on the bureau."

"Oh, for Christ's sake. It would be so nice not to have all my filthy little habits pointed out to me for once. I know there's a cigarette burning on the bureau."

Retreating into the bathroom, I slammed the door after me. But even a bath failed to soothe my nerves. I lit a cigarette and lingered in the tub.

"What on earth are you doing in there?" Joyce shouted.

"Writing a book."

"Isn't he witty?"

"And next time you use my razor on your blessed armpits, kiddo, I'll thank you to wash it and replace the blade."

"Now who's pointing out whose filthy habits?"

I don't like mirrors. I make a point of never sitting opposite one in a restaurant. But tonight I had a special interest in studying my face.

"Mortimer!"

Mortimer, of course, could be a Jewish name.

"What are you doing in there?"

I'm a tall man with a long horse-face. But my nose is certainly not prominent. Turning, I considered my face in profile. When I finally came out of the bathroom, I asked Joyce. "Would you say I had a Jewish face?"

She laughed.

"I'm serious, Joyce."

"As far as I'm concerned," she said, "there's no such thing as a Jewish face."

I told her about the lecture.

"If you want my opinion," she said, "you wouldn't mind Shalinsky's notion in the least if you weren't a sublimated anti-Semite."

"Thank you," I said, switching off the light.

An hour later, sensing that I was still awake, Joyce turned to me in bed. "I've been thinking, darling. Look, if — now please don't get angry. But *if* you were Jewish——"

"*What?*"

"I mean, if you have got Jewish blood I'd love you just as——"

"Of all the stupid nonsense. What do you mean, *if* I'm Jewish? You've met my parents, haven't you?"

"All I'm saying is that if——"

"All right. I confess. My father's real name is Granofsky. He's a goddam defrocked rabbi or something. Not only that, you know, but my mother's a coon. She——"

"Don't you dare use that word."

"Look, for the tenth time, if I had Jewish blood I would not try to conceal it. What ever made you think …?"

"Well," she said. "You know."

"Goddam it. I told you long ago that was done for hygienic reasons. My mother insisted on it. Since I was only about two weeks old at the time, I wasn't consulted."

"O.K.," she said. "O.K. I just wanted you to know where I would stand if——"

"Look, let's go to sleep. I've had enough for one day. Tomorrow first thing I'm going to settle this matter once and for all."

"What are you going to do?"

"I'm going to start a pogrom."

"Some of your jokes," Joyce said, "are in the worst possible taste."

"Yes. I know. I happen to be cursed with what Hy calls a Goyishe sense of humour."

The next morning I phoned Shalinsky.

"*Jewish Thought* here. Mr. Shalinsky is in Toronto. I'll have him get in touch with your office the minute he returns."

"Shalinsky, it's *you*."

"Ah, it's you, Griffin. I'm sorry. I thought it was Levitt the printer. He usually phones at this hour on Thursday mornings."

"Look, Shalinsky, I'd like you to come over here at three this afternoon."

"Good."

Taken aback, I said: "What do you mean, *good?*"

"I was hoping you'd want to talk. Speaking frankly, I didn't expect it to happen so soon."

"Just be here at three," I said. "O.K.?" And I hung up.

By the time Shalinsky arrived I had amassed all manner of personal documents — my army discharge papers, passport, driving licence, McGill graduation certificate, marriage licence, a Rotary Club public speaking award, my unemployment insurance card, vaccination certificate, Bo-lo Champion (Jr. Division) Award of Merit, three library cards, a parking ticket, and my bank book. On all these documents was the name Mortimer Lucas Griffin. Seething with suppressed anger, I watched as Shalinsky fingered each document pensively. He looked up at last, pinching his lower lip between thumb and index finger. "Facts," he said. "Documents. So what?"

"So what? Are you serious? All this goes to prove that I was born a white Protestant male named Mortimer Lucas Griffin."

"To think that you would go to so much trouble."

"Are you mad, Shalinsky?"

"I'm not mad." Shalinsky smiled, blinking his eyes against the smoke of his cigarette. "Neither do I want to make problems for you."

"What do I have to do to prove to you that I'm not Jewish?"

Shalinsky sifted through the papers again. "And what about your father?" he asked. "Couldn't he have changed his name without you knowing it? I mean, this is within the realm of possibilities, is it not?"

"Or my grandfather, eh? Or my great-grandfather?"

"You're so excited."

"I'd take you to see my parents, but they're both dead."

"I'm sorry to hear that. Please accept my condolences."

"They died years ago," I said. "A car accident."

"Is that so?"

"I suppose you think I'm lying?"

"Mr. Griffin, please."

"You're ruining my life, Shalinsky."

"I hardly know you."

"Do me a favour, Shalinsky. Cut my courses. I'll be grateful to you for the rest of my life."

"But your lectures are marvellous, Mr. Griffin. A delight."

"Some delight."

"Why, some of your epigrams I have marked down in my notebook to cherish. To memorize, Mr. Griffin."

"I've got news for you, buster. They're not mine. I stole them from my professor at Cambridge."

"So what? Didn't Shakespeare, may he rest in peace, steal from Thomas Kyd? The oral tradition, Mr. Griffin, is ——"

"Shalinsky, I beg of you. If you won't quit my courses, then at least don't come to classes. If you'll do that for me I promise to pass you first in the class."

"Absolutely no."

Emptied, undone, I collapsed on the sofa.

"You don't feel so hot?" Shalinsky asked.

"I feel terrible. Now will you please go."

Shalinsky rose from his chair with dignity. "One thing," he said. "Among all those papers, no birth certificate. Why? I ask myself."

"Will you please get the hell out of here, Shalinsky!"

My parents were very much alive. But I hadn't lied to Shalinsky because I was afraid. There were my mother's feelings to be considered, that's all. You see, I was born an indecent seven months after my parents' marriage. They never told me this themselves. They always pre-dated the ceremony by a year, but once I accidentally came across their marriage licence and discovered their deception. Not a very scandalous one, when you consider that they've been happily married for thirty-two years now. But the secret of my early birth belonged to my parents and, to their mind, had been carefully kept. There was something else. My father, a high-school teacher all these years, had been a poet of some promise as a young man, and I believe that he had been saving his money to go to Europe as soon as he graduated from McGill. He met my mother in his senior year, alas. I was conceived — suspiciously close to the Annual Arts Ball, I put it — and they were married. (A shock to their friends for, at the time, my mother was seeing an awful lot of Louis Cohen, a famous judge today.) Next year, instead of Europe, my father enrolled for a teacher's course. I have always been tormented by the idea that I may have ruined their lives. So I was certainly not going to open a belated inquiry into the matter for Shalinsky's sake. Let him think I was Jewish and that I was afraid to show him my birth certificate. I knew the truth, anyway.

But as far as Shalinsky was concerned, so did he.

Beginning with my next lecture he contrived to make life a misery for me.

"It seems to be your contention — correct me if I'm wrong — that Kafka's strict Jewish upbringing had a crippling effect on the man. Would you say, then, that this was also true of Hemingway, who had a strict Catholic upbringing?"

Another day.

"I may have misinterpreted you, of course, but it seems to me that you place Céline among the great writers of today. Do you think it possible, Mr. Griffin, that anti-Semitism goes hand in hand with literary greatness? Answer me that."

Shalinsky filled all my dreams. He attacked me in alleys, he pursued me through mazes and, in a recurring nightmare, he dragged me screaming into the synagogue to be punished for nameless iniquities. Many an afternoon I passed brooding about him. I saw myself being led up the thirteen steps to the hangman's noose, the despised strangler of Shalinsky, with — because of my ambiguous state — neither minister nor rabbi to comfort me. Because I was sleeping so badly, I began to lose weight, dark circles swelled under my eyes, and I was almost always in an unspeakable temper.

Fearful of Shalinsky, I cut *The Merchant of Venice* from Eng. 112.

"Ah, Mr. Griffin, a question please."

"Yes, Shalinsky."

"It seems to me that in our study of Shakespeare, may he rest in peace, we have so far failed to discuss one of the Bard's major plays, *The Merchant of Venice.* I wonder if you could tell me why."

"Look here, Shalinsky, I do not intend to put up with your insolence for another minute. There are other problems besides the Jewish problem. This is not the Jewish Thought Literary Society, but my class in English 112. I'll run it however I choose, and damn your perverse Jewish soul."

With that, and the sharper exchanges that were to come, my reputation as an anti-Semite spread. Soon I found myself being openly slighted by other lecturers at Wellington. Several students asked to be released from my classes. It was rumoured that a petition demanding my expulsion was being circulated among the students with, I must say, huge success. Eventually, Joyce found out about it.

"Mortimer, this can't be true. I mean you didn't call Shalinsky a meddling Jew in class last week …? "

"Yes, I did."

"Is it also true, then, that you've stopped taking our newspapers from Mr. Goldberg because … you want to transfer our business to a gentile store?"

"Absolutely."

"Mortimer, I think you ought to see an analyst."

"I'm crazy, eh?"

"No. But you've been overworking. I don't know what's come over you."

"Is this Hy's idea?"

She looked startled.

"Come off it. I know you've been seeing Hy and Eva secretly."

"Mortimer, how could you have written that article on Chagall for *Jewish Thought*?"

"What's wrong with it?"

"Did you have to call it 'A Jewish Answer to Picasso'? Hy's furious. He thinks that was so cheap of you. He——"

"I'll kill that Shalinsky. I'll murder him."

Joyce, holding her hands to her face, ran into the bedroom. Three days later, when I sat down to the tiresome job of correcting the Eng. 129 midterm essays, I was still in a rage with Shalinsky. But I swear that's not why I failed him. His essay on Kafka was ponderous, windy, and pretentious, and deserved no better than it got: F-minus. Unfortunately for me, Dean McNoughton didn't agree.

"Not only do I consider this failure unwarranted, Griffin, but frankly I'm shocked at your behaviour. For the past two weeks charges of the most alarming nature have been flooding my office. I've been in touch with your wife who tells me you've been overworking, and so I prefer not to discuss the charges for the present. However, I think you'd best take the second term off and rest. Hodges will take your courses. But before you go, I want you to mark this paper B-plus. I think Shalinsky's essay is worth at least that."

"I'm afraid that's impossible, sir."

Dean McNoughton leaned back in his chair and considered his pipe pensively. "Tell me," he said at last, "is it true you offered to mark Shalinsky first in your class if he only stopped attending your lectures?"

"Yes, sir."

"I'm afraid I have no choice but to mark this paper B-plus myself."

"In that case I must ask you to accept my resignation."

"Go home, man. Rest up. Think things over calmly. If after three weeks you still want to resign.…"

I started impatiently for the door.

"I don't understand you, Griffin. We're not prejudiced here. If you're Jewish, why didn't you say so at first?"

Pushing Dean McNoughton aside roughly, I fled the office.

Joyce wasn't home when I got there. All her things were gone, too. But she had left me a note, the darling. It said, in effect, that she could no longer put up with me. Perhaps we had never been right for each other. Not that she wished me ill, etc., etc. But all her instincts rebelled against sharing her bed with a fascist — worse, a Jewish fascist.

I don't know how Shalinsky got into the house. I must have left the door open. But there he stood above me, smiling faintly, a hand-rolled cigarette in his mouth.

"My wife's left me," I said.

Shalinsky sat down, sighing.

"Joyce has left me. Do you understand what that means to me?"

Shalinsky nodded his head with ineffable sadness. "Mixed marriages," he said, "never work."

All this happened two years ago, and I have married again since then. I don't earn nearly as much money in my new job, and at times it's difficult to live with my father-in-law, but next spring, God willing, we hope to rent an apartment of our own (not that I don't appreciate all he's done for us).

I don't see any of my old friends any more, but my new life offers plenty of rewards. I.M. Sinclair, for instance, composed a special poem for our wedding and read it after the rabbi's speech.

Lay your sleeping head, my love,
human on my faithless arm....

When the last issue of *Jewish Thought* appeared, imagine my delight when I read on the title-page: EDITED BY J. SHALINSKY AND M. GRIFFIN. Our circulation, I'm pleased to say, is rising steadily. Next year we hope to sell 1,500 copies of each issue. Meanwhile it's a struggle for Gitel and me. For me especially, as I am not yet completely adjusted to my new life. There are nights when I wake at three a.m. yearning for a plate of bacon and eggs. I miss Christmas. My father won't have anything to do with me. He thinks I'm crazy. Hy's another matter. He's phoned a couple of times, but I no longer have much use for him. He's an assimilationist. Last week my application for a teaching job with Western High School was turned down flatly — in spite of my excellent qualifications.

It's hard to be a Jew, you see.

THEIR CANADA AND MINE

A Memoir

Back in 1953, on the first Sunday after my return to Montreal from a two-year stay in Europe, I went to my grandmother's house.

"How is it for the Jews in Europe?" she asked me.

My uncles reproached me for not having been to Israel, but their questions about Europe were less poignant than my grandmother's. Had I seen the Folies Bergères? The changing of the Guard? My uncles were on their way to becoming Canadians.

Canada, from the beginning, was second best. It made us nearly Americans.

My grandfather, like so many others, came to Canada by steerage from Poland in 1900 and settled down not far from Main Street in what was to become a ghetto. Here, as in the real America, the immigrants worked under appalling conditions in factories. They rented halls over poolrooms and grocery stores to meet and form burial societies and create *shuls.* They sent to the old country for relatives left behind and rabbis and brides. Slowly, unfalteringly, the immigrants started to struggle up a ladder of streets, from one where you had to leave your garbage outside your front door to another where you actually had a rear lane; from the three rooms over the grocery or tailor shop to your own cold-water flat on a street with trees.

Our street, St. Urbain, was one of five working-class ghetto streets between the Main and Park Avenue.

To a middle-class stranger, it's true, any one of these streets would have seemed as squalid as the next. On each corner a cigar store, a grocery, and a fruit man. Outside staircases everywhere. Winding ones, wooden ones, rusty and risky ones. An endless repetition of precious peeling balconies and waste lots making the occasional gap here and there. But, as we boys knew, each street between the Main and Park Avenue represented subtle differences in income. No two cold-water flats were alike and no two stores were the same either. Best Fruit gypped on weight but Smiley's didn't give credit.

Among the wonders of St. Urbain, our St. Urbain, there was a man who ran for alderman each election on a one-plank platform (provincial speed cops were anti-Semites), a boy nobody remembered who had gone on to become a professor at MIT, two men who had served with the Mackenzie-Paps in the Spanish Civil War (they no longer spoke to each other), Herscovitch's cousin Larry, who had demanded kosher food when he was sentenced to six months in jail for receiving stolen goods, a woman who called herself a divorcee, and a boxer who had made the ratings in *Ring* magazine.

St. Urbain was, I suppose, somewhat similar to ghetto streets in New York and Chicago. There were some crucial differences, however. We were Canadians, therefore we had a King. We also had "pea-soups", i.e., French-Canadians, in the neighborhood.

While the King never actually stopped on St. Urbain, he did pass a few streets above on his visit to Canada just before the war, and many of us turned out to wave. Our attitude toward the Royal Family was characterized by an amused benevolence. They didn't affect the price of potatoes. Neither could they help or hinder the establishment of the State of Israel. Like Churchill, for instance. The King, we were told, was just a figurehead. "If he wants to put in even double windows at the palace, he needs a special act of Parliament." We could afford to be patronizing because among our own kings we could count Solomon and David. True, we wished the Royal Family a long life every morning in *shul*, but this wasn't servility. It was generosity.

"Pea-soups" were for turning the lights on and off on Shabbos and running elevators and cleaning out chimneys and furnaces. They were, it was rumored, ridden with TB, rickets, and diseases it's better not to mention. You gave them old clothes. A week before the High Holidays you had one in to wax the floors. The French-Canadians were our *"schwartze"*.

Our world was made up of five streets. Above Park Avenue came Outremont, where Jewish bosses and professional men were already beginning to make inroads on what used to be a middle-class French-Canadian reserve. Two streets below our own came the Main.

The Main was rich in delights. But looking at it again after an absence of many years I must say that it can also be sordid, it's filthy, and hollering with stores whose wares, whether furniture or fruit, are ugly or damaged. The signs still say FANTASTIC DISCOUNTS or FORCED TO SELL PRICES HERE, but the bargains so bitterly sought after are illusory — and perhaps they always were.

The Main was the sort of street narrow reform candidates were always clamoring about. It was described as vice-ridden, a hot-bed for Communism, and a breeding ground for juvenile delinquency. Well, I guess there was a patina of truth on all these clichés. But they overlooked a lot. Like the smell of fresh bagels on a Sunday morning and the pike floating glumly toward you in the window of YOUR MOST TRUSTFUL kosher butcher. The "war assets" store with the sign over the cash that read MEXICAN MONEY IS ACCEPTED IN MEXICO. And more, much more. Why, within one block you could have disfiguring blackheads removed, talk with a miracle-working rabbi, shoot a game of snooker with a stranger, bet on a horse, consult a matchmaker, read newspapers in six different languages, furnish your bedroom for twenty dollars down, send a food parcel to a relative in Warsaw, and drop in on a herbalist with a sure cure for the most embarrassing of all ailments.

The Main, with something for all our appetites, was dedicated to pinching pennies from the poor, but it was there to entertain, educate, and comfort us too. Across the street from the *shul* you could see THE PICTURE THEY CLAIMED COULD NEVER BE MADE. A little farther down the street there was the Workman's Circle and, if you liked, a strip-tease show. It was to the Main, once a year before the High Holidays, that I was taken along for a new suit (the itch of the cheap tweed was excruciating) and shoes (always with a squeak). We also shopped for food on the Main, and here the important thing was to watch the man at the scales. On the Main, too, was the Chinese laundry — "Have you ever seen such hard workers?" — the Italian hat-blocker — "Tony's a good *goy*, you know. Against Mussolini from the very first." — and strolling French-Canadian priests — "Some of them even speak Hebrew now. Well, if you ask me it's none of their business. Enough's enough, you know." Kids like myself were dragged along on shopping expeditions to carry parcels. Old men gave us snuff, at the delicatessen we were allowed salami butts, card players bought us candy for luck, and everywhere we were poked and pinched by the mothers. The best that could be said of us was, "He eats well, knock wood," and later, as we went off to school, "He's a rank-one boy."

After the shopping, once our errands had been done, we returned to the Main once more, either for part-time jobs or to study with our *melamed*. Jobs going on the Main included spotting pins in a bowling alley, collecting butcher bills and, best of all, working at a newsstand, where you could read the *Police Gazette* free and pick up a little extra short-changing strangers during the rush hour. But make no mistake. We were not sent out to work because we were poor, God forbid, like those no-goods next door. Work was good for our character development and the fact that we were paid was incidental. To qualify for a job we were supposed to be "bright, ambitious, and willing to learn". An ad I once saw in a shoe-store window read: PART TIME BOY WANTED FOR EXPANDING BUSINESS — EXPERIENCE ABSOLUTELY NECESSARY — BUT NOT ESSENTIAL.

Our jobs and lessons finished, we would wander the streets in small groups, smoking Turret cigarettes and telling bad jokes.

"Hey, shmo-hawk, what's the difference between a mail box and an elephant's ass?"

"I dunno."

"Well, I wouldn't send *you* to mail my letters."

As the French-Canadian factory girls passed arm-in-arm we would shout things like, "I've got the time if you've got the place."

Shabbos it was back to the Main again and the original Young Israel Synagogue. While our grandfathers and fathers prayed and gossiped and speculated about the war in Europe in the musty room below, we played chin-the-bar upstairs and told jokes that began, "Confucius say..." or "Once there was an Englishman, Irishman, and a Hebe, see. And they were all after this here dame...." We would return to the Main once more when we wanted a fight with the pea-soups. Winter, as I remember it, was best for this type of sport. We could throw snowballs packed with ice or frozen horse-buns and, with darkness coming so early, it was easier to elude pursuers. Soon, however, we developed a technique of battle that served us well even in the spring. Three of us would hide under an outside staircase while the fourth member of our group, a kid named Eddy, would stand idly on the sidewalk. Eddy was a good head-and-a-half shorter than the rest of us. (For this, it was rumored, his mother was to blame. She wouldn't let Eddy have his tonsils removed and that's why he was such a runt. It was not that Eddy's mother feared surgery but Eddy sang in the choir of a rich *shul*, this brought in some thirty dollars a month, and if his tonsils were removed, it was feared his voice would go too. Eddy sang sweetly.) Anyway, he would stand out there alone, and when the first solitary pea-soup passed he'd kick him in the shins. The pea-soup, looking down on little Eddy, would naturally knock him one on the head. Then, and only then, would we emerge from under the staircase. "Hey," one of us would say, "that's my kid brother you just slugged," and before the poor pea-soup could protest we were all over him.

These and other fights, however, sprang more out of boredom than from true racial hatred, not that there were no racial problems on the Main.

For if the Main was a poor man's street, it was also a dividing line. Below, the French Canadians. Above, some distance above, the English. On the Main itself there were some Italians, Poles, Yugo-slavs, and Ukrainians, but they did not count as true gentiles. Even the French Canadians, who were our enemies, were not entirely unloved. Like us, they were poor and rough with large families and spoke English badly.

Looking back it seems that it was only the English who were truly hated and feared. "Among them," I heard it said, "with those porridge-faces, who can tell what they're thinking. *If* they do think." It was, we felt, their country, and given enough liquor who knew when they'd make trouble?

We were a rude, aggressive bunch round the Main. Cocky too. Send round Einstein and we would not have been overawed. But bring round the most insignificant little Anglo-Saxon fire insurance inspector and even the most powerful merchant on the street would dip into the drawer for a fiver or a bottle and begin to bow and scrape and say "Sir".

After school we used to race down to the Main to play pool at the Rachel or the Mount Royal. Other days, when we chose to avoid school altogether, we used to take the No. 55 streetcar as far as St. Catherine Street, where there was a variety of amusements offered. We could play the pinball machines and watch archaic strip-tease movies for a nickel at the Silver Gameland. At the Midway or the Crystal Palace we could usually see a double feature and a girlie show for as little as thirty-five cents. The Main, at this juncture, was thick with drifters, panhandlers, and whores. Available on both sides of the street were "Tourist Rooms" by day and night, and everywhere there was the smell of French fried potatoes cooking in stale oil. Tough, unshaven men in checked shirts stood in knots outside the taverns and cheap cafés. There was the threat of violence.

As I recall it, we were always being warned about the Main. Our grandparents and parents had come there by steerage from Rumania or cattleboat from Poland by way of Liverpool. But no sooner had they unpacked their bundles and cardboard suitcases than they were planning a better, brighter life for us, the Canadian-born children. The Main, good enough for them, was not to be for us, and that, they told us again and again, was what the struggle was for. The Main was for *bummers*, drinkers, and (heaven forbid) failures....

During the years leading up to the war, the ideal of our ghetto, no different from any other in America in this respect, was the doctor. This, mistakenly, was taken to be the very apogee of learning and refinement. In those days there also began the familiar process of alienation between immigrant parents and Canadian-born children. Our older brothers and cousins, off to the university, came home to realize for the first time that our parents spoke with embarrassing accents. Even the younger boys, like myself, were going to "their" schools. According to them, the priests had made a tremendous contribution to the exploration and development of this country. Some were heroes. But our parents had other memories, different ideas, about the priesthood. At school we were taught about the glory of the Crusades and at home we were told of the bloodier side to that story. Though we wished Lord Tweedsmuir, the Governor-General, a long life each Saturday morning in *shul*, there were those among us who also knew him as John Buchan, the author of thrillers riddled with anti-Semitism. From the very beginning there was their history, and ours. Our heroes, and theirs.

Our school, Baron Byng High School, was under the jurisdiction of the Protestant School Board, but had a student body that was nevertheless almost 100 per cent Jewish. It became something of a legend in our area. Again and again we led the province in the junior matriculation (McGill entrance exams). This was galling to those on the left who held we were the same as everyone else, but to the many more who felt that at all times there's nothing like a Yiddish boy, it was an annual cause for celebration. Our class at BBHS, Room 41, was one of the few to boast a true gentile, i.e., a white Protestant. His name was Whelan — and he certainly was a curiosity. Envious students came from other classes to study and question him. Whelan was not too bright, but he gave Room 41 a certain tone, and in order to keep him with us we wrote essays for him and slipped him answers at examination time. We were, I'd say, as proud of Whelan's accomplishments (and no less condescending) as ever a Britisher abroad was of his African houseboy.

Our parents used to apply a special standard to all men and

events. "Is it good for the Jews?" By this test they interpreted the policies of Mackenzie King and the Stanley Cup play-offs (our equivalent of the World Series) and earthquakes in Japan. To take one example — if the Montreal Canadiens won the Stanley Cup it would infuriate the English in Toronto, and as long as the English and French were going at each other they left us alone: *ergo*, it was good for the Jews if the Canadiens won the Stanley Cup.

We were convinced that we gained from dissension between Canada's two cultures, the English and the French, and we looked neither to England nor to France for guidance. We turned to the United States. The real America.

America was Roosevelt, the Yeshiva College, Danny Kaye, a Jew in the Supreme Court, the *Jewish Daily Forward*, Max Baer, Mickey Katz records, Dubinsky, Mrs. Nussbaum of Allen's Alley, and Gregory Peck looking so cute in *Gentleman's Agreement*. Why, in the United States a Jew even wrote speeches for the President. Returning cousins swore they had heard a cop speak Yiddish in Brooklyn. There were the Catskill hotels, Jewish soap operas on the radio, and, above all earthly pleasure grounds, Florida. Miami. No manufacturer had quite made it in Montreal until he was able to spend a month each winter in Miami.

We were governed by Ottawa, we were also British subjects, but our true capital was certainly New York. Success was (and still is) acceptance by the United States. For a fighter this meant a main bout at Madison Square Garden, for a writer or an artist, praise from New York critics (Adele Wiseman for her novel, *The Sacrifice*), for a businessman, a Miami tan, and, today, for comics, an appearance on the Ed Sullivan show (Wayne and Shuster), or for actors, not an important part at the Stratford Festival but Broadway (William Shatner, Lou Jacobi) or the lead in a Hollywood TV series (Lorne Greene in *Bonanza*). The outside world, "their" Canada, only concerned us insofar as it affected our living conditions. All the same, we liked to impress the *goyim*. A knock on the knuckles from time to time wouldn't hurt them. So, while we secretly believed that the baseball field or the prize ring was no place for a Jewish boy, we took enormous pleasure in the accomplishments of, say, Kermit Kitman, a one-time outfielder with the Montreal Royals, and Maxie Berger, the boxer.

Streets like our St. Urbain and Outremont, where the rich lived, made up an almost self-contained world. Outside of business there was minimal contact with the gentiles. This was hardly petulant clannishness or naive fear. In the years leading up to the war neo-fascist groups were extremely active in Canada. You had Father Coughlin, Lindberg, and others. We had Adrien Arcand. The upshot was almost the same. So I can recall seeing swastikas and *"A bas les Juifs"* painted on the Laurentian highway. There were suburban areas and hotels in the mountains where we were not allowed, beaches with signs that read GENTILES ONLY, quotas at the universities, and serious racial fights on Park Avenue. The democracy we were being invited to defend was imperfect and hostile to us. Without question it was better for us here than in Europe, but this was still their Canada, not ours.

I was only a boy during the war. I can remember signs in cigar stores that warned us THE WALLS HAVE EARS and THE ENEMY IS EVERYWHERE. I can also remember my parents, my uncles and aunts, cracking peanuts on a Friday night and waiting for the United States, for those two unequaled friends of our people, Roosevelt and Winchell, to come off it and get into the war. We admired the British, they were gutsy, but we had much more confidence in the United States Marines. (Educated by Hollywood, we could see the likes of John Wayne, Gable, and Robert Taylor, making mincemeat of the Panzers, while Noel Coward, Laurence Olivier, and others seen here in a spate of British war films, looked all too humanly vulnerable to us.) Briefly, then, Pearl Harbor was a day of jubilation here, but the war itself made for some confusions. In another country, relatives recalled by my grandparents were being murdered. But out on the streets in our air cadet uniforms, we Baron Byng boys were more interested in seeking out the fabulously wicked v-girls ("They all go the limit with guys in uniform, see. It's patriotic like.") we had read about in the *Herald*. True, we made some sacrifices. American comic books were banned for the duration due, I think, to a shortage of U.S. funds. So we had to put up a quarter on the black market for copies of the *Batman* and *Tip-Top Comics*. But at the same corner newsstand we bought a page on which four pigs had been printed. When we folded the paper together as directed the four pig's behinds made up Hitler's hateful face. Outside Cooperman's Superior Provisions, where if you were a regular you could get sugar without ration coupons, we would chant "Black-Market Cooperman! Black-Market Cooperman!" until the old man came out, waving his broom, and chased us down the street.

The war in Europe brought about considerable changes within

the Jewish community in Montreal. To begin with, there was the coming of the refugees. These men, interned in England as enemy aliens and sent to Canada where they were eventually released, were to make a tremendous impact on the community. I think we had conjured up a picture of the refugees as penurious Hasidim with packs on their backs. We were eager to be helpful, our gestures were large, but in return we expected a little gratitude. As it turned out, the refugees, mostly German and Austrian Jews, were far more sophisticated and better educated than we were. They had not, like our immigrant grandparents, come from little villages in Galicia. Neither did they despise Europe. To the contrary, they found our culture thin, the city provincial, and the Jews narrow. This bewildered and stung us. But what cut deepest, I suppose, was that the refugees spoke English better than we did and, among themselves, had the gall to talk in the hated German language. Many of them also made it clear that Canada was no more than a frozen place to stop until a U.S. visa was forthcoming. So, for a while, we real Canadians were hostile. (This has long since died down, of course, and the refugees of 1940-41 have been assimilated into the community. They have done much to enrich its cultural life, too.)

For our grandparents who remembered those left behind in Rumania and Poland the war was a time of unspeakable grief. Parents watched their sons grow up too quickly and stood by helplessly as the boys went off to the fighting one by one. (They didn't have to go, either, for until the very last days of the war Canadians could only be drafted for service *within* Canada. A boy had to volunteer before he could be sent overseas.) But for those of my own age the war was something else. I cannot remember it as a black time, and I think it must be so for most boys of my generation. For the awful truth is that for many of us to look back on the war is to recall the first time our fathers earned a good living. Even as the bombs fell and the ships went down, always elsewhere, our country was busting out of the depression into a period of hitherto unknown prosperity. For my generation the war was to hear of death and sacrifice but to see with our own eyes the departure from cold-water flats to apartments in Outremont, duplexes and homes in the suburbs. It was when we read of the uprising in the Warsaw Ghetto and saw, in Montreal, the changeover from small *shuls* to big synagogues-cum-parochial-schools with stained glass windows and mosaics outside. During the war some of us lost brothers and cousins but in Canada we had never had it so good, and we began the run from rented summer shacks with outhouses in Shawbridge to Colonial-style summer houses of our own and speedboats on the lake in Ste. Agathe.

The war was when the concept of the ghetto became even more rigid in Montreal. German Jews, the argument went, were the most assimilated, and look what happened to them. Our antipathy for the *goyim* quickened. We wanted no part of them.

Back in Montreal, living within the Jewish community once more, this time after an absence of seven years in Europe, I found the changes come about in so short a time astonishing.

As far as I can see it's still a matter of their Canada and ours, but on all levels, even among older Jews, there has been a disheartening adjustment to what we Canadians defensively call the American way of life. When I was a boy, we had already begun to discard anything that made us appear different. Some business and professional men anglicized their names: Rabinovitch, let's say, was reborn Rice, and Lipschitz, Lane. But the children were still given sturdy Old Testament names. Today I find the children of even the most Orthodox families are, just as in the U.S., more likely to be called Neal, Stuart, Michele (for *Malke*, this), and Eugene. Naturally, the rabbis who serve such an up-to-date community are no longer severe men with splendid beards. Today's clean-shaven young rabbi, as you well know, is not so much a descendant of Hillel, Shammai, or the Baal Shem Tov, as a regular guy, like Norman Vincent Peale. He no longer threatens the community with God's terrible wrath but, instead, organizes father-and-son breakfasts, golf tournaments, and musical-comedy-type Bar Mitzvahs.

Just as Americans come up here to look for hockey players, we scout the U.S. for modern rabbis. So, probably, the rabbi has come to Montreal or Toronto from, say, Cleveland. Most likely he has a Ph.D., his weekly column in the Toronto *Telegram* or Montreal *Star* is signed Dr., and deals with everything from "What Is True Happiness" to, say (for National Sports Week), "Jewish Athletes from Bar Kochba to Hank Greenberg." The most envied congregation would be the one with the rabbi who has appeared most often on television panel games.

Still, there is a definite dichotomy of feeling about the U.S. here.

For even as the big city Jews here hasten to imitate the U.S., they also, as Canadians, have become more and more fiercely nationalistic in recent years. So, while the tone may be set for them by New

York, they are aggressively proud that the Canadian dollar was, until recently, worth 103 American cents. Miami may still be necessary but, as Canadians, the Jews object to being pushed around by Washington. This is true socially too. For even as the community insists that its rabbis emulate the up-to-date Protestant minister, it is determined that the children should attend parochial schools. Jewish-sounding names may be abandoned, the children may very well have a tree for Christmas, but they will still live in ghettos. Yesterday there was one ghetto, today, as the Jews have moved out to suburbia, there are a series of such enclaves. No longer with much excuse, however. But when I put this to a seemingly assured young man, he replied, "Well, I just wouldn't feel comfortable living next door to a *goy*. All this brotherhood crap is meaningless. Underneath, they're still anti-Semites."

The same man told me that because many golf courses are still restricted the Jews have constructed clubs of their own. Recently, there was a crisis at one of these clubs. A young Jew brought along a friend of his, a gentile, to play with him. The gentile liked the course and the people he met there so much that he applied for membership. After much heart-searching his application was turned down. "Why?" I asked.

"Well, it wasn't that they had anything against him personally. But they did feel that if they let him in the others would apply. Soon, they'd all want to get in … and we'd be pushed into our own corner again."

"What if a Negro applied?"

"He'd be turned down. But not because he was colored. Only because he's a *goy*."

Well, in a sense it's amusing, even gratifying, to know that we Jews so recently off St. Urbain can now kick the *goyim* off our own golf, curling, and yacht clubs, but it's also very depressing. We've adjusted splendidly, sure. We're Canucks now, still a little off-white perhaps, but no longer as different as we were.

"It's no longer the same, is it?" an old friend said to me. "When we were kids if we came home from school and said our teacher was picking on us, we were told, 'if he's picking on you he has a good reason.' Today my oldest goes to the child psychiatrist twice a week. It's twenty-five bucks a crack." He had other, more damaging criticisms to make about the community. But like so many others he was careful to add, "Listen, it's sad. For all I know it's even shameful. But you mustn't tell the *goyim*. For them, it's ammunition."

234

So while our Jewish political leaders fatuously proclaim our Canadianism, even as they protest how very much at home we feel here, the Jews still live apart and in fear. It's still a question of their Canada, and ours. The Jews, assured in their own suburban camps, have only to step into the outside world to feel conspicuous and insecure.

All this may sound dreadfully familiar, and it should, for the Canadian Jew is (not unjustifiably) a would-be American. However, there are some subtle differences in our condition as compared to yours. The Jews in Canada have never taken as integral a part in the political and cultural life of their country as have the American Jews. True, we have been handed some political lollipops. There's a Jew in the Senate, another is an MP, and, in Quebec, there are now two Jewish judges, but there is no Jewish politician of stature in Canada, and, as I said before, our cultural capital is New York. This is not to say that the cultural bastions of Toronto — the book and magazine publishers, the CBC, what little theater there is — is anti-Semitic; far from it, but it is in *their* hands. Whereas, looking down on the cultural life of New York from here, it appears to be a veritable yeshiva. I won't even go into the question of Broadway or television, but from *Commentary* by way of *Partisan Review* to the *Noble Savage*, from Knopf to Grove Press, the Jewish writers seem to call each to each, editing, praising, slamming one another's books, plays, and cultural conference appearances. So many of the talented young writers are Jews, and I'm sure, in New York, not one of them has been asked as I was recently asked at a party in Montreal, "When are you going to stop writing about the Main Street and Outremont? I mean, aren't you ever going to write about Canada?"

I have, since my return to Montreal, been back to the Main again and again.

Today the original Young Israel Synagogue, where we used to chin the bar, is no longer there. A bank stands where my old poolroom used to be. Some familiar stores have gone. There have been deaths and bankruptcies. But most of the departed have simply packed up and moved with their old customers to the nearest of the new shopping centers at Van Horne or Rockland. And what are these centers if not tarted-up versions of the old Main, where you could do all your buying in a concentrated area and maybe get a special price through a cousin's cousin? Yesterday it was a dollar off because it's you, today it's the shopping stamp.

Up and down the Main you can still pick out many restaurants and steak houses wedged between the sweater factories, poolrooms, cold-water flats, wholesale dry goods stores, and "Your Most Sanitary" barbershops. The places where we used to work in summer as shippers for ten dollars a week are still there. So's Baron Byng High School, right where it always was. Rabbinical students and boys with sidecurls still pass. These, however, are the latest arrivals from Poland and Rumania and soon their immigrant parents will put pressure on them to study hard and make good. To get out.

But many of our own grandparents, the very same people who assured us the Main was only for *bummers* and failures, will not get out. Today when most of the children have made good, now that the sons and daughters have split-level bungalows and minks and winters in Miami, many of the grandparents still cling to the Main. Their children cannot in many cases persuade them to leave. So you still see them there, drained and used-up by the struggle. They sit on kitchen chairs next to the Coke freezer in the cigar and soda store, dozing with a fly-swatter in hand. You find them rolling their own cigarettes and studying the obituary column in the *Jewish Eagle* on the steps outside the Jewish Library. The women still peel potatoes on the stoop under the shade of a winding outside staircase. Old men still watch the comings and goings from the balcony above, a blanket spread over their legs and a little bag of polly seeds on their lap. As in the old days the sinking house with the crooked floor is often right over the store or the wholesaler's, or maybe next door to the junk yard. Only today the store and the junk yard are shut down. Signs for Sweet Caporal Cigarettes or old election posters have been nailed in over the missing windows. There are spiderwebs everywhere.

Joseph Sherman

FOR MORDECAI RICHLER'S SHALINSKY WHO SAID "A JEW IS AN IDEA"

In the days before
the synagogue's fire   when I was thirteen
I would take such a thought as this
a problem worth a morning's pondering
to the Shul
to the dusty corner next the Ark
where sat Epstein
beneath his grey homburg   *reading*
tucked within the folds of his yellowing Tallith
(a shawl that could canopy a wedding party)
I would go to his seat before opening prayers
and put it all to him   this man
who could love his people no more
if he lived as long again
And I can see old Epstein place his finger
in the book of prayer   close it
and look up
Epstein who was master of a good six tongues
not counting Yiddish and Hebrew
would say   with a confidant's smile
so I could understand
"You know, eh, that the Creator
(whose Name we cannot pronounce)
made the heaven and earth in six days,
and before He rested on the seventh
which He made especially holy, eh, as He should,

you know this? that on the morning of the sixth day
He rubbed the dust between His fingers and said,
and this I tell you now He said, 'You know,
I have got a Wonderful Idea!'"

SCARECROW MAN:
A LITANY

for Martin Demaine

(Glass figure/nine inches high/cruciform arms/hand-blown)

All men who examine Scarecrow Man see themselves

All men who observe his facelessness	know their own
All men who note his translucence	know their own
All men who plumb his hollowness	know their own
All men who sense his brittleness	know their own
All men who perceive his grotesquerie	know their own
All men who feel his insularity	know their own
All men who find the blade at his heart	know their own
All men who see the stars in his head	know their own
All men who know his crucial asymmetry	know their own
All men who understand his beauty	know their own
All men who discover his purpose	know their own

All men who dare glance upward
        to the skrew
        of descending ravens   know their own

William Weintraub

SPORT IN THE OLD TESTAMENT*

They arrived at the synagogue just as Rabbi Sheldon Cohen finished shining his riding boots. The handsome, beardless cleric had been a three-letter man at Rabbinical College and his zeal for sport had never died. He was getting a bit old now for water polo and jiujitsu, but he still played his daily eighteen at the golf club and wielded an eager broom at the curling club. And he had just been elected Master of Fox Hounds of the Disraeli Hunt, Montreal's first Jewish pack. It was currently being organized and would be restricted to those of good character and extreme wealth.

Still wearing his new scarlet hunting coat, the Rabbi crossed the broadloomed floor of his study to greet his two visitors.

"Shalom, shalom, peace be with you," he said. "Please sit down. What can I do for you?"

"Well, Reverend," said Erskine, "it's about the speech you'll be giving tomorrow." He took his copy of the text from his briefcase.

"Oh?" said the Rabbi. He had been worrying about this.

Harry watched carefully, aware that he was about to see public relations in action.

"I'm just wondering, Reverend," said Erskine, "whether you've picked the right topic."

"Well," said the Rabbi, "I chose a Talmudic subject because of the conference's intellectual nature. Let me have a look at it again, will you?" He took some typewritten pages from his desk and leafed through them. Damn it, he shouldn't have bought this thing from Rabbi Epstein without reading it all the way through. But then again, the old man had assured him that it was extremely intellectual.

"To be quite frank, Reverend," said Erskine, "I wonder whether the reporters covering this speech will be able to understand it. And what's the point of a speech if it doesn't hit the papers?"

"Hmmm...the Talmud is very complicated, Mr. Erskine."

"For instance," said Erskine, "this section where you tell about a

*Chapter 18 of William Weintraub's novel
Why Rock the Boat?

239

theological argument those two old men had in Lithuania in 1654. That runs to about ten pages, doesn't it?"

"Yes...hmmmm...." The Rabbi sat down at his desk and looked distastefully at the script, badly typed and phrased in Epstein's sketchy English. To think he had paid the old chiseler ten dollars for this wretched thing.

"Have you ever heard of Rabbi Epstein, Mr. Erskine?" he said. "The great Talmudic scholar."

"Can't say that I have."

"A fascinating man. He has a very colorful little congregation over in the Jewish part of town. I've incorporated a few of his ideas." With disgust, the Rabbi looked down at the old man's cabalistic fulminations; Erskine was right, this thing was totally incomprehensible. He must have been out of his mind even to buy it, let alone deliver it to a big convention. What could he have been thinking of? This fox hunt was taking up too much time.

"Actually," said Erskine, "I was rather hoping you'd give us your 'Sport in the Old Testament'. I've heard it several times, Reverend, and personally I never tire of it."

The Rabbi got to his feet and thoughtfully examined the riding breeches that lay folded on a chair.

"Upon reflection, Mr. Erskine," he said, "I shall be pleased to address the BUMTA convention on 'Sport in the Old Testament'. In our troubled times, I feel — excuse me——" His telephone was ringing and he picked it up and engaged in a long argument with someone at the other end regarding how often foxhounds should be fed.

"So many details," the Rabbi sighed, hanging up the phone. "Today's clergyman is so beset by detail that he has no time left for policy matters. I sometimes envy the medieval rabbinate, in their quaint black caftans and their funny old hats. No telephones, no broadcasting, no committees. Yes, in the ghetto a man could sit down and concentrate on the big picture."

"Well, then, Reverend," said Erskine, "I wonder if you could let us have a text of your speech."

"But I don't use a text. I know that speech fairly well, you know."

"In that case," said Erskine, "I wonder if you could deliver it now."

"Now?"

"Yes, right here. Young Barnes will take notes and write some releases. We'll hand them out to the press in the morning."

"I suppose I could do that," said the Rabbi.

"Fine," said Erskine. He rose to go. "Here's two dollars, Barnes," he said. "When you're finished, grab a cab down to the hotel."

Erskine left and Harry took out his notebook. "Whenever you're ready, Your Reverence," he said.

The Rabbi paced up and down, flirting his riding crop self-consciously. "It's strange," he said, "giving a speech to only one person."

"Just pretend I'm a large crowd, Your Reverence."

"Very well then." The Rabbi took up his stance behind his desk and cleared his throat. "Mr. Chairman," he said, "Ladies and Gentlemen, Friends. As we forgather here today in the spirit of interfaith, I am reminded of — excuse me——" The telephone was ringing again and Harry waited, pencil poised.

"Don't argue with me, Solly," the Rabbi was saying into the phone. "There's a wholesale and a retail price for everything and horses are no exception. We are definitely not buying our horses on the retail level. Now you just go back to the dealer and make that quite clear to him."

The Rabbi hung up and continued his speech. As his pencil flew over the paper, Harry realized what a fine professional Larry Erskine must be in the field of public relations. In just a few minutes he had completely changed the course of events, and for the better. The Rabbi was happier with his new speech, the conference would probably also be happier, and the public would most certainly be happier.

"And so, friends," the Rabbi was saying, "we must face up to the very sad possibility that our beloved Montreal Canadiens may fail this year to win the Stanley Cup, emblematic of hockey supremacy in this broad land of ours. And in the heaviness of our hearts we will wonder if it is righteous to place the blame squarely on a coach who has very seldom shown even the slightest familiarity with his business. If we turn to the curious old pages of the Book of Deuteronomy...."

No wonder this speech was popular, Harry thought. The Rabbi was being highly partisan about the biggest of all sports controversies. Spoken in a tavern, these words would cause fisticuffs.

"And in conclusion, dear friends, let us remember those old prophets who many many years ago walked the sun-baked hills of Judea, let us remember that those prophets were pondering the very problems we ponder today, at this important BUMTA conference: how to build a healthier, happier community; how to achieve peace of mind and sound mental health; how to formulate a meaningful program for teen-agers; how to choose between the many worthy causes that make such demands on our time; how to keep the Arabs out of Israel.

"And as they pondered these problems, those colorful men of yore, they realized one thing: that man does not live by bread alone. No, our daily toil must be complemented by meaningful use of leisure. And what builds better bodies, for a better future in this broad land of ours, than sports?

"And so it was that those bearded old prophets questioned themselves, in their heart of hearts. 'Why do we play?' they asked. 'Do we play to win? For the glory? For the spoils?.... No,' they said. 'No, we play for the sake of the game. Play up, play up, and play the game!' And they wrote it on their parchments, in their squiggly old Hebrew letters.

"So today, as then, let us be good sports, ladies and gentlemen. For remember — a good sport is a good Canadian. Thank you. Shalom. Peace be with you."

"If I may say so, Your Reverence," said Harry, "that was very good."

"Thank you, thank you. By the way, do you think this fits me?" The Rabbi took off his skullcap and tried on a hunting cap with an extravagantly long peak.

"A perfect fit, sir."

Erna Paris

GROWING UP A JEWISH PRINCESS
IN FOREST HILL

The boundaries of our world were in our heads — in the clothes we wore, in the lilt of our voices, in the way we walked along our streets — but they were also physical. Unspoken but real. The centre of the universe was the juncture of Bathurst Street and Eglinton Avenue. (I still figure out north and south in any city by imagining myself at those crossroads.) The northern boundary fell somewhere around Elm Ridge Drive, a few blocks north of Eglinton; the southern boundary was definitely St. Clair Avenue. No one spent time east of Spadina or west of Rosebury Road and remained respectable or "safe" either, though that, of course, had never been proved.

Inside that self-imposed ghetto (for that's what it was) we grew up in the Forties and Fifties, "spoiled Forest Hill snobs" as we were known on the outside, the children of the children of immigrants from Russia and Eastern Europe. Our grandparents still spoke Yiddish and went to orthodox synagogues and suffered often silently that their children were taking on the contours of this WASP land, becoming Canadians and maybe not Jews so much any more, while their grandchildren, me, for instance, slept through Sunday-morning classes at Holy Blossom Temple and never learned either Hebrew or Yiddish or much of anything Jewish except that six million of us had died in Europe. The day that knowledge burned through my head I wrote my first heroic adolescent poem about Jewish girls my age (of course) who had chosen to die rather than be "used" and I cried with shame and disbelief and finally terror over my desk in my parents' mansion on Rosemary Lane (what a name) with the all-Canadian pennants (FHCI rah-rah) pinned up on the walls.

My friends and I knew the scars of that knowledge were permanent and since we could neither assimilate it emotionally nor understand it any other way in the context of our privileged lives, we tacitly agreed to forget. Years later I stumbled through a guided tour of a concentration camp, images flattening themselves against a picture screen inside my head.

I am sipping Spanish sherry in the warmth of my parents' living room beside a bright fire; the curved back of my armchair encircles me, caressing; a hatted Renoir child aglow in rich reds and blues smiles down at me from her place on the wall; a bell tinkles. Dinner is served. We stop to gape at the camp dissection tablet — god — it's a huge well and tree platter, the one my mother serves meat on; they have brought me back from the showers, blood, my blood, swirls along silver canals into a deep well; mother smiles at me, scoops up the juices with a curved silver spoon; later, the meat will be incinerated.

I make a first real connection between the child of Forest Hill and the collective past of every Jew. I am twenty-two years old.

After a few years of marriage, my grandmother was left alone to raise five children in this strange country whose language she did not speak and only barely understood. She did people's sewing and her boys sold newspapers, and when the oldest one finished school and went to work, the others were able to continue. My father was skinny, shy and determined. He became a chartered accountant and won the Ontario gold medal that year but remained jobless until the only Jewish firm in Toronto took him in. He did very well and moved from Havelock Street where we wintered with my grandmother and from the summer cabin on Centre Island (Jews were asked to leave) to Walmer Road near Casa Loma where I attended Hillcrest Public School. My Grade 2 teacher (a hateful bag, as I recall) evidently filled my head with stories of Jesus Christ. My parents panicked (assimilation loomed spectre-like, they did not see it had already overtaken them) and withdrew to the warm uterine closeness of Forest Hill, which not only boasted the best school system in Canada in the Forties but celebrated both Christmas and Hanukkah. (A Jewish child would play Mary, a gentile child would play Judah Maccabee; later at Holy Blossom Temple we would sing, "We'll soon be one world.")

I guess the school was good enough, though all I remember of those early years was my Grade 6 teacher who taught us the word "potential" in vocabulary class. There was also the microcosmic capitalism of the schoolyard where wholesale buyers and sellers in the marble business bargained and shouted at each other. "Three alleys here," sang the retail vendors, tempting skeptical customers, "from the second line." Once in a while a rich philanthropist who had suddenly tired of his glittering wealth would climb the steps of the outside fire escape and announce a scramble; then all commerce would cease as it rained biggies, peewees and puries.

My family, though *nouveau riche* like everyone else, remained puritanical in outlook. My mother was a pianist and preferred concerts and books to coiffures and coffee klatches. My father hadn't forgotten the hard years. I couldn't have many clothes for fear I might become a "clotheshorse", a dreaded affliction, I was led to understand.

We talked a lot at the dinner table. Between gulps, my father would give us vocabulary tests and ask us to act out different emotional states. ("How would you mime joy, sorrow, pain, surprise?") Sometimes he would read aloud from American plays or Orwell's *Animal Farm* and orchestrate conversations in which everyone, including my five- and six-year-old brother and sister, was expected to have an opinion. That was fun, and I grew up loving "discussions" though being "on" so much of the time was often intolerable. Literature was an integral part of our lives and I just assumed it was for everyone else. I listened to stories at the public library long before I could read. My father loved to make up fairy tales with permanent characters and serialized episodes and when I was still a baby he would use them to get me to eat. "Just as the slimy crocodile slithered toward the beautiful princess who was struggling to free herself from the net.... " My eyes would widen, my mouth would open, and in would pop a spoonful of spinach.

Like many Village families, my parents cared deeply about child-rearing, and in their zeal I was raised according to the psychology textbook and was expected, somehow, to conform to the "norms" for my age. I remember reading Gesell's *The Child From Five To Ten* and shouting to my parents when I discovered how "normal" I was. Whew! There was little room for individual differences in that philosophy; normal adolescent pursuits of "finding out who you were" were tacitly discouraged. (What if you found out you were the wrong person?) Education in my family was an ongoing process. Now I feel lucky I had it. Then I wished I could relax.

Forest Hill parents believed in education, though I didn't know another family quite like mine. My friends' parents were mostly articulate, confident (in their own space), and the Home and School Association became a formidable pressure group that teachers respected and dealt with out of necessity. Education had a lot to do with making money and status — a passkey to the outside world — but it wasn't just that. Intellectual excellence was also worthwhile in itself. In Europe, the scholars, the men of the

Torah, were the most highly respected of men, and in Forest Hill, even among the kids of my generation, it was okay to be smart in school. (In other neighborhoods, top students were considered finks.) Outside school, we learned liberal humanistic values. Why, right in the Holy Blossom prayer book it said, "As Thou hast redeemed Israel ... so mayest Thou redeem all who are oppressed and persecuted." We grew up with a strong feeling for the underdog (though purely theoretical and never tested) and when the black civil rights movement came along, we felt it deeply.

I always admired the liberalism of the community, quite emotionally, in fact, but sometimes it became absurd. In the Sixties, Stokely Carmichael came to Toronto to raise money. In an enormous Forest Hill home he talked to a sympathetic audience about growing black anger. Rumors of militant black anti-Semitism hung in that room, heavy and unspoken. White uniformed catering ladies passed tidbits; Carmichael passed a hat ("cheques will be fine"). Then someone asked for the mike and said it. Everyone looked embarrassed. The men signed the cheques. Last year I listened to René Lévesque tell a Holy Blossom audience why the Québécois must separate. A hundred hearts beat in sympathy. Rumors of Québécois anti-Semitism hung there, heavy and unspoken. Someone took a floor mike and said it. The audience murmured a bit, and many hissed the questioner. Liberalism is a fine tradition that no one wants to abandon.

Our lives in the Forties and Fifties were insular and "unreal" — unconnected to the WASP reality of Toronto, unconnected to the rural reality of Canada. We knew almost nothing beyond the Village, the downtown department stores where we'd sometimes wander on Saturday afternoons and charge clothes to our fathers' accounts, and the bits of northern Ontario where we summered and wondered at the people who stayed there after Labor Day. Our grandparents had moved to Canada, to Ontario, to Toronto, to Forest Hill, caught in a spin of ever-narrowing concentric circles until we, their children, were pin-pointed, wriggling, then paralyzed and out of touch. Our parents did not settle this land, feel its earth, grow crops out of its blackness; they did other things. They stimulated business in its towns and enriched its intellectual and cultural life. Within Forest Hill they hoped we would never know the hardship and pain that had touched other generations. But we grew as hothouse flowers and more than one of us has had trouble "outside" — unable to go back, never quite making it elsewhere.

"I'm writing about growing up in the Village," I recently told an old friend. "We didn't," she said.

I first left the ghetto when I was fifteen to take a summer job that struck my friends as unusual. I worked in the kitchen at Sunnybrook Hospital. I met girls who were there because they had to work. They were very different. Their teeth didn't flash silver bands implanted there to work silently day and night, correcting, perfecting, and they didn't lope confidently or move their bodies the way my friends did. I had a boyfriend called Ronnie who was eighteen and he used to drive me home sometimes, and my working friends, too. One day we had an argument and Ronnie took me home first. I knew the girls musn't see my Rosemary Lane home. I spoke to him, feeling quite desperate, but he didn't hear. I was right. Their mouths fell open — they hadn't known — and it wasn't the same at work from then on.

My friends were inordinately interested in clothes, encouraged by their mothers who were grooming them as poised and beautiful Jewish Princesses (it must be said) from an early age. I was a Jewish Princess, too, in my own way. I was small and I suppose I was "cute" and vivacious, because I became a cheerleader and danced in school shows and did all those Fifties things which meant, naturally, that I was popular with the boys. Jewish Princesses didn't "go all the way". Neither did other teenage girls in the Fifties, but Jewish Princesses had to "save" themselves to hook Mr. Right who would be a doctor or a lawyer if you played your cards right, or a rich businessman if you weren't so classy. Mr. Right also expected purity and spent his wild young seed on "shiksas" (gentile girls, definitely not Princesses) which was okay with everyone, but if a Princess dated a "shaygitz" (gentile boy, definitely not a Prince) she indeed shocked the community.

The boys "respected" the girls from the Village and mostly we played those demi-virgin petting games until we were sick with guilt and desire (will he think I'm cheap?). Respect was a funny thing. I had one friend called Bob who had a reputation for having lots of experience. He took me out off and on for several years and never tried a kiss, though I knew he liked me. One evening we had a bit to drink and we sat in his car and talked for a long time. The next day he called and in hushed tones asked me if he'd done anything "wrong".

Princesses were not to be toppled from their thrones.

I was eleven years old when I entered junior high school and plunged into a flurry of social activity for which I was quite un-prepared. We had Friday-night dances at FHJH. We also had tea dances at noon. In 1950, the style was long skirts, but my crowd of eleven- and twelve-year-olds wore their skirts two inches longer than anyone else. So it went with everything. When we weren't having school dances we had Temple dances and I went to my first formal ball when I was thirteen.

My boyfriends shot around in their fathers' cars and had lots of money, and by age seventeen I was already bored with the Royal York Ballroom, the Cork Room, the Old Mill, the Colonial and most of the other so-called glamor spots of the city. I was also bored with staid formal dances and preliminary "coketail parties" (how we aped our parents), and I still have a closet full of those pink, frothy strapless dresses that I eventually conned my parents into buying.

Thursday evenings we would go to the sneak preview at the old movie theatre on Spadina Road. After school and on weekends, we would hang out at the Egg or the Townhouse on Eglinton, and the kids from Vaughan Collegiate or Oakwood or the boys from further south (with an eye on upward mobility) would happen by. We'd stroll by those shops that sold overpriced everything from bananas to gilded china and we'd sometimes pass our parents who were strolling, too. There was and still is a family feeling on the north side of Eglinton between Bathurst Street and what is now the Spadina Expressway pit. When someone double-parked to run in for a dozen bagels he knew that the car he'd boxed in also belonged to a Jew who was probably in that same store *eating* bagels. There'd be no "what do you think you are doing blocking my car" scene with alien WASP accents. Eglinton was safe if you didn't venture too far.

Most of us wanted to get married. Period. I never thought much about my life beyond my wedding day, that magical moment of supreme joy (and glory) when all adolescent miseries would be settled forever. Many of my friends did marry Princes and they settled down to the serious business of bearing children, buying a home in the Village or the suburbs (more of the same) and joining the Temple as young adult families. Some "escaped" by moving to Rosedale, that alternate bastion of privilege. A few of the boys dreamed of becoming writers and drinking absinthe in Montparnasse à la Hemingway. Some did. We liked ideas and talked endlessly, but careers and dreams were not encouraged in

Village girls. We were educated, yes, but almost never in the professions. A solid liberal education would prepare us to become good mothers to our children. We bought that mostly (some years later I held my new-born in my arms and played Beethoven's Ninth Symphony for her benefit). But I was vaguely troubled through four years of university. Was this so I could nurse babies and prepare dinners and please my man in bed once I had "graduated"? It made me cynical; it made me feel unreal. My education was preliminary (irrelevant?) to what was to be my "real" life, the final packaging of the product. It never connected me with the outside world.

I wanted a husband, too, but the conventions of Princes and Temple membership and the suburbs terrified me. Parachute into the vortex of the circle and erase all the outer lines so that even the memory of escape becomes a vague, once-held notion. Harden, darken, become brittle there, a tiny dot in the centre of forgotten thoughts. No. I went to Paris "for a year of postgraduate French", met a French Catholic and brought him back to Forest Hill where I married him at Holy Blossom in full view of the community before I returned with him to France.

I made a lousy expatriate. Forest Hill hadn't prepared me for life outside the Village, let alone a foreign country. My first year in France I became obsessed with concentration camps, with anti-Semitic graffiti on the walls of the Metro, with acquaintances who asked me why the Jews killed Christ, with sickness and alienation. I stayed and I stayed. Then I came home.

Ten years have passed and I'm once again living on the outskirts of the Village. I tell myself that I'm here because the rent is low, but it is really home I seek. I do some of my shopping on Eglinton, sometimes I buy bagels. I keep meeting the girls I went to school with, at the bank, at the grocery store, the ones who didn't leave. They look the way I remember their mothers. Their hair is perfectly groomed, their clothes exquisite. They winter in Florida and summer at the cottage or in Europe. Their kids sit in Sunday-morning classes at Holy Blossom and go to camp in northern Ontario. They live all around me, these girls I knew. When the Sixties happened they hesitated because they were young, then they turned against "youth" and were middle-aged.

I'm back, in touch with my roots, faced with the familiar ambivalence that will not go away. Still attracted to the rich emotional qualities of my people, to their warmth, their humor, still drawn by the comfort of predictability, aware that this indeed is home. Still disturbed by an unbearable provincialism in which every subject is reduced to its lowest common denominator ("Is it good for the Jews?"), still repelled by the smug features of excess. I may not stay for long — but on down days, it's still "safe" on Eglinton Avenue.

Larry Zolf

BOIL ME NO MELTING POTS, DREAM ME NO DREAMS

When the fathers of Confederation built this country in 1867, there was universal agreement among *all* Canadians, English- and French-speaking, that there was no place for the American Dream on the northern half of this continent. In 1776 we embraced the United Empire Loyalists and rejected George Washington's Revolutionary Army by force of arms. We booted Uncle Sam in the pants in 1812 and slapped his wrists in the Fenian Raids of the 1880s. We rejected slavery and provided sanctuary for American Negroes fleeing that "peculiar institution".

We rejected republicanism, the American idea that the people in and of themselves can shape their own ends and destinies. We countered Jacksonian democracy with the responsible government of a constitutional monarchy and made it plain to our southern neighbours that there were higher forces shaping our destinies than the untutored rabble of the untouched West. And while we did agree with the Yankee that life and liberty were inseparable, we differed in our pursuit of happiness. In Canada, that pursuit didn't necessarily entail *égalité* and *fraternité*. We flatly rejected the American egalitarianism of the Western frontier and the American fraternity of the melting pot.

Canada was conservative country, the land of particularity. The entity known as Anglo-Saxon British Canada was prepared to tolerate the particularity of French Canada and the Slavic-German-Jewish-Oriental particularities of the Golden West, provided all accepted the British monarchy, the British connection, the British rules of the British game as the *summum bonum* underlying all these particularities.

This, then, was the lay of this land in the year 1926 when an obscure ex-Tzarist draft-dodger and ex-infantryman in Alexander Kerensky's Revolutionary Army decided to emigrate to these shores. That dashing, mustachioed, bulbous-nosed Polack of the Judaic persuasion was none other than Yoshua Falek Zholf, son of Reb Yisroael Zholf, husband to Freda Rachel Zholf, father to Meyer, Reisel, and Judith Zholf, and father-to-be to son-to-be yours truly.

My father was a dreamer. In his youth he dreamed of a Russia where life and liberty were inseparable, where a Jew could freely pursue happiness. In 1914 he was a draft-dodger, moving from city to city and village to village.

When the Tzar was toppled in February, 1917 and Alexander Kerensky proclaimed liberty and equality, my father came out of hiding, drafted his own personal revolutionary manifesto, and presented it to a recruiting officer in Kerensky's army. It read:

> To the Russian Revolutionary Army:
> Dear Sirs: Whereas, I, Falek Zholf, have hitherto refused to shed my blood for the bloody Tzar Nikolai the Second, enemy of my people, and, whereas, the great Revolution has freed my people, and all other peoples that inhabit Mother Russia, I today present myself in payment of my holy debt of loyalty to my fatherland.

My father's revolutionary dreams of brotherhood quickly came to naught. He was sickened by Kerensky's execution of soldiers with Bolshevik sympathies, sickened by Bolshevik execution of nationalists, and soon he and his family were threatened by the vicious anti-Semitism of the Polish government of Pilsudski and Sikorski.

Still my father continued to dream. There was the pastoral dream of life on the land in communion with the sky and the stars and all that, but the Polish government took his land away. There was the dream of pioneering in Palestine, but the Zionists wanted only single men. There was the dream of America, the new homeland of his three brothers, but the goddess Liberty had shut her eyes and gates to Europe's teeming, huddled masses.

Suddenly along came Canada, the British colony that dreamed no dreams and offered Pa, the peasant, a chance to join the Gallician garlic-eaters that were cultivating the flatlands of the Canadian Golden West.

All this is by way of introduction to a fundamental confusion in my father's life which led to a subsequent fundamental confusion in my life. My father ultimately drifted into Winnipeg and renewed an occupation he once pursued secretly in Poland at some risk to his own life — the teaching of Jewish liberal-socialist values to Jewish children. He became first a teacher and then the principal of the Isaac Loeb Peretz Folk School in Winnipeg. This school was a branch of a school system and school curriculum with central headquarters in New York City.

Herein lay the rub. My father, unaware of all the trouble Sir John A. and the Fathers had gone to, just naturally assumed that Canada was part of the American Dream. His admission to this country he regarded as a miracle. He looked on Canada as a place where Americans sent people they didn't really want to have *now* but might take in later on, provided that while here they were always on good behaviour. In a sense, he regarded Canada as America's Australia — a temporary penal colony for temporary undesirables.

As my father's English was not very good and his reading material was strictly confined to Yiddish books and newspapers that came from New York, it was not surprising that Pop soon came to regard Winnipeg as just another borough of Gotham-on-the-Hudson.

The more he read his New York Yiddish newspapers the more he got excited by the American Dream! Who could blame him? The New York paper told of Jewish wonders that poor old Pop could scarcely have imagined in the dreary Polish village that was once his home. Not only could Jews own land in the U.S.A., but, miracle of miracles, wonder of wonders, Jews were actually trusted in America. In the Soviet Union they were purging Trotsky, Kamenev, and Zenoviev. In America they were electing Herbert Lehman governor of New York State. Didn't Roosevelt have a Morgenthau in his cabinet? Weren't Felix Frankfurter, Sam Rosenman, and Ben Cohen FDR's bosom buddies? America was indeed the land of milk and honey; its streets were paved with Jews.

It was natural, almost proper, that my father should have passed the American Dream on to me, his youngest and the first to be born on the very soil of Canada-America. Until I was thirteen years old, I was enrolled in the day school section of the Isaac Loeb Peretz Folk School. My father was my teacher. There I learned to read from a Yiddish Dick and Jane, Max and Molly primer. It was in Yiddish that I first read *Huckleberry Finn*, *Tom Sawyer*, and *Moby Dick*. For extra grabbers my father threw in a Jewish *Children's History of the Life and Times of Eugene V. Debs*, *The Life and Times of Samuel Gompers*, and *The Life and Times of Emma Goldman*. At the tender age of nine, I knew that Franklin D. Roosevelt was God the Father, David Dubinsky of the International Ladies Garment Workers' Union was God the Son, and Sidney Hillman of the Amalgamated Clothing Workers of America was God the Holy Ghost.

At the tender age of twelve, I won my first essay contest. The subject was Statue of Liberty poetess Emma Lazarus, as described by the then Wunderkind of Winnipeg, borough of Manhattan, in these immortal words: "Emma Lazarus was not only a daughter of Israel but a daughter of the world." The next year I capped my success with a bar mitzvah speech triumph that extolled the virtues of Meyer Levin, bombardier on Captain Colin Kelly's *Spirit of America* and the only Jew decorated for bravery at Pearl Harbor. Knowing a good thing when I saw it, I spoke these immortal words: "Meyer Levin was not only a son of Israel; he was a son of America."

And so was I. As I listened in my teens to my father telling horror stories of gas ovens and lamp shades and watched his heart slowly breaking as the news drifted in of the death of his entire family overseas, it was nice, almost comforting, to cast my eyes south of the border. There I could thrill to the athletic exploits of Barney Ross and Hank Greenberg. I could drool at the succulent beauty of Bess Myerson, Miss America, 1946. I could cry tomorrow with Lillian Roth and call my house a home with Polly Adler.

I can remember staying up all night with the old man, crying and cheering as Harry Truman, who gave us Israel, was given four more years. In high school I defended America in the Korean War and argued that the West Germans were good and the East Germans bad. In college, NATO was groovy, the Marshall Plan divine, McCarthyism a minor aberration.

Today, as I reflect on the validity of my American Dream then and now, a certain sense of nostalgic silliness seems to overtake me. I can understand the validity of the American Dream for my father. In the bitter anti-Semitism of Tzarist Russia and Sikorski's Poland, he was considered sub-human. In Auschwitz and Dachau, he and his fellow Jews were not human at all. In the American melting pot, he was not only human; he was an involved participant, an equal.

As my father saw the American Dream, to be Jewish and human was to be American. Today as I see the American Dream operating in black America and yellow Vietnam, I am forced to conclude that somehow to be *really* human is to be neither Jewish nor American. Today the Jewish community in America is indeed a participant and more than an equal in the power elite of white America. The Jews are close to the top in education, affluence, status. But to black America the Jew is as much whitey as anyone else. The lessons of persecution and humiliation that the Jew picked up on his way to affluence and success he is not prepared to pass on to the Negro way, way below. The American Jew lives in a white neighbourhood, worships in a white, cavernous temple, eats white kosher Chinese food at white Chinese restaurants, has white directors for his white bar mitzvah movies. He likes it that way and is sure *everyone* will understand.

Having richly benefited from the American Dream, he is eager to pass the message, not the benefits, to those less fortunate people abroad. The patriotism of today's American Jewry is awesomely wholesome. American-style democracy has been good for the teeming, huddled Jewish masses. How can it help but be good for the teeming, huddled masses of Vietnam? Our Hebrew boy, Walt Whitman Rostow, is today's Emma Lazarus, offering Lyndon Johnson in true Statue of Liberty style as sanctuary to the misguided peasants of South-east Asia. Our Hebrew boy, Dr. Edward Teller, Pop to the H-bomb, is today's real-life Dr. Sivana, just itching to say "Shazam" and watch the world disappear.

I must admit that my stomach feels queasy when I hear Nicholas Katzenbach and Dean Rusk gloating over the Viet Cong kill toll, the damned dead of American-style democracy. And I must admit to a similar type of queasiness when I hear Jews gloating over Arab losses in the Six-Day War, the damned dead of Zionist-style democracy, even though I know you shouldn't compare the two and that Nasser will fry me whenever he gets the chance. I also feel queasy whenever I hear bigots, Birchers, and Lubor Zinks praising to the skies the Jewish victory over "Arab communism".

It saddens me to see how the American Dream and the melting pot have coarsened and vulgarized my racial confrères. The gentleness of East European Jewish Hassidism, the sweet music of the soft, humane Yiddish culture is no longer there. I guess I prefer the schlemiel wisdom of Gimpel the Fool to the Sammy Glick-shtick of Norman Podhoretz. I'd rather walk the crooked, narrow streets of Chagall's shtetl than drive through Forest Hills or Shaker Heights.

That brings me to the lay of this land in 1968. Canada has not yet bought the American Dream. It's still conservative country, the land of particularity. I know the Hebrew particularity ain't quite as yet the equal of other particularities. I know that living here is still a trip backwards in the time tunnel.

Still, I'm glad to be here and to be a Canadian, whatever that word means. I'd rather be somewhat of an outsider in Canada than an equal, accepted participant in the American nightmare.

I am aware that we have avoided American pitfalls more by accident than by design. I realize that we don't have America's responsibilities and therefore her problems. Well, huzzah, I'm glad we don't and to hell with the reasons.

Huzzah, we're not in Vietnam. Huzzah, we won't go there. Huzzah, we never will. Huzzah, we have no Watts-Newark-Detroit.

Huzzah, we don't intend to build them.

I'm also aware that my country is in a state of disarray and flux. The old order is crumbling, and all institutions are open to criticism and review. I like that. In my own little way, here in Canada I can be a minor revolutionary, albeit a gutless one, a sort of chicken-hearted Trotsky.

I know that my country has not quite made up its mind about what it wants to be. It has ceased being British and, thankfully, has not yet become American. If there is anything still valid to the British heritage left us by the Fathers of Confederation, let it be this:

Let the country continue to be a land of un-American activities. Boil me no melting pots and dream me no dreams. Worry not, rumour has it that God is Dead. If so, he can't bless America.

Avi Boxer

NO ADDRESS

I am late.
I have missed the wedding.
My father descends
the synagogue stairs
with my dead mother
veiled in white.

What shall I do?
I cannot cross the street.
The trafficlights will not change.
The snow falls like confetti.
They do not see me.
I shout.
They do not hear me.
Gone.

A talith of snow
slips from a branch
over my shoulders.
My hands tremble,
open before me,
like a prayerbook.

A patrol car stops.
A policeman questions me,
discovers
I have no address.

Helen Weinzweig

HOLD THAT TIGER

The blue slip inside my envelope directed me, this year, to a
converted warehouse on Harbour Street. I hadn't been in Toronto
for years and looked forward to seeing old landmarks in the city
where I was born. For the occasion I bought a grey suit, a new shirt
and tie. All the employees, all 53,969 of us, all over the world, must
take the Company's ADAPT exam: Annual Development and Ad-
vancement Program Test. The objective of Personnel, we have been
assured, is entirely a paternal one, stemming from the Company's
interest in each and every one of its workers: It wants to know
merely that we are happy in our work and leading productive lives.

I entered a doorway beside a Scandinavian furniture store. I
ascended four flights of stairs so narrow I had to let my arms hang
lest I bump an elbow. Three men preceded me; a woman was
behind me; we were ten minutes ahead of the hour. I followed the
procedures of those in front; she would do the same when I was
finished. A handprint on the door caused it to open. We entered
singly, allowing the door to click shut each time. In my turn, I stood
in the exact centre of a long empty corridor, with a single window at
each end. In front of me was a plexiglass box mounted on a beam. I
stood before it and spoke my Social Insurance Number, whereupon
a card was ejected. It had the same number I had just voiced,
together with the letter M and the number 6. I held the card and
looked around for M and 6. I saw a forest of plywood partitions,
stained brown, arranged in such a way as to appear as a classical
maze. Rats and rewards came instantly to mind. Here and there in
the labyrinthine entrances and exits a letter and a number appeared. Great confusion set in as dozens of us searched for our
places. By the time I found my letter and number and sat down in
my cubicle, I was in a sweat.

The Minotaur in this labyrinth was a large writing pad with
yellow sheets, lined. Every page had my Social Insurance Number
printed at the top right-hand corner. Instructions were on the cover:
Answer the following questions in strict numerical order, starting
with Number 1 and ending with Number 10. Refrain from giving
false or misleading information: Replies will be verified by Person-

nel. No partial answers. No equivocation. No talking or consorting
with other candidates. A box lunch will be provided at 1200 hours.
A bell will ring for breaks at 1000 and at 1430 hours. Remember
your aisle and seat number. Good luck.

Although the partitions were only about five feet high they were
three feet off the floor, so that you could not see over them. Anyone
wishing to check on us could peer under the partitions and see
pairs of feet at desks. But, of course, that would not be necessary. It
came to me that the fire sprinklers, located overhead between the
fluorescent lights, were not all vertical: Some were pointed at angles
and their ends were closed off with a shiny, black material. These
were cameras.

In each cubicle were two desks facing in opposing directions,
against the partitions, so that we sat back to back. I was curious to
know who shared my part of the maze but did not dare turn around.
I dropped my pen. I went down on all fours, pretending to search,
and saw a woman's slim legs from under a black skirt, her ankles
locked around her chair. She was already writing rapidly, a cheek
resting against her left palm.

All ten questions were printed on the first (unlined) page.
Quickly I read them, as I had at school, to test my knowledge against
that of my inquisitor. But these questions were unlike any in the
past. Their purpose was not clear; there was no logical sequence.
A sense of desperation came over me; I would spend the day providing answers for a computer. For some reason, today, I could not
bring my mind to address itself again to a machine. I shall imagine
that you, young woman scribbling away behind my back, will be the
reader of my words. I will talk to you.

Question 1: Do you have any obsessions that are likely to interfere
with your daily duties?
Answer: There are certain preferences I have that, I suppose, have
become obsessive. But since these inclinations, as I prefer to think
of them, are part of my daily life outside of my time with the
Company, they do not interfere with my work. I do have certain
fixed habits: I shave with a strop razor; all my socks are black, even
the two pair I wear inside my jogging shoes; I eat my salad last; the
top sheet of my bed must be securely tucked in at the foot, tucked
in all the way up the far side and halfway up on the near side; I
use shirt cardboards for telephone numbers, holding them together
with three loose-leaf metal rings. The foregoing are examples of a

few routine habits, but since I am not given to unreasonable behavior, further cataloguing would be of no interest.

On second thought, I do have one obsession — at least everyone has called it that. No one must touch, that is, move in any way, my three toy replicas on my desk.

Question 2: Are you afraid of any of the following: Mice, Lice. A man's arm around your shoulder. A woman's screams.
Answer: All of the above. I am terrified of mice and rats. In the places we lived there were always mice and sometimes rats. I hid under the blanket for fear of the rats I heard all night, even in my sleep. I keep my hair cut as short as possible, a crewcut it's called, because of my fear of lice. In Grade 2 I was accused of having brought lice into the classroom. My head was covered with them, the nurse said. I had to have my head shaved. If anything in my life could be deemed to be obsessive, it is the fear of a man's arm about my shoulder. This had to do with a policeman holding me back from running to my mother who was being taken away, screaming.

There was the sound of a bell, a lovely, light tone, the kind one hears in a temple. It was the first break. I turned my head to the left, in the direction of the exit from our cell (I have come to think of this cubicle as our cell), pretending to be ruminating on the next question, but hoping to catch a glimpse of my companion. I listened intently. In the silence I could hear the hum of the air conditioner, the occasional cough or clearing of a throat. She sighed a long, drawn-out sigh, but did not go out. Visions of an Ariadne, of a young and beautiful princess, whose perfume even now reached me, who would love me at sight and lead me safely out of the labyrinth — thoughts of an impossible love distracted me from the real business.

Question 3: The psychological profile established by Personnel indicates that you have been in the past, and most of the time still are, a steady, intelligent and productive employee; at other times, most markedly since the 1964 Select Employees' Conference in Amsterdam, your profile graphs are erratic. Can you account for the variations in performance?
Answer: In the fifteen years I have been with the Company I have tried to be a loyal worker. Above all, I have tried to be honest and truthful. But my work has gone unnoticed. Moreover, I am often called in to elucidate what did I mean by this memo, that letter or

some phone call. Soon after my third ADAPT exam I was transferred to the Leamington office. About a year later I became aware that my telephone doodles were being taken out of the wastebasket while I was in the washroom; that my brown paper bag containing my lunch was being opened and the contents examined; a typist from the typists' pool would bring a tape recorder instead of a notebook. The following year I was moved from the front office to a windowless inside room.

At home our usually convivial evenings were spent in the exchange of monosyllables. We slept back to back. My wife sensed that our difficulties were due to my work and began to ask questions. I said very little because I am not in the habit of taking anyone into my confidence. This is due, perhaps, to the fact that I have always had to fight my own battles. Just the same she used her considerable intelligence to put together a picture of frustration. She thought I ought to protest such cavalier treatment. I said, "So long as I am being paid by the Company I have no right to object." In reply, she quoted Ambrose Bierce: "Fidelity is a virtue peculiar to those who are about to be betrayed." But to whom should I complain and of what specifically? Then I hit upon a solution, the exercise of which accounts, possibly, for the changes in my graph.

When I was in my early teens, my foster mother used to say, Never lie: A liar becomes a thief, a thief becomes a murderer! Images of being hanged, drawn and quartered; images of my hands being cut off; images of being seated in a chair with wires to my shaved head; images that made me resolve never to tell a lie.

There are people who believe that Truth, like Time and Space, is relative. I say, tell that to the boy in the orphanage who lines up for adoption, his face aching from the smile he holds. That boy knows Truth Absolute.

Still, to live is to manipulate the truth. For myself, I devised a system of compromise. On Tuesday, Thursday and Saturday I always tell the truth as I see it. Those are the days with the accusatory "u's" in them. On those days I face the memory of my foster mother's troubled eyes. You, they blaze, are lying! At the end of each Tuesday, Thursday or Saturday I feel cleansed. I am at peace. But on Monday, Wednesday and Friday I suspend the truth. I dissemble, hedge, misrepresent, evade, disguise the facts. I sometimes lie outright. Paradoxically, it is often on a Monday, Wednesday or Friday that I am invited out for a drink after work by my superior.

In this manner a balance is struck between conscience and

necessity. A flexibility in regard to Truth may appear as instability on my psychological profile.

Do you think, young woman in our cell, I have been prolix? But Saturday is truth day and I must adhere to some principle, even one of my own invention. Incidentally, just between us, do you not find it reprehensible that this annual exam is held on our, not the Company's, time...?

Question 4: Did you report in sick this past year? If so, how long were you absent and what was the nature of your illness?
Answer: On May 22 (it was a Wednesday) I had the apartment super phone the office to say that I had a sore throat and fever and could not come in to work. I took that time off in order to see an old friend. I had read in the newspaper that Frederick Childerhouse would be in Toronto for a few days to negotiate a takeover. I couldn't get through to him on the telephone, even with person-to-person calls. Finally I dialled direct, whatever the cost, and told three secretaries that I was a reporter from *The Globe and Mail* wanting an interview for the front page of the business section. Fred called me back. I heard that hollow echo one gets from one of those phone arrangements where there is no receiver to hold against the ear: One speaks into the air while facing a machine on the desk, and it, the machine, replies into the room. It said, Jack, you old son-of-a-gun, how are you? I could tell he was pleased as punch to hear from me. It invited me to lunch the next day.

I took my time getting ready, choosing a tie carefully. I even went to the bank so that I could face Fred with money in my pocket.

We lunched at the Toronto Club. I liked the hushed atmosphere, the dark, polished wood, the heavy silver, the obsequious service. Fred said he would have known me anywhere. I said he hadn't changed at all, except for a little grey at the temples. His hair was thick, his frame lean. He was as handsome as I remembered him. Just a few thin red veins down the sides of his nose were the only signs of the attrition of time.

Mostly we spoke of the decision we had made, solemnly and ceremoniously, to deliberately fail our last year in Jarvis Collegiate. Neither of us knew then how to change our lot in life: his being to go to the university and success; and mine to go to work and uncertainty. That last year of high school Fred played drums in a jazz cellar and I went to hear him. Sometimes I took Rose-Lynn with me. Fred remembered her.

"She liked you. She liked you a lot. I thought for sure you two would wind up getting married," he recalled.

"Rose-Lynn was sent away to school in Switzerland at the end of our last year at Jarvis," I told him. "I never saw her again."

"In those days...," he began, then fell silent. After a while he said, "I haven't picked up a pair of sticks since I graduated."

By three in the afternoon he was telling me about his two marriages, the two divorces and how he manages to keep in touch with each of his eight children.

In my turn, I told him about Vivian; that like myself she felt alone in the world; that we got married three months after we met at the Adult Resources Centre.

"She died in childbirth, eight years ago," I said simply.

Our visit ended with pleasantries but with no reference to the future.

As to the "nature of your illness" ... I suppose it could be termed a kind of sickness, this persistent illusion that somehow I would be transformed from a clerk in Leamington, riding on the Number 18 bus daily, into one of Fred's vice-presidents flying on the Concorde.

Question 5: Upon hearing a dance beat that goes: *tee*-dum-dum, *tee*-dum-dum, *tee*-dum-dum, *tee*-dum-dum; and upon receiving instructions and diagrams that indicate dance steps, *one*-two-back, *one*-two-side, *one*-two-back, *one*-two-side — would you:

(a) Do the fox trot or the cha-cha?

(b) We have in our files a photograph of you holding a dance trophy and shaking hands with Trump Davidson at the Palace Pier in 1948. Explain.

Answer: (a) I no longer dance.

(b) Through Fred I became interested in, then addicted to, jazz. I discovered I could dance as naturally as I could breathe. Every Saturday night Rose-Lynn and I went dancing at the Palace Pier. She was slight, blonde and, like me, lived to dance. I was eighteen, she was sixteen. So well-matched were we that other dancers would stop to watch us. Our favorite dance, which became our contest number, was *Tiger Rag*. And when the trombone repeated *Hold That Ti-ger!* over and over, we charged down the length of the dance floor, returned to the bandstand in a variety of steps, and charged down again to the other end. Life could offer no more: I had a job and a beautiful dance partner; I won prizes.

Ah, my unknown love, I feel your concentration, your rigid spine behind me. Are you wondering, at this very instant, who cares about your replies? In all these years I have never discovered what happens to my print-outs. There has been no sign, ever, that I have made an impression on anyone. The man who, possibly, holds my future in his hands is someone not unlike myself, with a fresh haircut, clean shirt and a discreet tie. He reads with understanding and sympathy, as he recalls his own exam that took place recently or will take place soon. In my imagination he makes some sort of entry on my dossier, then passes it on, together with this print-out, to the next authority. It is my hope, dear colleague, that you fare better than I. Take your time; don't fret; do not attempt to influence the results: We reveal ourselves no matter what we say.

Question 6: Describe a community activity in which you have participated, the nature of your contribution and outline the relevance it had for you.
Answer: When I was twenty I lived in a rooming house on Clinton Street. There I was befriended by an older man, Wilhelm Schroeder. He was an idealist. He believed that the working class would one day own the means of production. He was editor and printer of a Marxist newspaper called *The New Proletarian*. Bill, as I called him, urged me to give up my job with the capitalist exploiter manufacturer. (His words.) That didn't take much persuasion because I worked in the factory basement as a shipper. For a while I was out of work, but Bill shared everything he had with me. We were like father and son. He gave me a present of his most precious possession, all that he had left of his childhood: toy miniatures of Hitler, Goering and Goebbels. Naturally I was startled at first — the verisimilitude was frightening. Bill noted my hesitation. He said that they were after all only toys; that he had spent many happy hours playing with them. I promised I would never part with them. You must understand that these replicas were the first gifts I had ever received. I see now that it is very important to face things that one is afraid of in order to conquer fear. But I digress.

I helped Bill set type. I also delivered copies of the paper. My territory was bounded by Bathurst and Dufferin, Bloor and King streets. One day a week I was stationed on the corner of Queen and

Spadina handing out leaflets. This community activity ended when Bill left for Montreal because his typewriter, filing cabinet and printing machine were smashed with axes by vandals one night. He claimed it was the work of communists.

For me, the relevance of this community activity was that I was offering hope with inspiration to the poor and the dispossessed.

Question 7: If you were a Company scout and had to stake out the Hotel Krasnapolsky in Amsterdam, would you disguise yourself as:
    (a) a waiter
        a salesman of Perrier
        a reporter covering the meeting of the Club of Rome
        other
    (b) Why?

This was going to take some thought. My fingers were cramped; I pulled them one by one. While I was deliberating on giving an honest answer to imagining myself as someone else, I became aware that a cart had stopped in the aisle beside us. I wondered if she knew the procedure for obtaining lunch. I stood up and tapped her on the shoulder. She turned, and I took advantage of the next moment to look into her face. She had a small nose and mouth and a broad forehead; large dark eyes and straight brows that almost met and which gave her a worried look. She smiled at me. I pointed to the sign on the robot: FOR LUNCH RAISE RIGHT HAND IN FRONT OF ELECTRONIC EYE MARKED "E". She did. The ticking sound was replaced by a whirring noise. She watched in fascination as a box lunch was deposited at the corner of her desk. Then it was my turn, and the arm released a box from its claw onto my desk.

I ate out of the cardboard box. A baloney sandwich on white bread; yellow mustard on the side; tiny yellow biscuits in the shape of fish and marked Goldfish, two to a package and two packages in the lunch; a piece of yellow cheese marked Colby and a white paper napkin. All were individually sealed in plastic. There was a can of pop called Fresh Up. I nibbled and considered. The question may have something to do with the 1964 meeting in Amsterdam. I was one of the specially chosen employees from the Company's worldwide plants and subsidiaries. Had we been infiltrated by an industrial spy? By the CIA? By the RCMP? Was I supposed to know something…?
Answer: (a) I would disguise myself as a reporter for a chain of

American newspapers and cover the meetings of the Club of Rome.

(b) Since I am experienced in the field of newspaper publication, I feel I would succeed in the guise of a reporter. I could have been a writer, everyone said so at school. At any rate, I have always read a great deal and am well-informed and could ask the correct questions. And since the Club of Rome produces large-scale computer studies, resulting in massive amounts of data, I am certain I could elicit information useful to the Company.

Question 8: Point out, briefly, which aspect of the Select Employees' Conference in 1964 you found to be most valuable to your career.
Answer: The second day's presentations and subsequent discussions on *Interdependence* were most illuminating. I realized then that each and every one of us in the Company performs a function vital to someone else. Without my input, another person cannot do his or her job.

They know. The fear of discovery has gnawed at my mind. I thought I was off the hook; no one ever said anything to me about that last day. Now I see that they have just been biding their time….

Ariadne, my love, are you at this very moment complying with simple requests that you tell them who your favorite movie stars are? What suggestions you have for the improvement of the food in the cafeteria? Perhaps you have hopes, illusions, desires. You think your answers will bring a recognition of your great potential. Beware. You are being lulled into a feeling that all is well at the palace. In time, should you work for the Company long enough, you will be asked questions that force you to dredge up the mold and the miasma from the dungeons. The computer is not only the confessor, but also the judge-executioner.

The bell sounds. You raise your head. Your chair scrapes. I see you leave. You walk briskly.

Question 9: When your wife stood in the doorway to the living room where you were sitting with the newspaper, and she stood there, half-turned to come into the room or half-turned to leave, and asked you, Do you love me? — what was your reply?
Answer: In my heedless youth, the question angered me. Perhaps because it confused me. I thought that everything pointed to my love for Vivian — I worked, I saved, I was faithful: I came home every night, ate, unbuckled and slept. On Monday, Wednesday and

Friday, I said, Of course I love you, my darling. On Tuesday, Thursday or Saturday, I had to tell her, I don't know what love is; perhaps it is only a chemical charge for the propagation of the species.

Ah, my Ariadne, you're back, your hair combed, lipstick renewed. You dare not look at me, you lower your eyes, you bump against your chair. As for me, I am not afraid to stare at you openly and frankly. I may even speak to you when we are finished. Nothing I do from now on will make any difference. The die is cast; my fate is sealed.

Question 10: Why are there no asides or soliloquies in Ibsen's play *Ghosts*?
Answer: Because the facts speak for themselves. The sins of the fathers. Sin. An illicit pleasure — once only — and the drama unfolds, inexorably, inevitably. No chorus of comments is necessary.

It was the last night of the 1964 Select Employees' Conference in Amsterdam. At dinner I sat beside Sam Milner of our Windsor plant. Just before coffee and the final lecture, we slipped outside for a breath of air.

We found ourselves on an old narrow street behind the hotel. We kept walking, stopping now and again to examine with fatal curiosity the displays in the "Love Shops". We also stopped in front of old houses, high and narrow, in whose ground-floor windows sat smiling women, beckoning. In one window, built over the street, sat a young blonde woman, knitting under a lamp, a ball of blue wool secured between her thighs. She looked like any housewife, resting on a chair with lace doilies, behind a sparkling window with starched curtains.

And while we strolled and gaped and poked one another and made lewd remarks like schoolboys, Vivian, a thousand miles away, alone in our house, went unexpectedly into labor. A mother fell at a bus stop and broke her wrist and did not reach her daughter in time.

Sam and I dared each other. It was the first time either of us had been in Europe. We went back down the street and bought prophylactics. And while the other 198 specially selected employees were sitting in the Hotel Krasnapolsky, being hectored on marketing methods, we entered the houses.

And while I was paying a stranger for the act of love, Vivian's dark head was tossing in agony. While I was exhausting myself on that compliant woman, the lifeblood of my wife was ebbing away. Vivian died. The baby died.

Back home, I picked up our wedding picture, my three toy figures and a few books and left everything behind.

Do you, Ariadne, hold the thread that will save me? The monster still stalks this labyrinth; he will not be slain: He is memory.

Tom Wayman

JEWS

A weird family to come from
like most families. And if you trace it back
you have to stop at the great-grandparents:
the most distant lives anyone remembers.
Behind them, only a few names
can be recalled.

Herschel, born in 1897
my father's mother's brother
remembers *his* father
Louis Altschuler, born 1859
in Russia, lived in Mglin
also known as Amlin.
Louis trained as a rabbi
but decided it was the rich
who ruled the synagogues.
So he gave it up and in 1899
emigrated to Bracebridge
Ontario, where he worked as a pedlar
carrying all the objects he sold door-to-door,
farmhouse-to-farmhouse, laid out and
wrapped in one huge square of cloth
gathered at the four corners and hoisted
onto his back. By 1904
he had saved enough to bring over
his wife and five children, including Herschel,
so he quit peddling as unsuitable
for a family man and worked
at a number of jobs
and moved to Barrie, and then in 1913
to Toronto, by this time with a sixth child.

Herschel remembers the other Jew in Bracebridge:
a man who made a living
by selling the labor of certain immigrants
for whom he translated, arranged jobs,

collected wages and provided bad housing
while taking a large percentage of what they earned.
Eventually one man protested
and roused up the others
so the labor broker fired the troublemaker.
But before he left, the broker
slipped money into his pocket
and then had him arrested for theft.
As the court needed a translator
one of Herschel's brothers was asked.
The broker went to Herschel's father
and appealed to him as a fellow Jew
to order his son to falsify the accused's story
during the trial. Herschel's father refused
saying *this*
is a matter of justice.
But later when the laborer was acquitted
and the broker himself charged,
Herschel's father would permit no word
to be translated against him.
After all, he said, he *is* a Jew.

And isn't this the idea of a family?
You don't want any member to cause harm to somebody else
but at the same time you don't want one of us hurt.

On the other side of my life
it was a similar pattern to get to North America.
My mother's mother, Margaret Matusov
was born near Vitebsk about 1870
and eventually married a carpenter.
They left Russia together,
spent six months in Berlin
and arrived in England about 1895
settling in Newcastle
until 1910, when Joseph left for Canada.
His wife and, by now, four children
went to Liverpool to wait
while he earned the passage money,
lost it gambling, and by 1912 had it again
and the whole family arrived in Toronto.

At every stage of these journeys: life
and death. Margaret's sister
a woman whose name no one I talked to recalls
was with the family as it waited in Liverpool
and met and married a man named Bailey, *Uncle Mushka*,
and stayed. Herschel identifies
an old photograph as one of his brothers
dead of T.B. in northern Ontario before the First World War.

So many people have become
just a name on a chart I made
or at most a few anecdotes and odd facts.
An important date in a life
shrinks from being a particular incident
on a certain day in one of the months
— a moment during which someone
was probably even aware of the weather —
to being just a reference to some hazy
approximate year.

And the family is dwindling: couples now mostly have
one or two children
moving apart on the map, and in their lives.

But is it only the words of a priest, or lines
on a form from the State, or the birth of a child
that can make a family? Over the decades
people have also tried religion and class,
race and the tribe. Myself
I think we have come to another kind of family.
Perhaps now it is just ourselves and our friends
— some of whom we like a lot, and others
we see as little as possible of like any unpleasant relative.

One list I have of my friends
includes a nurse, a seaman, a clerk,
a builder, a printer, a logger, a teacher
and so on. But this doesn't explain who they are
any more than if I wrote down their names:
each with its own family
that can also be traced across this continent to where
it leaps backward over an ocean into another world.

I meet so many people, enjoy them,
live with them or around them for years
and then some turn into words on paper
in a letter, or on a chart.

I believe all these people form a family.
And now I've said that
I think it is up to someone else to worry about
which of them are Jews.

Mark Sarner

BEYOND THE CANDLES OF CHANUKAH

When I was a boy in the '50s, we would go downtown every year to usher in the Christmas season by watching Santa Claus take that long ride down Yonge Street to his installation at Eaton's. My brothers and I would take turns sitting on my dad's shoulders for a better view of the floats and of the crowds, more people than I believed could be in one place at one time. A week or so later my mother would take us down to the store for our obligatory visit to Santa's lap for a photograph and the difficult question of what it was we wanted him to bring us on Christmas morning. Some of those pictures of Santa and me survive. I don't look quite comfortable.

At South Preparatory School in lower Forest Hill, we would honor the Christmas spirit by moving out into the halls after opening exercises to sing carols. Most of my friends would sit there silently through it all, their mouths resolutely shut. There was an unspoken understanding among us that this whole Christmas thing had little to do with us. We tolerated it, just as we tolerated the Lord's Prayer, read each morning by the teacher. We accepted the Christmas tree in the back of our room, and we brought money from home as our contribution to its purchase; we exchanged presents with our classmates, and we took our Christmas holidays like the next kid. But we were not quite like the next kid. We were Jewish children. We had little idea of exactly what that meant, but at least we were relatively clear on the irrelevance of Christ to our immediate lives.

Instead of Christmas, we had Chanukah, the Festival of Lights. Each night, for eight nights, my brothers and I would wait anxiously for my father to get home from the office so that the family might gather around the *Menorah*. We would rush through the blessings and then fight amongst ourselves for the privilege of kindling the Chanukah candles. There was a certain mystery in that moment when the whole family stood in the dark as the first candle was lit, the attention of everyone directed at that single flame. In that moment Judaism seemed a warm place that bound us all together. But we never talked about such things. The candles lit, my brothers and I proceeded directly to the living room and the pile of carefully

273

wrapped and sequentially numbered gifts in front of the fireplace. Each night we were permitted to open only one present each. It was simple coincidence that Chanukah came at roughly the same time of year as Christmas; yet, somehow, the coincidence was especially gratifying to our young minds. Christmas lasted only one day; our holiday went on for more than a week.

The nightly Chanukah ceremony was just another part of the business of being Jewish, a distinction that carried with it a large number of rites and observances throughout the year. There were the High Holy Days in the fall: Rosh Hashonah and Yom Kippur, during which we did not go to school and my father did not go to work. He and my mother went to services and, when we were old enough, my brothers and I joined them, only to find it difficult to stay awake. There was Passover at the Easter break, and the long ordeal of the *Seder* meal; and there was the weekly ritual of the Sabbath on Friday when my father came home early from work and my mother laid out the special tablecloth and good dishes in the dining room.

Besides the celebrations, however, there was also considerable inconvenience. Two afternoons a week I went to Hebrew classes after school and one morning on the weekend was allotted to attendance at religious school, where we learned Jewish history. If we tolerated the Lord's Prayer in public school like good little children, we tolerated our religious education hardly at all. The classes always seemed to proceed in an atmosphere just this side of open student revolt. In public school we were by and large a well-behaved and attentive lot; in the study of Judaism, the good student was the exception.

I always felt torn. I don't think I understood any better than anyone else why these Jewish studies were important enough to take up valuable time that seemed better spent playing hockey or football, but I did come to appreciate and to stand in awe of the miracle of Jewish survival over the course of more than 5,000 years.

This survival was clearly important and inspiring. In it lay the sense of being a part of a people that was different, a people that had chosen and been chosen by God and had struggled to maintain faith in the face of almost unbroken hardship and persecution. I was fascinated, and all of this excited me more than anything I was studying in regular school.

Yet the lesson of childhood was not that of Judaism. Along the way I learned that all of this was peripheral and relatively unimportant compared to the real concerns of life. The Jewish past was antique; it was European; it was Eastern. It seemed at once wholly absorbing and inconsequential. Survival in the present did not depend on this extracurricular study, but rather on more basic concerns such as doing well in public school and being good-looking. The promise of our young lives seemed to be that we would grow up and in the process would be relieved of what was inconvenient and burdensome about being Jewish. At age thirteen the *Bar Mitzvah* would bring the freedom of having no more Hebrew classes; at sixteen, around the time of the driver's licence, we would be confirmed and so finally have our weekends free.

That, more or less, is how it went for me and for the vast majority of the children I grew up with in Toronto. We grew out of things like Chanukah. So, too, we grew out of Judaism itself. The process of gradually weaning ourselves from the traditions and the observances of Jewish life seemed to continue more or less unabated through the 1960s.

What lingers now is the remnants of tradition, the habit of observance and the concentration of Judaism into a mere handful of Jewish rituals. The reality of being Jewish in Toronto in 1978 is far from an experience common to all Jews. As I look around I see a sprawling community that on the surface seems united — but not around the tenets of Judaism that once defined the Jewish experience. On these subjects there is considerable fragmentation. Some Jews have withdrawn into the shell of traditional belief; some have achieved an uneasy settlement in the middle ground; others have forsaken the whole business in favor of unbridled secularity. For me, things are by no means clear. This is a time of turmoil. North America, the modern world in general, and recent Jewish history in particular, have made it difficult to be a Jew in pursuit of a well-defined and desirable form of Jewishness.

The centre of Jewish life has shifted from the home and the family to the synagogue and a relative handful of public occasions; the Jewishness of Jews has been reduced to a simple ethnicity, a part of our heritage not quite in keeping with the modern reality of our participation in the feast of material wealth that rules Toronto. We Jews, the people of The Book, have become the people of the bond — the Israeli bond. Our "personal quarrel with God", as Elie Wiesel described the essence of Jewish history, has become a quarrel with Arab and other states as even from Bathurst and Eglinton we live for the Promised Land. We are no longer preoccupied with the

Jewish past and the maintenance of our sacred tradition; instead we find ourselves swimming in the confusing, swirling present.

In three short generations we have worked out our own particular and uneasy peace with ourselves and we have transformed Jewish life in the process. The first generation of eastern European Jews poured into North America from 1880 to the early 1920s, seeking the land of promise. Amazingly, their sons and daughters fulfilled that promise, making the transformation swift and almost universal. Yet, in 1978, the long road up from poverty has deposited us at the highest levels of the middle class only to leave the third generation, my generation, with a disconcerting sense of loss.

On the holiest day of the Jewish year, the Day of Atonement, I sit with my mother at the evening services of Yom Kippur. While Chanukah and other minor religious holidays may have slipped off into nonexistence, affecting me only because the YMHA is closed, the High Holy Days maintain their hold. I cannot resist them. In fact, I look forward to them as an opportunity to confront my Jewish identity — or lack of it.

This year there is a new rabbi and a new prayer book. The service has been changed. There is more Hebrew in it, injected, no doubt, to bring us back to the experience of a heritage otherwise lacking in our lives. But everything proceeds according to a peculiar logic. In the past, with more English, the congregation was more the participant. If the words meant little to the readers as they sat in their pews, at least they were heard to pass through their mouths. Now, there is less to do and more to listen to. The rabbi reads, the cantor sings from the pulpit, and the choir responds. It is beautifully stylized, an orchestrated interpretation of the service to which the congregation is more audience than ever before. We need not pray; we need only witness as others pray for us, in a melodic language we need not understand.

It is during the Day of Atonement that we ask God's forgiveness for all the sins we have committed in the preceding year. It is a time of assessment and of resolution. The core of Judaism is the covenant with God. It is a covenant between God and His people, a covenant between God and each individual Jew. First made with Abraham, it was renewed at Mount Sinai when Moses delivered the law, the word of God. It is the covenant which, we are told, made us a people distinct from other people by the single fact of our unique relationship with the one and only God. The Jews accepted the law; ever since, we have been struggling to understand it. It is the covenant and the law that have sustained us throughout a long and painful history.

The central concern of Jews, however, is no longer the reaffirmation of the covenant and the adherence to, or interpretation of, the law. So the sermon is not concerned with such matters. Nor does it serve to enlighten our tradition or the sanctity of this holy ritual of repentance that is Yom Kippur. The new rabbi addresses what his predecessor addressed in each and every year of his tenure: the survival of Israel. If it is difficult to believe firmly in God or even to question Him about His role in the modern Jewish world, it is a simple and automatic matter to take this opportunity, when there are more Jews gathered together than at any other time, to define our responsibility as the support of Israel. Israel takes precedence over all other issues; our responsibility to provide for it is foremost. We are then given the opportunity to raise our pens and pencils in unison and pledge money to buy Israeli bonds.

I watch my mother as she fills out her pledge card but look away so as not to be able to see what amount she has decided to give. The ushers come around to collect the envelopes. I too am an adult and a wage earner capable of making my own commitment, but I have never done so — not because I am protesting but rather because I am befuddled by the whole process. Clearly Israel has replaced God as the very foundation of Judaism. Our religious heritage has been ceded to our role as funders of the state, and the amount of our contribution seems the barometer of what kind of Jews we are. The decision is private; it is personal, the way our relationship with God used to be. I always wonder how much is enough. I wonder, too, what the rabbi gives and if his giving would provide a realistic answer to the question of faith. I find it impossible to imagine our lives without Israel and her imperiled existence.

After the service we go back to my mother's, where my two brothers are watching a baseball game. The World Series is always mysteriously congruent with the High Holy Days. There's usually an Argo game thrown in there somewhere, too. For a couple of years the Canada/Russia hockey series was another major competitor. If timing like this is a test of our piety in the modern world, then we are scoring very low indeed. I sit down in the den, loosen my tie, and watch the Yankees take another one from the Dodgers. Jews are different, I think. Not so much different from other people now, but different from what they used to be. The change is irrevocable.

The Toronto version of modern Jewish life got its start in the years between 1880 and 1920. In those years, the Jewish population of Toronto grew from 548 to over 34,000.

A voluntary ghetto sprang up in the heart of downtown, just west of University Avenue, and eventually spread to Spadina and the Kensington area, once known as the Jewish market. The Toronto community lacked the coherence provided by the old-world experience. Suddenly the Jew found himself an individual whose relationship to the world around him was no longer automatic.

My grandfathers were both scholarly men in Europe. One, when he came to Canada and settled in Winnipeg before the First World War, remained wed to his past; his relatives proceeded to make their fortunes while he worked for community institutions and maintained his righteous poverty. The other, who came later, found his way into the garment business and eventually did well enough to move his family into Rosedale before he died at an early age.

Basically, those were the choices: either to cling to the old ways and treat the new world as an opportunity to sustain a traditionally Jewish life without threat of attack; or to cast off what was cumbersome about the past and accept Canada's invitation to achieve success. Most chose the latter approach; those who didn't saw their children do so. The sense of inevitability that characterized this transformation of Jewish life made the process seem almost preordained. There was something, indeed, in the notion of this being the Promised Land; and if not the Promised Land, then at least it was the land of promise.

The struggle was hard, but it had always been hard. At least here there was the genuine prospect of success. The Jews did not hang their hopes on becoming assimilated into the Anglo-Saxon world of Toronto. Instead, they rallied around a pragmatism meant to hold the community together while availing its members of maximum opportunity. They embraced a fateful concept: a Jew at home, a man abroad.

This was not the first time that Jews had split themselves in two in order to preserve their Jewish identity. In fifteenth-century Spain, during the time of the Inquisition, the Marranos had chosen to convert to Catholicism and perform in public like good Catholics. At home, however, they maintained their Jewish customs. Judaism is a religion of observance that requires only the individual and his personal covenant with God. It was painful to have to give up living openly as Jews, but the loss of the synagogues and public religious rites did not circumvent this essential Judaism.

Toronto Jews were not the Marranos. In Spain the lines were clearly drawn; to be a Jew was to face possible death. To assume the appearance of the Christian majority was to acknowledge that the threat came from without; within, the Jew could remain a Jew. Here, the threat was more subtle. It required self-discipline in order to maintain the distinction between the private person and the public one.

The cost of success became the gradual surrender of what it meant to be Jewish. To be Jewish at home gradually lost ground to the idea of being successful abroad. There was no substitute for hard work and relentless study, both of which Jews displayed in large quantities. Men who could have known the *Torah* in Europe learned the intricacies of modern business methods. Boys who might have spent their youth poring over the *Talmud* in another time and place now applied themselves to the mastery of subjects that would carry them into the professions of medicine, law and accounting.

In many ways it was a story of mundane heroism as a generation of parents sacrificed their lives for their children in what has come to be a stereotype of immigrant history. The children accepted their end of the bargain by achieving monumental economic success. They planted themselves in Forest Hill and in the new Jewish suburbs that spread endlessly up Bathurst Street.

If God had been moved to one side, along with a large part of Jewish observance, He could not be forgotten entirely, partly because what happened in Europe in the 1940s called His existence into serious question. European Jewry was all but obliterated by Hitler. There were many questions to ask of God and of what Jewish life could possibly be in the aftermath of the Holocaust.

Had it not been for Israel, those questions might have been answered by that tireless process of inquiry that had characterized the now-distant Jewish past. Jewish scholarship still had its place along with Jewish theology. But it was as if these central Jewish concerns were no longer within the realm of the individual Jew. The Holocaust was a devastating reminder of the need for Jewish solidarity and cohesion — but not based on a return to God. In 1948, when Israel became a reality, the focus of modern Jewish belief was firmly in place.

I sit in Temple with my father on the morning of the Day of Atonement, my presence beside him confirming a sacred bond between father and son as we read together the *Kaddish*, the prayer that honors the deceased and praises the living. All the lights are lit today on the memorial plaque against the wall.

There are so many factors that impinge on Jewish life. The golf season or the tennis season. The cottage season. The necessity of winter vacations and of maintaining a standard of living that makes them possible. There is the responsibility to Israel and the cost of new cars. Generally, the whole catastrophe of living in the material world overshadows the idealism necessary to live a true Jewish life.

The congregation's younger rabbi addresses this issue indirectly with a sermon on synagogue affiliation. It represents, he says, the way to affirm one's place in the Jewish community and to remain a part of Judaism as it is now practised. He talks about the many Jews who are not in synagogues today and so can be assumed to be neglecting their duty as Jews. I am surprised that he's so bold on such an issue.

But it all makes sense in the contemporary situation. Just as Israel can replace God as our central concern as Jews, so membership in the synagogue can replace, as a criterion for religiosity, the quality of observance by the individual. We cannot, after all, be depended upon to carry out the traditional observances ourselves because we have neither the inclination to do so nor the knowledge required to know what they are. I think it is just not feasible to call for a return to the law because it is so clearly lost to expediency — or, at the very least, dying off with the loss of my grandmother's generation.

There are, of course, still significant numbers of the pious, old-fashioned Jews around. No shift in history is ever so complete as to obliterate completely what has gone before. We can still see them praying together, people alone with God in the early morning hours of *Shabbat* at synagogues that open early on Saturdays. And we can be certain of adherence to the law from those Jews we see on north Bathurst Street, the ultraorthodox who pray three times a day as is required and who have chosen the religious over the secular life.

They are the living reminder of the heritage we have abandoned. Their lives contain the message that the Jews may have been chosen to live outside the context of whatever world surrounds them and inside that very special relationship of God and His people that has defined our history until recent times. It is entirely possible that we were chosen to be without land — the wanderers, the riders of the blinds of the world; and without a voice — silent and incomprehensible in the face of all the oppression vent upon us; and without golf and tennis clubs and the condominium in Florida, and the rest — barred from the country clubs and exclusive shopping establishments of the world and from the difficulty of resolving economic reality against the tradition of a total commitment to God and His law.

It is all possible, but such a possibility is untenable from our current position. It is anachronistic, antiquated. We are no longer wanderers, only tourists at best. And we are no longer trapped, like the Soviet Jews, in the oppression of the modern world. We are settled here amongst our things. They weigh too much to carry. They mean too much to be abandoned.

"It has been said," writes Leo Rosten in *A Treasury of Jewish Quotations*, "that whereas the core of Christianity is the figure of Jesus, the core of Judaism is the Law — as set forth in the *Torah*, the Oral Tradition, the *Talmud*. It was a Christian scholar who made this interesting distinction: Christianity is a religion built around an ideal person; Judaism is a religion of ideals."

Such clarity seems impossible now. More acceptable is another line of Jewish thought that says Judaism is whatever the Jews at any particular time in history choose to make it by the nature of their practices. In other words, everything is all right. The Jews, like society in Thomas Jefferson's view, can reconstitute their Jewishness in every generation without an allegiance to the past.

Many Toronto Jews seem devoted to the Jeffersonian approach, safe in the knowledge that this is the trend of Jewish life elsewhere in the Western world. We need not worry about assimilation into the Christian majority, for the City of Churches is not what it once was. It too has given way to rampant secularity. We are free from the need to conform; we are free, too, from the need to maintain distinctions between Christian and Jewish principles.

The sustaining power of Jewish life today lies in its social/ cultural environment — the pleasantries, the Jewish food and the

Jewish celebrations that can proceed with only the loosest facsimile of observance. We are a warm and an enthusiastic people and thankful for that. We are comfortable enough to be able to enjoy what the world has to offer; and we are still in the habit, though removed from the reason, of aspiring to an ethical life.

We are liberal politically. We support all manner of good causes, including the culture of the city itself. But most of all we love the good show, the finished product that comes to the Royal Alex. We Jews are voracious consumers of culture; our humanist past has prepared us for it more than for anything else and we are still full of the energy of a people partaking of the world's delights for the first time.

What is unusual about the Toronto Jewish community, however, is that it has produced so little cultural product of its own. The secularization of Jewish life in New York, even in Montreal, has produced at least one generation of Jewish writers and intellectuals who have taken their humanistic tradition out into the world and from the encounter have produced significant work to enrich the cultural climate, even if such creations have sometimes made the local Jewish community uneasy. The list of New York Jews is endless — from Norman Mailer to Bernard Malamud, from Alfred Kazin to Lionel Trilling, and on and on. In Montreal there have been Mordecai Richler, Irving Layton, Leonard Cohen and the whole left-wing movement of poets and writers that grew up in the 1940s. It is through such people that Jewish life becomes a general subject and it is through their work that an understanding is forged between the socially isolated Jewish ghetto and the world around it.

But Toronto has not produced its generation of Jewish writers. The Toronto community cannot be proud of anyone who has achieved significant success nor can it be angry at anyone for being publicly critical. Possibly our story is too late or too similar to those of Montreal or New York and so it is not necessary for us to tell it. Instead, we can proceed with our ever-escalating upward mobility. It seems a conspicuous absence; yet it also seems consistent with the life of the city itself and how a people becomes a part of it. Or doesn't.

It is as if everything here conspires against self-criticism. Our unbridled support of Israel takes care of our responsibility as Jews; and our commitment to ensuring that our children get the basics of a Jewish education takes care of our responsibility to keep Judaism alive. We do not have to worry about the question of split loyalty because it is sanctified by the national policy of multiculturalism that permits us to hold dual citizenship. In America there is always the dilemma of whether one is an American Jew or a Jewish American; in Canada we can be both without having to ask any questions.

Judaism now demands almost nothing at all. For a branch of a people whose past is the unceasing argument and the endless search for truth that will tell us what God meant and so how to act, we are remarkably docile and unquestioning. Jewish life now is essentially a matter of loyalty. What separates Toronto Jews is the degree of tradition they still observe or avoid; what unifies them and cuts across almost all the generational barriers is Israel.

In 1948 with the War of Independence, and again in 1956 with the Suez crisis, and once more in 1967 with the Six-Day War, we have identified ourselves with the plight of Israel and have reveled in the image of a tiny nation holding strong against the forces of destruction. The modern image of the Jew is the Israeli, the hero of Entebbe; we feel our emotional fate inextricably bound up with the Holy Land.

In 1967, the radio was on all the time at my father's store on Spadina as we listened to a play-by-play of the June war. We cheered every victory as if we ourselves were under attack and as if we ourselves were acting. In 1973, when the Egyptians attacked on Yom Kippur, it was as if history had turned against us again. But our despair turned to celebration once the audacious Israelis marched toward Cairo on the one front and Damascus on the other.

We are a sensitive people; history has given us some justification. Who can fault us for such blind loyalty and nationalistic fervor where Israel is concerned? But how can we accept so totally this revival of Jewishness through a Zionism that is devoid of religion and of God?

When *Holocaust*, the television version of the real thing, was broadcast last spring, the Jews of Toronto were riveted in front of their sets. Children who had no idea what had happened found even this cleansed version horrific and impossible. For many of them, the series was the closest they have ever come to the downside risk of being a Jew in a world that has not shown much tolerance for Jews. It is all beyond comprehension. Nor can we truly appreciate the defiance, small as it may seem now, of the millions who went into those chambers with the *Sh'ma*, the words of the sacred covenant, on their lips. We are unlikely candidates to do the same.

For those of my generation, born around the birth of Israel and the first Jewish children in the world after the Holocaust, Jewish life has imposed few hardships. We have not deserted the community in favor of assimilation; it has never really become necessary because the nature and the structure of the community have changed so dramatically. We have not rejected it; but it has not made all of us a part of it. There is the distinct feeling of being wanderers once more, but this time on a barren, internal landscape. The experience is not discussed. Possibly because all attention is directed outward to Israel and the shifting political realities of Jews in the world at large. Possibly because there are no words yet to describe the experience. Possibly because such feelings do not fit into the mainstream of Toronto Jewish life.

Two questions were asked about the television program *Holocaust*. They are the questions that are constantly in the minds of Jews when trying to assess the impact of an event: Was it good? Was it good for the Jews?

They are questions that can also be asked about what has happened to us in Toronto. Yet in the world of contemporary Jewish life, my generation, the next generation to assume the mantle of Jewish responsibility, has no personal knowledge of anything ever being any different and even less idea of exactly what could be wrong with what is happening. There is ambivalence and there is frustration; and a sense of atrophy that is internalized and inarticulate. And there is the habit of survival that keeps the ideal and the possibility of a resolution alive like a dim, flickering light.

Ray Shankman

At my wedding there was no
red haired madman fiddling,
no Uncle dancing with two bottles
of schnaps cradled in his arms,
no Grandmother hiking up her skirts
to dance the Blackbottom;

At my wedding there were 100 plates
invited: how many from our side
how many from that side, arguments
over which is better square tables
or round tables, friends I've never seen
mooching a meal underneath the Circus tent;

A silly photographer who grieved
when the Bride wouldn't smile,
a supercilious Rabbi who droned text
without feeling, a mother whose iron will
never melted before the potential
of Divine Union.

At our wedding we had flowers and tears,
this egomaniac of a Bridegroom indignant
full of passionate conviction screaming
to the guests, "I hope you'll all be as happy
as we are going to be" and a pissed Aunty
shouting back, "we'll wait and see, we'll wait and see."

At our wedding the song ended before it began,
the dance faltered before the mirror
of wilting flowers and tearstained make-up
and the guests, now dead, plotted the marriage course
with deft fingering minds.

David Lewis Stein

FRESH DISASTERS

I have had enough of dying. All the best people are going. A whole generation is sinking into the earth. I have stood now at too many gravesides. Sometimes I have wept and sometimes I have looked down at my shoes and wondered why I could not cry. But always I have been there; I have done my duty. Now I want an end to it. I want a truce, a lull. I need time for the bleeding inside to stop. I will sit here quietly sipping martinis until it no longer seems so terribly important that we buried Alec Reisman this afternoon. If I am very still, if I disturb no one, make no demands, perhaps the gods will be kind. I will not start thinking about my wife's face. Susan was standing in her place of honour before Alec's open grave. I looked at her expecting the usual cold detachment, or better still, a healthy sneer, something to help get us both through the day. But when she turned to me, Susan's face was gaunt, grey, worn down like a piece of driftwood. She looked at me with pity in her eyes.

In the past year I have lost my mother, my grandfather, and two uncles. Then I have been a surrogate, a dutiful agent from the past, at funerals for three of my father's friends. Now Alec. There is no one left of my parents' generation. In my family, I am now the eldest male child, and if there were any family left worth speaking of, I could claim to be the head of it. But my sisters are scattered from Montreal to San Diego, and I have not seen my cousins in years. We are, as I tell my students in "Sociology 127", split at last into nuclear units.

The peasants have made their final break with Europe. It has taken three whole generations and God only knows how much labour and thwarted love but now, a triumph of sorts — a little triumphant music, please, as we fan out to our townhouses and suburban estates — now we are independent and free. No more loyalty demanded to those grotesquely extended families, those smelly ranks of uncles and aunties our history obligated us to love, honour, and, if necessary, support all the rest of our days. It has taken three whole generations to heal the trauma of separation from the Old World but now, at last, we are free. A few dances of liberation please, romantic *pas de deux* and tap-dance solos. The only people who can command our love now, as a legal and moral right, are our spouses and our 2.3 children. Or, as in my case, since Susan and I are waiting only for the final decree of our divorce, we are responsible only to ourselves.

This is not what my grandfather came to this country seeking. It's not what my father struggled all his life to achieve. I'm not even sure it's what I really want. One does not always choose to be part of great historical movements. But I do have it and I am trying to make the best of it.

I have begun to live in historical time. All the people I know and care about, I have known for at least twenty years. How much have I changed in twenty years? How much did the world change between 1900 and 1920? Or between 1930 and 1950? How much have I changed since I first brought Susan to the roof of the Park Plaza Hotel and grandly told her this was my local pub? Outside, there have been wars and revolutions and liberations and oil embargoes and voyages into space. But in here Harold and Ray, the waiters who have always been here, came gradually to distinguish our faces among the happy-hour crowd and to stop by our table to say hello.

We were still graduate students then and it was terribly important to be recognized by ordinary people outside our tight little campus world. Acceptance by Harold and Ray was proof we had not yet become ivory tower academics. After we got married, Susan and I liked to sit alone at the corner table in the early evening and watch the golden lights of the skyscrapers come on, a floor at a time. We liked to look out at the thickets of hammerhead cranes hoisting up still newer, higher slabs and towers. I suppose we identified with their assertion of power. We were coming of age, expanding very fast, and a new city was growing up to receive us. We never dreamed it would turn into a cold, taut city. Just as we never dreamed we could grow bitter as well as old.

When the kids started coming, Susan was too tired to sit in bars any more. She was too tired for anything, if it came to that. But sometimes, maybe once every six months, we'd make it back up here after a movie. We'd find the place almost empty, even on Saturday nights. The smart people had moved on. Those hammerhead cranes had put up too many big new hotels with smart, new bars on their ground floors. The people who mattered were spread too thin; the community unravelled. Not even a trained sociologist like me can keep track now of where and when the interesting people pitch camp.

When Susan and I did come up here, we'd make for our corner table and order martinis like the old days and talk about the film we'd just seen. Then I'd recognize the signs. Susan's eyes would begin to close and her head would nod. It was a toss-up whether she could finish the drink before her eyes closed and she began to drool and snore. Harold always walked with us out to the elevator and told us we should come up more often.

Well, he must be pleased now. The roof bar has been remodelled, tarted up really, but at least one of the old gang doesn't seem to mind. I've become a regular again. Harold and Ray are very discreet. When I come with a date — I still can't get used to the idea, a man my age going out on dates — they give me the big hello and show us to our table and ask how things are going. Then, after I've introduced my date to them, they quietly slip off so we can chat with uninhibited intimacy. My dates are always impressed. I am still in what my friends tell me is the Lolita/Pygmalion stage of being single. Later on, they say, when I have proven myself, I will be ready for mature women again. I certainly hope so. I'm bored already. Only when I am alone does Harold stop by as in the old days for a good long chat about handball and people and the state of the world. All this has taken twenty years of historical time.

I despise talking so much about Susan and my personal life. Broken marriages abound. They have become a cottage industry. Every person is unique, of course. How I love it when my students solemnly inform me that every single person in the world possesses his own special, unduplicable combination of qualities. There's nothing like a touch of education to over-extend the adolescent ego. Ah, yes, I tell them. It's true that every person is unique but every divorce is exactly the same, just like every happy family. So how do you fit that into your conceptual framework, eh? No matter whether they begin with violence or sweet reason over candles and wine, they all end in bitterness. It does not matter whether the parties begin by hating each other, they will surely hate each other by the time it is all over. They announce with a giant sigh of relief that at last they are free and, poor dears, they will never be free again.

I really should go home. But I am afraid someone will telephone me with news of some fresh disaster. Have I heard whose marriage has just broken up? In my circle of friends I count five marriages, including my own, that have gone down the drain this year alone. And do I know that so-and-so has gone psychotic? Yes, he tried to kill the *au pair* girl with nail scissors and his mother had him committed to the Clarke. And somebody has just lost his job and such-and-such firm of hot-shot young lawyers is coming apart like a shattered glass, and somebody else has just been denied tenure at the university. His wife's pregnant and what's the poor bugger supposed to do? Teach public school? And someone else has died. The funeral is tomorrow, ten o'clock at Benjamin's. Shiva at the daughter-in-law's. In lieu of flowers please send contributions to the cancer fund. This has been a very bad year, and I can't take too much more of it. I have become very thin ice and the pressure of a child's sob could shatter me.

The trouble is, if I stay here much longer, I will become a fresh disaster myself. It does not matter that I have known Harold and Ray for twenty years of historical time — if I become embarrassing, they will throw me out. And if I make a public fool of myself, how can I come back here? There are so few places now where I feel safe.

Still, this is a risk I will have to take. I do not want to close my eyes until I have drunk so many martinis I can see only the cozy black insides of my own eyelids. I do not want to close my eyes and hear again Alec Reisman's dry, sardonic voice like slippers trampling over eggshells.

"Everything we produce gets turned into capital. In a capitalist society, we are all businessmen. Look at the poet! What does he do, after all? He takes his nice feelings, he packages them with a pretty title, and he sells them in the marketplace. You think you're so much better than me because I'm in the real-estate business and you're a big shot university professor. But, personally, I see no difference between us. You package your brains and the university puts them on the shelf like you were a box of corn flakes. The university peddles you just the way I sell condominium apartments."

"The difference is, I am still trying to improve my life, to become a self-conscious human being. And you've given up. You sold out years ago. Yeah, you're so rich now, so cultured, eh? You can quote Karl Marx chapter and verse. But in your soul you're still a little peasant boy from Europe, mean and bloody-minded."

"Did I ever deny it? This country is no different from Europe.

The only difference is, in Canada the peasants have all the money."

Alec Reisman was my father's best friend. A few facts. They grew up together, sold newspapers together, played basketball together, went to high school together, and, I think, even lusted after the same women together. I suspect my mother must have been one of them, although God knows why she chose my father. But something traumatic happened very early on in all their lives. As close as my father and Alec were, Alec was never welcome in our house. I never remember our two families sitting down to supper together. It was always my father going out to play golf with Alec or Alec coming over very late at night, after my mother had already gone to bed, to kill a bottle of whisky and argue with my father. I would lie in bed listening to them shout at each other and bawl each other out, and I would wonder how they could still say they were friends.

They joined the Young Communist League together. Looking back, my father used to say he was young and foolish but it was the Depression and the world was going to hell and only the Communists seemed to have any idea how to save it. And he was a Jew and the only leader in the world standing up to Hitler then was Stalin. Besides, he used to say with a chuckle, the Communists gave the best parties. If my mother was close by, he would pat her bottom and she would blush and wriggle away. It was the only sign of affection he ever allowed himself to show her in public.

Alec was more like what the Communists had in mind. He liked to tell people that when he was growing up, "There were the poor people, and then there was the Reisman family. We were the lowest of the low." My father used to tell a story to illustrate what Alec meant. One summer they were both supposed to be going off to a camp for two weeks. Some church was getting kids off the street because of the polio epidemics that used to hit the city every year. So Alec and my father signed up and the morning they were to go to the country they came with their mothers to the church steps. Everybody got on the buses and they began to pull away — all except the last bus, with Alec and my father inside. They wondered what was going on. Finally the door opened and the bus driver got out. When he came back, he called out Alec's name. Alec had to get off and my father and the bus went away to summer camp without him.

It turned out that even though this was a charity camp, the kids were supposed to bring two dollars. This was to cover the cost of chartering the bus. Neither Alec nor my father had explained this to their parents. They were about eight years old at the time. My grandmother always had a few bills in her little black coinpurse. But in Alec's family, two extra dollars was unheard of. His father was a plasterer but he had a crooked spine and seldom was able to work a full week. In her whole life, I'll bet Alec's mother never had two dollars to spare. And apparently, there was nobody around that day, neither from the camp, nor the bus company, nor the church, who would let her off the hook. So they kicked Alec off the bus and he never did get to go to a summer camp.

"My mother cried all the way home," Alec told me. "It didn't bother me so much. I was an active kid; I could always find things to do in the street. But the humiliation for my mother, that was something I never got over."

My father and Alec didn't last long as Communists. The Hitler-Stalin Pact finished off my father. If Stalin could join with his worst enemy, then how could anyone ever trust the Communists again? What was going to happen to the Jews in Europe? What was my father to say to the Norman Bethune Club he organized among the medical students? My father stomped out of the Party, bellowing curses at Stalin and Tim Buck. Alec, however, simply shrugged off the Pact. If Tim Buck said the alliance was nothing more than a shrewd tactical manoeuvre by Stalin, that was good enough for Alec. When Hitler atacked Poland and the party was outlawed in Canada because of the Pact, Alec went underground. He used to talk about that as though he had been in the wartime underground, but really, not much happened. Alec changed his job and shortened his name but he stayed at home, living with his mother. The cops never bothered him. I don't think they were very serious about catching the Communists and, anyway, Alec wasn't very important. When Hitler attacked Russia and Stalin was a hero again, Alec joined the Air Force. After the war, he never went back to the Communists, not for ideological reasons but because he was too busy. The war made all the difference for Alec.

When it started, he was just another kid from Spadina Avenue hanging around pool rooms and shooting craps in alleys. If it hadn't been for the Young Communist League he would probably have wound up a bookmaker or worse. Then the Air Force took him and made him a radar technician. Alec said the Air Force was the first time he realized he was smarter than most other people. After he got out, he used his credits to study accountancy and open his own office. Later, he went into partnership with one of his clients and they were spectacularly successful. Their Happy Times Development Co. built shopping centres and apartment buildings all across Canada and in Florida and Texas.

Yesterday, the newspapers told with such eloquence the story of how Alexander Charles Rice, the poor immigrant boy from Lithuania, had risen from his humble origins to become one of the wealthiest men in Canada. Nobody mentioned that Alec had once been a member of the Young Communist League. The editorial writers didn't even talk about the time Alec organized the famous three-day student strike at Long Road Technical School. Yet Alec always credited the Communists with teaching him how to be a successful businessman.

"The only philosopher who ever understood human nature was Karl Marx," Alec liked to say. He said it so often it sounded like a speech to a service club. "Marx taught us that everything that exists in the whole world is produced by human labour. And everything is for sale. There is only one question still to be decided: who is going to get all this wealth everybody is producing? The Communists used to say they should make that decision in the name of the working class. But one day I thought, 'Why them and not me? Why should the big shots in the party have all the fun?' So now I'm a capitalist and a miserable exploiter of the working class. But I'll tell you something: I give away more money to charity every year than the Communists collect in dues from their whole membership. And I'll tell you something else: I do a thousand times more good with my money than they do."

Yet for all his talk about hard times and the Communists, the closest Alec ever got to a real revolutionary situation was when he came to visit me during the Columbia student strike. I was quite a shock to him; I enjoyed it thoroughly. My head was wrapped in bandages and blood caked my face. I told Alec the world was never going to be the same again. It sounds funny now, but it was real enough then. The Students for a Democratic Society had taken over five buildings and held them for a week. Finally the administration sent for the cops. The cops busted the students inside the buildings and then smashed everybody they found on campus, the left, the jocks, the liberals — even the campus rabbi got his head cracked. Next morning the cops were everywhere, like an occupying army. There were so many student factions Columbia felt like a civil war. Even

Alec was impressed. When he found me, he held me at arm's length and then embraced me. He even kissed me.

What they only talked about, I did. The Communists waited for the revolution like hitchhikers waiting for a ride. But I was there. I screamed "Up against the wall, motherfucker" at the cops and I held my ground when they came at me with the blackjacks. I was lucky to get away with my life. I was there. I have eleven stitches in my head to show for it. I was part of a real uprising and nobody will ever be able to take that away from me.

Spring in New York that year, 1968, really did feel like the beginning of a revolution. Years of anti-war demonstrations had finally driven Johnson to announce he would not run again. Incredible as it may sound now, the president of the United States was afraid to show his face in the streets. Then an assassin shot Martin Luther King. Blacks rioted in ten American cities. The country was on fire. It hadn't come to New York yet, but everybody knew it would. Everybody was into some kind of politics. They went all the way from the sweet, ancient pacifists of the War Resisters League to the underground guerrillas who were already holding seminars on how to plant bombs. There was even something called "Dial-A-Demonstration". You could call up and find out how many things were going on that weekend. I used to go every Sunday to the big anti-war demonstrations in Central Park. I was doing research for my doctoral thesis; my subject was the kinship relations between members of the traditional left and the so-called New Left. My research showed that most of the new leaders were children of old-time Communists and party sympathizers. They inherited their radicalism just the way the Young Americans for Freedom inherited their conservatism. Newspapers used to say there were 50,000 or 75,000 demonstrators at those Central Park rallies but the newspapers lied. Newspapers always lie. We filled the whole Sheep Meadow. Sometimes it felt like half a million people. Most people stayed in those very tight little groups — the feeling of paranoia was very high in those days — but the overall feeling was still very communal. People smiled at each other and shared their joints. There was so much smoke in the air you could get stoned just sitting there. Everybody sang about love, and talked about love; some people even tried to look loving. Love was the only defence against the war. I wrote in my notebook, "The children of the middle class have been denied power so long they no longer want it. They insist on their right to remain children." That's a good one, eh? It's really a pity I never finished my book about the New Left.

I was in Fayerweather Hall the night of the "Big Bust" at Columbia. I'd been going from building to building that night, taking notes on people's state of mind, when we got the word: the pigs were on campus. By the time they got to Fayerweather, the noise outside had grown to a roar of battle with sounds at the edge of breaking glass and people screaming. Through our high windows we could see television lights going on and off somewhere like a lighthouse beacon. And suddenly the police were there. They clubbed down the people on the steps of our building and pulled away our pitiful barricade of furniture and they were inside the building. For a moment, I remember, the roaring stopped. Everyone froze; there was absolute silence. We were all sitting on the floor and the cops facing us looked terrified, ready to kill us. Then somebody yelled, "Up against the wall, motherfuckers!" and we all yelled it. It was a wonderful moment of defiance. I have felt ever since that I can face anything because I faced death that night in Fayerweather Hall.

I never even saw which cop hit me or what he hit me with. All I remember is somebody throwing me through an open door. I guess some cops on the other side were supposed to catch me and take me to a paddywagon. But no one did. I just went on and on with my head bent over and streaming blood until finally I collapsed on the grass. Some medical students in white coats found me and got me off to a hospital.

I was lucky. No bones were broken. But it still took eleven stitches to close the wound and they hurt like hell. I still get migraine headaches along the scar. In the morning, Alec found me and took me to his hotel. He was in New York raising money for his umpteenth apartment house. I was all set to quit school and join the guerrillas but Alec talked me into coming down to his hotel and resting for a few days. I suppose it was a good idea. I was in no condition to think clearly.

"I almost went to Spain," Alec told me over a bottle of Scotch in his room.

"What stopped you?"

"Who would look after my mother? My brothers were still babies."

"You should have gone," I told him. "You really should have gone."

"What difference would it have made if I had?" Alec said.

Poor Alec, he could only evaluate experience by how much it increased or diminished his power; he never understood the concept of individual growth. One thing I was sure I had got out of the Big Bust was a whole new understanding of education. My notebook journal said, "Education is only the last moment before the cops come." In the liberated buildings at Columbia — or "occupied", depending on your age and orientation; I still think of them as "liberated" — everybody talked. Words became actions. The students themselves decided what had to be done and they did it instantly. But it wasn't only politics that occupied us: we listened to music; we talked about literature, psychology, films, everything under the sun. The tension was unbearable; everybody knew the cops would have to come. But at the same time, we were serene, our minds were open. We easily absorbed ideas it would have taken us years to assimilate in the boredom of a classroom. There was even a wedding in Fayerweather Hall when I was there. We stood in the stairwell holding candles and a minister with a dog collar performed a real ceremony. The couple were dressed in white and the bride had a little veil. The minister told them they were "children of the new age".

I wish I had kept the notes I made in Alec's hotel. I was working on a way to translate my great insight into practical teaching methods. I wanted to recreate the Columbia strike every time I entered a lecture hall. I was going to make every lecture I gave a confrontation. The job of being a teacher was to challenge students to the roots of their being.

I suppose that all sounds terribly pompous now. The truth is, I've become a very different kind of teacher and I don't have any theories of education any more. Pedagogical theories don't last long when you're facing students every day. Still, I don't think I was so wrong then. And I'm not ashamed of anything I did at Columbia.

In a way, I'm fortunate I never finished my book on the New Left. The scene changed so fast everything I had to say would have been outdated by the time the book came out. I know a lot of people who used to talk about "going into the street" and "picking up the gun". They get very angry now if you remind them of the things they said then. Some of them have even gone the other way; they've become full-time reactionaries. They seem to think the New Left collapsed just to confound their predictions and spite them personally. So they've turned reactionary to spite their old leaders. Or to spite themselves. I don't know. It's an idea I should work on some time.

The only long-term advantage of a book would have been to give me one more emotional card to play on Alec. I tried for years to make Alec respect me. I suppose I even wanted him to love me. But the only person Alec respected unconditionally all his life was my father. He used to tell me my father was a saint — even if he did get rich on other people's misery. But my father was not a saint; he was not even kind. And Alec must surely have known this. But even when I was a grown man myself and came to visit him with children of my own, Alec would never talk honestly to me about my father.

As I remember my father, he was always angry. The world was populated by fools, con men, thieves, pimps, bookies, rackos, hoods, and on and on. Raging, that was my father; raging long into the night. The only acceptable people were his patients, and for them he would drive himself into a frenzy. On their behalf he fought with hospitals, insurance companies, landlords, even other doctors. A woman told me once how she came to him for a second opinion about an operation on her legs and he saved her life. Her own doctor wanted to tie off her veins and that would have left her a cripple for the rest of her life. My father examined her and decided the problem had something to do with her thyroid and he could cure her with medication. He called up her own doctor while she was still sitting in his office and bawled him out for giving such a sloppy diagnosis. Years later, the woman still recalled it all with amazement and delight. Right in front of her, my father called her doctor a pimp, a butcher, a money-grabbing whore, and every other name he could think of.

I suppose my father was loved by his patients. Or maybe they just respected him. Anyway, dozens of them came to his funeral, people I'd never seen before. But except for Alec, few people spent much time with my father. His outrage was too overwhelming. I always thought my father had the power to cast a black spell around him, making everybody he talked to angry at him or angry at the world. I've often pictured my father moving through life enveloped in a cloud of acid that burned anyone who got too close. The only place he felt completely happy was the operating room. There, nobody could talk back to him. My father loved the science of medicine and he was good at it. But he hated sick people. He hated weakness of any kind. Other doctors have told me how much they admired his skill but they were afraid to work with him. He'd rant and scream and bawl them out right in front of the nurses. Still, they all sent him patients and my father made a lot of money. Most of it he lost because he insisted on playing the stock market himself and he'd never listen to Alec's advice. But the other doctors told me there wasn't a surgeon in the city who worked as cleanly and as quickly as my father. There wasn't a surgeon in Toronto who did less damage to the patient than my father.

My father died at the age of fifty-two. Perhaps, if he had lived longer, he would have mellowed and become a crusty but lovable old curmudgeon. But his life didn't work out that way. He was sitting with my mother one night after supper telling her what a useless bunch of whores the new surgery nurses were when he keeled over. His heart had stopped and he was dead within minutes. The firemen didn't even try to revive him. My mother was the only one there at the end. My sisters had all married and I was at Columbia. We had all cleared out of that rich, fearful house as quickly as we could. But my mother stayed on there alone for another twelve years. She finally died in January, diabetes and cancer of the bowel.

My father never paused long enough in his life to examine the roots of his anger. And I suppose there was really no reason for him to. He found the emotional energy generated by his sense of outrage a very useful tool in the practice of medicine. The closest I have been able to come myself to developing a consistent theory of his behaviour is to say that from the day he left the Communist Party to the day he died, my father was trying to prove that the Communists and Alec Reisman were wrong. My father insisted they acknowledge that there is such a thing as an unselfish man in the world. There are non-commercial, non-exploitative relations between people. "Look!" my father seemed to be saying, "I'm living it, aren't I? So what if other people are stupid, weak, and greedy! Look at me! Am I not all the proof you need?" What ate my father up alive was the realization that neither the Communists nor his old friend Alec cared much what he did. They knew they were right. Dialectical materialism and human nature were on their side. I don't think anything my father could have done would have impressed them.

Alec gave me the money to finish my Ph.D. He paid off the mortgage on my mother's house and put me on the payroll of one of his companies. Then he took me out to lunch at his club and explained why he was doing it that way. He wanted me to have income free of my father's insurance so I wouldn't feel I was taking money from my mother in her time of need. And he wanted me on the payroll so he could claim the tax deduction of my "salary".

I collected that salary for five years. It carried me through the rest of my Ph.D. and a year of post-doctoral research in Vienna when I was supposed to be working on my book. I even used the money to get married on. I consoled myself by making silent promises to pay Alec back as soon as I was earning enough money of my own. I even approached him once with a first installment. He said that hurt him more than anything else had in years. Accepting his money was the least I could do in memory of my father. And, anyway, it gave Alec such pleasure to see me get a good education. Who was I, Alec wanted to know, to deny him such a small enjoyment in his life?

"I have lived too long in your debt, Alec. You should not have expected me to be grateful. Surely the business world taught you that much. Nobody loves the landlord."

"You're still worried about the money? That's too bad; that kind of worry will keep you from growing up. I guess it's because you always worked for a salary, selling yourself off a little piece at a time. You're always afraid you'll run out of stock. It's only when you go out and actually make the money from other people — yes, like the Communists say, from the sweat of the workers — that you know what money is worth."

"It's not the money and you damned well know it. It's the idea. I know I have moved far beyond you. People can change with a single generation if they put their minds to it. I have left Europe far behind, I have risen far above the mean, frightened peasant class I sprang from. Yet you persist in your stubborn, irrational insistence that I am no better than you."

"If your life was such a big success, perhaps I would take you more seriously. But look at yourself, sitting alone in a bar on the day you helped bury the last man in your father's generation who could have explained anything to you. *Regardez!* A paunchy romantic, slopping down martinis like a character in a bad love song. Look at yourself, middle-aged and getting fat, divorced and desperately needing the comfort and support of a woman, yet not knowing how to pay — there's that damned word again! — not knowing how to pay for that support by giving freely of yourself. Look at the mess of your life: an assistant professor of sociology who has just been granted tenure by the university and instead of celebrating, you're terrified."

That's true enough. I've been working all my adult life to gain a secure teaching position and now that I've got one, I'm more afraid than ever. Now that I'm a tenured member of the staff, the university will never fire me. I can stay there until I retire. But what if Alec is right, what if ideas are only commodities we buy and sell? And what if I have no more ideas to market? What will I teach for the rest of my life? What will my students think of me when I'm fifty years old? What will they say of me at sixty?

Right now, I am still a good teacher. I wish I had been able to impress Alec with that before he died. When students are asked to evaluate their professors at the end of the year, they always give me the highest rating in the whole sociology department. I told Alec that a couple of times but he only smiled and said "That's nice." The only kind of success that counted with Alec — besides making a pile of money — was approval from above. Only if somebody rich or somebody powerful said you were good would Alec believe it. Alec died a fabulously wealthy man but he stayed a Communist and a peasant all his life. He never believed anything unless somebody in authority told it to him.

My relations with students were too intangible for Alec to appreciate. And anyway, these changed from year to year. Now that I am a tenured professor and I no longer need their approval, I am afraid that my attitude toward students is going to change permanently. I have lost my compulsive need to succeed with them. I am dreading what may happen in my classes this year. I am afraid I may already have begun to lose my nerve.

For a long time, I tried to treat my students as people. I listened to their troubles and I took them seriously even when they knew themselves they were not being very serious. Then it all came apart in my hands. And I don't know why. I didn't do anything foolish like start an affair with one of my students. But it did just hit me one day that I was enjoying all this a little too much. I saw suddenly that I was living vicariously off the energy of my students. It was what made me in their eyes a good teacher. But in my own eyes I suddenly saw myself as dishonest.

I was already into my late thirties. And there I was, spending all my time worrying about the problems of twenty-year-olds. I was good for them because I had some experience of the world and I was a sympathetic listener. I could foresee consequences of decisions they had to make and I gave them useful advice.

The catch was, I had stopped dealing realistically with my own problems. I was so absorbed in, and so good at understanding, the troubles of the twenty-year-olds, that I got no pleasure at all out of coping with the demands life makes on a man who is getting down to the wire, almost forty years old. I simply stopped handling my own life and instead became the very model of the always available, always sympathetic, altruistic university teacher. I think of it now as the Dracula syndrome. I had stopped living in my own historical time. I was poaching on my students' time.

I can hear Alec's broken, panting laughter as I say this. It was emphysema that finally killed him. But after thirty years of two packs a day, I suppose it was only a question of whether the emphysema turned his lungs to marble before the lung cancer turned them to ditchwater.

Alec would have said I was merely selling bits of myself to my students as well as to the university. Instead of letting the university package and market everything I had to offer, I kept back a little and went into business for myself. I was like one of those Russian peasants who produces three times as much on his own tiny plot as he does for a state-owned collective farm. There's a thought that would have amused Alec.

It would have amused my wife, too. She inherited Alec's sense of humour. We had a fair run at destroying each other, Susan and I. But as much as I have been — or probably ever will be — married to anyone, I was married to Alec Reisman's eldest daughter. I suppose that adds an extra dimension to my relationship with Alec — overtones, undertones, semi-tones, half tones. I don't know.

I don't think so. Susan and I managed to create quite a perfect little hell for ourselves without any encouragement from Alec. We didn't live with each other; we lived off each other. I don't think Alec ever fully understood how destructive we got. It was something we kept from him, a kind of tacit mutual agreement. That silence was the only honourable thing we did together in our six years of marriage.

No, the way I see it, Alec entered my relationship with his daughter directly in only two ways. The first was that Susan never knew the first two years of our marriage and the idyllic year we spent in Vienna were all paid for by my "salary" from Alec's company.

And the second is that Susan is living now with an architect and probably she is going to marry him. She knows very well that I consider architects the most hypocritical collection of prostitutes in our society. They talk all this jargon about "planes intersecting" and "tensions between spaces" and so on, trying to give people at dinner parties the impression they are so terribly concerned about aesthetics and "human values". Then they take commissions from ruthless little developers like Alec Reisman and put up cheap, horrible, ugly slab towers all over the city. The higher and more costly the building they put up, the bigger their commission. Alec always used to say architects were even easier to buy off than politicians. Architects were greedier. They'd cut any corner Alec told them to, as long as they got their money off the top. Then the architects go back to their cozy little associations and give each other prizes and gold medals for good design. As a social scientist, I find it highly significant that Alec's daughter should wind up marrying an architect. It shows that despite education and cultural conditioning, parental influence is still the dominant factor in her life. Susan Reisman is still a peasant.

I have coffee with her when I bring the kids back from my weekly outing. She tells me how happy she is. She says she is learning at last how to love another person. I have a hard time not to burst out laughing — as old Alec himself would have.

I wish Alec had lived longer. Or died earlier. As it is, he went at a particularly bad time. I have grown to depend on those lunches with him and those long talks into the afternoon. My own life is a little shaky right now. The future looks a little bleak. I have developed a great desire to explore the past. It is not just nostalgia. I despise nostalgia. But I would like to see my own roots more clearly. And feel them more. But now Alec Reisman is dead and my last connection with the past has been broken. There is no one left from my father's time to whom I can explain my life. There is no one left to give me a blessing.

I think I should go home now. Tomorrow is visiting day with my kids and I don't want to go in feeling hungover and sick. Besides, it's closing time, right? Trying to get a drink after the last call is undignified. Harold and Ray would have to refuse me and I don't want to lose face with Harold and Ray. Not after all these years. I have a public face and I will not allow it to slip. That's something I learned from both Alec and my father. They practised it all their lives, a kind of old school stoicism. Keep a tight grip on your emotions. Never let anyone know what you really feel, especially if they've managed to hurt you. Susan used to call it "cheap machismo" and I suppose she was right. She used to sneer at me for trying to be like Alec and my father. But once that kind of pride has been drummed into you, it's not so easy to give it up. I sometimes think I have reached a state of communion with my appliances, a mystic bonding with my microwave oven, my colour TV, and my quadraphonic sound system. Like them, I am solid state. I have no moving parts. I produce incredible amounts of work and the world applauds. But nobody ever sees how I do it. I am opaque. Unfathomable. Yes. But underneath, yes, I know only too well, the dry rot has set in. It's beginning to spread too — but slowly. I still have time left, I think. The dance of death is very lethargic. That's an image that seems to occur to me quite often these days. The waltz of death takes place in slow motion. That's my final thought for to-night. It takes longer than one thinks to die.

I really must go. I want to have some energy left for my kids tomorrow. Sometimes I wonder if I look as large to my son as my father and Alec Reisman once looked to me. I'd like to think so. But I suspect I'd be kidding myself if I believed it.

Avrum Malus

I AM A MODERN JEW

I do not put on *tefilin*
I run each day

I put on my running shoes
heavy sweatsocks
and limp or fly
or do something between limping and flying
around the track

around and around the track I go
a modern Jew
on running shoes
limping and flying

ACKNOWLEDGEMENTS

"The Pact" first appeared in *Prism International*. Used by permission.

"To My Mother" is used by permission of Seymour Levitan.

"At My Wedding" was first published in *Tamarack* and reprinted in *The First Five Years*, Oxford, 1962. "Teaching Yiddish" was first published in *A Treasury of Yiddish Poetry*, eds. Irving Howe and Eliezer Greenberg, Holt Rinehart & Winston, 1969. Copyright Miriam Waddington.

Crackpot was first published by McClelland and Stewart in 1974. The New Canadian Library edition of the book was published in 1978. Used by permission.

"Once In a Year," "Sonnets Semitic — V", "Psalm xxxvi: A Psalm Touching Genealogy," "Autobiographical" are from *The Collected Poems of A. M. Klein*. Used by permission. *The Second Scroll* was first published by Alfred A. Knopf, Inc. in 1951 and was reprinted by McClelland and Stewart in 1961 and 1969.

"For A. M. Klein (1909-1972)" was first published in *Canadian Literature* No. 59. The poem is copyrighted by Seymour Mayne.

"The Rich Man" was first published by McClelland and Stewart in 1948. The New Canadian Library edition of the book was published in 1961. Copyright 1948 by McClelland and Stewart Limited. Copyright, Canada, 1961, by Henry Kreisel.

"A Birthday Party" was first published in *The Canadian Journal of Fiction* (1972) and is included in the collection *A Pyramid of Time* (Porcupine's Quill, 1979). Abraham Boyarsky holds the copyright.

"The Watchmaker" was first published in *Columbus And The Fat Lady* (McClelland and Stewart, 1972), and is included in *The Expatriate: Collected Short Stories* (1981).

"Uncle Nathan" and "Ichthycide" are from *Topsoil*, Press Porcépic, 1976. Used by permission.

"Lies My Father Told Me" is used by permission of Ted Allan.

"Jewish Christmas" is from *Raisins and Almonds* by Fredelle Bruser Maynard. Copyright 1964, 1967, 1968, 1972 by Fredelle Bruser Maynard. Reprinted by permission of Doubleday and Company, Inc.

"December: Our Store Window" is from *Most of the Time*, Barton Press 1981. Used by permission.

"A Basket of Apples" was first published in *The Atlantic Monthly* (1969). Copyright Shirley Faessler.

"The Nineteen Thirties Are Over," "The Bond," and "Why Should I Care About the World" are from *Driving Home: Poems New and Selected* (Oxford, 1972). Used by permission.

"Estevan 1934" and "near Hirsch a Jewish cemetery" are from *Out of Place*, Press Porcépic, 1977. "On the 25th Anniversary of the Liberation of Auschwitz" is from *Stony Plain*, Press Porcépic, 1973, and "In My 57th Year" is from *Life Sentence*, Press Porcépic, 1981. Used by permission.

"Diaspora (Lipton, Sask.)" was first published in *Aurora: New Canadian Writing 1979*, Doubleday. Copyright 1979 Robert Currie.

The Noise of Singing was first published by Golden Dog Press (1975). Copyright Abraham Ram and Michael Gnarowski.

BIOGRAPHIES

Ted Allan (1916–) was born in Montreal. His fiction and articles have appeared in a number of magazines, including *The New Yorker, Harper's*, and *Reader's Digest*. He has published a novel, *This Time A Better Earth*, and is co-author of *The Scalpel and The Sword: The Story of Dr. Norman Bethune*.

Solomon Ary (1911–) was born in Bialystok, Russia. He immigrated to Canada in 1930 and eventually settled in Montreal where he owns a paint store. Since beginning his writing career at age sixty-five, Ary has published several of his stories in *J.I.A.S. News* and *Prism International*. He also writes Yiddish folk songs.

Avi Boxer (1932–) was born in Montreal, where he has lived off and on ever since. He is presently writing for TV and producing documentary films. *No Address*, a collection of his poems, was published by DC Books.

Abraham Boyarsky (1946–) was born in Poland and came to Canada in 1951. He grew up in Montreal. He has published a collection of stories, *A Pyramid of Time*, and a novel, *Shreiber*. Boyarsky is a professor of mathematics at Concordia University in Montreal.

Leonard Cohen (1934–) was born in Montreal and studied at McGill and Columbia universities. Since the appearance of his first volume of poetry, *Let us Compare Mythologies*, he has published several collections, including *The Spice-Box of Earth*, *Flowers for Hitler*, and *The Energy of Slaves*. In the 1960s he published two novels, *The Favourite Game* and *Beautiful Losers*, and began a successful career as a popular composer and singer. *Death of A Lady's Man* is his latest collection of poetry.

Matt Cohen (1942–) was born in Kingston, Ontario, the town near which his novels *The Disinherited*, *The Sweet Second Summer of Kitty Malone*, and *Flowers of Darkness* are set.

Robert Currie (1937–) lives in Moose Jaw, where he spends his time teaching and writing. He has published three chapbooks and two books of poetry, *Diving into Fire* and *Yarrow*.

Shirley Faessler was born in Toronto and grew up in the Kensington Market area, then almost entirely Jewish, that she uses as the setting for most of her stories. She has published a novel, *Everything in the Window*, and is completing a collection of stories.

Phyllis Gotlieb (1926—) was born in Toronto and has lived there ever since. She has published four novels: *Sunburst, Why Should I Have All the Grief?, O Master Caliban!*, and *A Judgement of Dragons*. The latest of her four volumes of poetry, *The Works*, collects nearly all of her published poems.

A.M. Klein (1909—1972), the son of Russian immigrants, was born in Montreal. He received his B.A. from McGill in 1930 and was called to the bar in 1933. From 1939 to 1955 he edited the *Canadian Jewish Chronicle* and from 1945 to 1947 he was visiting lecturer in poetry at McGill University. His first collection of poetry, *Hath Not A Jew*, appeared in 1940. Klein's subsequent work includes his best-known collection, *The Rocking Chair and Other Poems*, for which he won the Governor General's Award, and a novel, *The Second Scroll*. After a severe illness Klein lived in seclusion from 1955 until his death in 1972.

Rochl Korn (1898—) was born in Poland. She lived in Uzbekistan, U.S.S.R., during the Second World War, in Sweden just after the war, and settled in Canada in 1948. She has published eleven volumes of poetry and fiction and was awarded the prestigious Manger Prize for Literature in 1974. Her work has been translated into Hebrew, French, German, Polish, and English. Her latest collection of poetry is *Farbitene vor*. Rochl Korn lives in Montreal.

Henry Kreisel (1922—) was born in Vienna, came to Canada in 1940, and now lives in Edmonton, where he is University Professor of Comparative Literature and Drama at the University of Alberta. He has published two novels, *The Rich Man* and *The Betrayal*, and a collection of stories, *The Almost Meeting*.

Irving Layton (1912—) was born in Roumania and grew up in Montreal. He taught at a parochial school and at Sir George Williams University before accepting a position as Professor of English at York University. He published his first volume of poetry, *Here and Now*, in 1954 and since then has published more than twenty collections, including *A Red Carpet for the Sun* which won the Governor General's Award. His most recent volume is *Europe and Other Bad News*.

Norman Levine (1924—) grew up in Ottawa. He lived in England from 1949 to the late 1970s and now lives in Toronto. He has published ten books, including *Canada Made Me, From a Seaside Town, I Don't Want To Know Anyone Too Well*, and *Thin Ice*.

Seymour Levitan (1936—) was born in Philadelphia and lives in Vancouver, where he teaches elementary school. His translations of Yiddish stories and poems are included in *Canadian*

Yiddish Writings, The Best of Sholem Aleichem, and the forth-coming *Oxford Book of Yiddish Poetry.* He is currently trans-lating a collection of Rochl Korn's stories and poems.

Jack Ludwig (1922—) was born in Winnipeg, did his under-graduate work at the University of Manitoba, and completed his Ph.D. at the University of California. He teaches English at the State University of New York on Long Island. Ludwig has published two novels, *Confusions* and *Above Ground.* His short stories have appeared in such magazines as *Tamarack* and *Atlantic.*

Avrum Malus (1943—) was born and raised in Montreal. He currently teaches literature and conducts a writing workshop at the Université de Sherbrooke. *I Set the Fire Which Destroyed Our Home* is his first book of poetry.

Eli Mandel (1922—) was born in Estevan, Saskatchewan, and now lives in Toronto where he is professor of Humanities and English at York University. Mandel has written literary criti-cism, has edited anthologies, and is the author of eight collec-tions of poems including *Idiot Joy,* which won the Governor General's Award in 1967. His most recent collection is *Life Sentence.*

Fredelle Bruser Maynard (1922—) was born in Foam Lake, Saskatchewan. Her childhood experiences are recounted in *Raisins and Almonds.* Dividing her time between New Hamp-shire and Toronto, she has taught creative writing and has written for several magazines.

Seymour Mayne (1944—), a native of Montreal, is a professor of English at the University of Ottawa. He has edited a number of critical texts in Canadian literature (including books on the poets A. M. Klein and Irving Layton) and is the translator of *Burnt Pearls: Ghetto Poems of Abraham Sutzkever.* One of his collections, *Name,* won the J.I. Segal Prize. His most recent book, a volume of new and selected poems, is entitled *The Impossible Promised Land.*

Jerry Newman (1935—) was born in Montreal and now teaches in the Creative Writing Department at the University of British Columbia. Two of his novels, *We Always Take Care of Our Own* and *A Russian Novel,* were published in Canada and England. His stories, one of which received a Martha Foley Award, have appeared in a number of literary magazines.

Erna Paris was born in Toronto and raised in Forest Hill. She is the winner of four awards from the Media Club of Canada for feature writing and radio documentary. She is co-author of *Her Own Woman: Profiles Of Ten Canadian Women,* and the author of *Jews: An Account of Their Experience in Canada.*

Lela Parlow (?—1978). Lela Parlow wrote in 1975: "I was born into the depression in Toronto, to Roumanian-born parents ... I've been a botanist, English teacher, am now a graduate student at York University. Liberated husband and four independent children." Lela Parlow died of cancer in 1978. Her poems have appeared in many Canadian magazines. A chapbook titled *Most of the Time* was published posthumously by Barton Press.

Abraham Ram who was born in Montreal, teaches literature and creative writing at Concordia University. He has written radio drama for the CBC and published poetry and fiction including three parts of a five-part prose series — *The Noise of Singing, Dark of Caves,* and *Once in Woods.*

Mordecai Richler (1931—) was born in Montreal and educated at Sir George Williams University. In 1959 he moved to England where he worked as a screenwriter and novelist. He returned to Montreal in 1972. His novels include *The Apprenticeship of Duddy Kravitz, St. Urbain's Horseman,* and *Joshua Then and Now,* and his essays have been collected in *Shovelling Trouble* and *Hunting Tigers Under Glass.* He is a judge for the Book-of-the-Month Club.

Joe Rosenblatt (1933—) was born in Toronto. His books include *The LSD Leacock, Bumblebee Dithyramb, Dream Craters,* and *Top Soil.* Rosenblatt was awarded the Governor General's Award for Poetry in 1976.

Mark Sarner (1948—) is a contributing editor of *Toronto Life.* He is also a partner in Sarner Young Inc., a communications company, and Radiant Pictures Inc., a film production company.

J. I. (Jakov-Itzchok) Segal (1896-1954) was born in the Ukraine. He settled in Montreal in 1911 and remained there until his death. He worked as a tailor but later became a teacher in the Jewish Day Schools. His poetry collections include *Fun Mayn Velt, Sefer Yiddish,* and the posthumous *Letste Lider.* Though he wrote some poems in Russian and Hebrew, the bulk of his work was written in Yiddish.

Ray Shankman (1940—) was born in Toronto and educated at Dalhousie University. He has taught at the Ben Gurion University of the Negev, Beersheva and now teaches poetry and the Bible at Vanier College in Montreal. His poems have appeared in a number of little magazines.

Joseph Sherman (1945—) was born in Bridgewater, Nova Scotia, and grew up in Sydney. His poems have been included in a number of anthologies. Two collections of his work have been published: *Birthday* and *Chaim the Slaughterer.*

David Lewis Stein (1937—) was born in Toronto, where he still lives. He has published a number of short stories and two novels, *Scratch One Dreamer* and *My Sexual and Other Revolutions*. His stories were recently collected in *City Boys: Stories* (Oberon).

Morley Torgov (1928—   ) was born in Sault Ste. Marie and now lives in Toronto. He is author of the Leacock Award winning collection of stories *A Good Place To Come From*, and the novel *The Abramsky Variations*. His new novel, *The Outside Chance of Maximillian Glick*, will be published in 1982.

Miriam Waddington was born in Winnipeg and attended the Peretz Shule there. She is a professor of English at York University and the editor of A. M. Klein's *Collected Poems*, as well as the author of a critical study of his work. She has published eleven books of poetry, the most recent of which are *Driving Home, The Price of Gold, Mister Never,* and *The Visitants*.

Tom Wayman (1945—   ) was born in Hawkesbury, Ontario. His family moved to British Columbia in 1952. He currently teaches Creative Writing at David Thompson University in Nelson, B.C. Wayman's works include *Waiting for Wayman* and *Money and Rain: Tom Wayman Live*. His latest collection of poetry is *Living on the Ground: Tom Wayman Country*.

William Weintraub (1926—   ) was born in Montreal, where he still lives and works. A former newspaper reporter and magazine writer, Weintraub has written and produced documentary films. Weintraub's writing includes the novels *Why Rock the Boat* and *The Underdogs*.

Helen Weinzweig (1915—   ) was born in Poland and came to Toronto at the age of nine. She did not begin writing until she was forty-five. Weinzweig has published two novels, *Passing Ceremony* and *Basic Black With Pearls*. Her stories have appeared in *Canadian Forum, Jewish Dialog, The Tamarack Review, Saturday Night,* and *Toronto Life*.

Adele Wiseman (1928—   ) was born in Winnipeg. After attending the University of Manitoba, Wiseman travelled extensively. She taught at McGill University and at Sir George Williams. Her first novel, *The Sacrifice*, won a Governor General's Award. *Crackpot* is her latest novel. She has also published a play, *Testimonial Dinner,* and a biography, *Old Woman At Play*. She now lives in Toronto.

Larry Zolf (1934—   ) was born in the North End of Winnipeg and now lives in Toronto where he is a CBC television producer. He is the winner of a Wilderness Award for best TV journalism and is the author of the extended essay *Dance of the Dialectic*. His reviews and articles have appeared in such magazines as *Saturday Night* and *Maclean's* and in major newspapers across the country.